PUBLIC HEALTH IN THE 21ST CENTURY SERIES

SMOKING RELAPSE: CAUSES, PREVENTION AND RECOVERY

PUBLIC HEALTH IN THE 21ST CENTURY SERIES

Family History of Osteoporosis
Afrooz Afghani (Editor)
2009. ISBN: 978-1-60876-190-6

Cross Infections: Types, Causes and Prevention
Jin Dong and Xun Liang (Editors)
2009. ISBN: 978-1-60741-467-4

Health-Related Quality of Life
Erik C. Hoffmann (Editor)
2009. ISBN: 978-1-60741-723-1

Swine Flu and Pig Borne Diseases
Viroj Wiwanitkit
2009. ISBN: 978-1-60876-291-0

Biological Clocks: Effects on Behavior, Health and Outlook
Oktav Salvenmoser and Brigitta Meklau (Editors)
2010. ISBN: 978-1-60741-251-9

Infectious Disease Modelling Research Progress
Jean Michel Tchuenche and C. Chiyaka (Editors)
2010. ISBN: 978-1-60741-347-9

Firefighter Fitness: A Health and Wellness Guide
Ernest L. Schneider
2010. ISBN: 978-1-60741-650-0

The Making of a Good Doctor
B. D. Kirkcaldy, R. J. Shephard and R. G. Siefen
2010. ISBN: 978-1-60876-449-5

Handbook of Disease Outbreaks: Prevention, Detection and Control
Albin Holmgren and Gerhard Borg (Editors)
2010. ISBN: 978-1-60876-224-8

Sexual Risk Behaviors
Luigi Passero and Cecilia Sgariglia (Editors)
2010. ISBN: 978-1-60741-227-4

Avian Influenza: Etiology, Pathogenesis and Interventions
Salomon Haugan and Walter Bjornson (Editors)
2010. ISBN: 978-1-60741-846-7

Heavy Metals: A Rapid Clinical Guide to Neurotoxicity and other Common Concerns
Kenneth R. Spaeth, Antonios J. Tsismenakis and Stefanos N. Kales
2010. ISBN: 978-1-60876-634-5

Physical Activity in Rehabilitation and Recovery
Holly Blake (Editor)
2010. ISBN: 978-1-60876-400-6

Smoking Relapse: Causes, Prevention and Recovery
Johan Egger and Mikel Kalb (Editors)
2010. ISBN: 978-1-60876-580-5

PUBLIC HEALTH IN THE 21ST CENTURY SERIES

SMOKING RELAPSE: CAUSES, PREVENTION AND RECOVERY

JOHAN EGGER
AND
MIKEL KALB
EDITORS

Nova Science Publishers, Inc.
New York

For permission to use material from this book please contact us:
Telephone 631-231-7269; Fax 631-231-8175
Web Site: http://www.novapublishers.com

Library of Congress Cataloging-in-Publication Data

Smoking relapse : causes, prevention, and recovery / editors, Johan Egger and Mikel Kalb.
p. ; cm.
Includes bibliographical references and index.
ISBN 978-1-60876-580-5 (hardcover : alk. paper)
1. Nicotine addiction--Relapse. 2. Smoking cessation. I. Egger, Johan. II. Kalb, Mikel.
[DNLM: 1. Tobacco Use Disorder--prevention & control. 2. Tobacco Use Disorder--therapy. 3. Recurrence--prevention & control. 4. Smoking Cessation. WM 290 S6705 2010]
RC567.S637 2010 616.86'506--dc22 2009041948

Published by Nova Science Publishers, Inc. ✢ New York

Contents

PREFACE

Smoking relapse can be defined as the resumption of smoking at any time after the quit date so a relapse prevention intervention can not clearly be distinct from an extended cessation programme. Although entirely preventable, smoking is one of the most common causes of morbidity and mortality in the United States. Patients in certain socioeconomic and demographic groups are uniquely vulnerable to tobacco dependence for many reasons. In this book, the authors evaluate some relapse prevention interventions. Special interest is shown for certain subpopulations such as pregnant women or respiratory patients. Furthermore, the authors present an evidence-based approach for providers that helps identify the most at-risk patients. The authors then offer specific clinical strategies for approaching tobacco cessation which are proven to be the most effective in overcoming these systematic barriers. A number of health policy recommendations are also proposed which can assist with breaking down barriers to care for each patient group and result in more effective cessation programs on the population level. In addition, it has been found that cigarette smoking is associated with an increased risk of suicide.

Chapter 1 - Cigarette smoking is associated with an increased risk for suicide (ideation, plans and actions). However, findings regarding this relationship are not yet consistent. Despite the fact that the prevalence of smoking is higher in suicidal individuals, it is not clear that smoking itself (or the effect of nicotine on brain function) is directly involved in suicidality or whether other factors associated with both suicide and smoking are implicated in this relationship. Indeed it has been found that several suicide risk factors are more common among current smokers than among those who have never smoked.

The authors identified the main hypotheses for explaining this association, focusing on the effect of nicotine exposure on the neurobiological system as a causal mechanism influencing suicidality in long-term smokers. Then they examined the association between tobacco and psychological problems (such as depression, alcohol use and schizophrenia) as possible determinants of an increased risk of suicide in smokers. Finally they reviewed the magnitude of smoking during adolescence.

Despite the large literature available, the findings are not yet consistent. Most likely, several factors contribute to the increased rate of suicidal behavior in current smokers. Future research is required to provide guidance in suicide prevention among smokers.

Chapter 2 - Although entirely preventable, smoking is one of the most common causes of morbidity and mortality in the United States. As a result it creates a significant financial burden on the health care system. This creates an obligation and urgency on the part of health care providers, public health officials, and government leaders to address the causes of smoking and identify the populations most susceptible, common barriers to quitting smoking, and strategies for improving success rates of cessation. Tobacco policy must address all of these concerns. To most effectively accomplish these tasks we must better understand influences that encourage smoking and barriers to successful cessation in at-risk patient populations. This requires a multifaceted, individualized, and culturally-sensitive approach.

Patients in certain at-risk cultural groups are uniquely vulnerable to tobacco dependence for many reasons. Factors such as directed and aggressive tobacco industry marketing techniques, barriers to accessing health care providers who provide treatment for tobacco dependence, inequitable access to pharmacological treatment options, and a limited availability of culture-specific support resources play significant roles. In this chapter, the authors identify six distinctive patient subpopulations, each with unique cultural characteristics to consider during the effective treatment of tobacco dependence. These include patient groups based on a patient's gender, age, race and ethnicity, native language, and sexual orientation. They first present an evidence-based approach for providers that helps identify the most at-risk patients. They then offer specific clinical strategies for approaching tobacco cessation which are proven to be the most effective in overcoming the existing cultural barriers. Lastly, they propose a number of health policy recommendations which can assist with breaking down barriers to care for each cultural group and result in more effective cessation programs on the population level.

Chapter 3 - Tobacco dependence is a chronic illness with severe, adverse implications on the smoker's health and well-being. Additionally, the public health impact of tobacco-related illness is staggering. The highly preventable nature of this disease spectrum makes smoking cessation a major public health priority. Health care providers must address smoking on the level of the individual patient, while policy makers and government leaders need to address the issue on the population level. To make the biggest impact on tobacco-related disease, the authors must better understand the influences that encourage smoking and the barriers to successful cessation in the most at-risk patient populations.

Patients in certain socioeconomic and demographic groups are uniquely vulnerable to tobacco dependence for many reasons. Barriers within the health care system at-large play a significant role, as do geographic and economic factors, insurance status, ability to read, and the presence of underlying mental illness. Other factors include directed and aggressive tobacco industry marketing techniques, barriers to accessing health care providers who provide treatment for tobacco dependence, inequitable access to pharmacological treatment options, and a limited availability of or access to support resources. In this chapter, the authors first present an evidence-based approach for providers that helps identify the most at-risk patients. They then offer specific clinical strategies for approaching tobacco cessation which are proven to be the most effective in overcoming these systematic barriers. Lastly, they propose a number of health policy recommendations which can assist with breaking down barriers to care for each patient group and result in more effective cessation programs on the population level.

Chapter 4 - Despite 50+ years of public health campaigns to reduce the rates of smoking in the United States, approximately one-quarter of the adults living in this country continue to use tobacco. Most of these persons have tried to quit smoking, typically more than once in their lives. This chapter examines the factors associated with trying to quit or cut down on tobacco use in a community-based sample of 485 adult persistent smokers recruited from the Atlanta, Georgia metropolitan area between 2004 and 2007. Both active and passive recruiting approaches were used, along with a targeted sampling strategy.

The data revealed that 90.9% of the smokers interviewed said that they had tried at least once before to quit or cut down on their smoking, with the "average" person having attempted to do this seven previous times. Multivariate analysis of the factors associated with the number of times that people reported having tried to quit or cut down on their tobacco use yielded three similar but not identical models. All three models contained two items in common, age (older age = more cessation/reduction attempts) and the number of reasons for wanting to quit/cut down on smoking (more reasons = more cessation/reduction attempts). Model 1 contained one additional item pertaining to viewing oneself negatively as a result of one's smoking and/or viewing one's tobacco use behaviors negatively (greater negative perception = more cessation/reduction attempts). Model 2 contained a different third measure, pertaining to the number of tobacco dependency symptoms that had been experienced (more symptoms = more cessation/reduction attempts). Model 3 contained both of these additional measures.

Chapter 5 - Exposure to drug-associated environmental stimuli (cue), drug priming, and stress have been thought of as the major risk factors contributing to relapse in abstinent subjects. The authors' recent animal studies along with reports from other laboratories have demonstrated that nicotine cues reliably reinstate nicotine-seeking behavior. However, investigation of nicotine-seeking elicited by nicotine priming and stress exposure as well as their combination with nicotine cues is limited. This study, using a response-reinstatement procedure, examined the motivational effects of a nicotine-associated cue, nicotine priming, pharmacological stress, and combination of the cue with priming or stress. Male Sprague-Dawley rats were trained in 30 daily 1-h sessions to intravenously self-administer nicotine (0.03 mg/kg/infusion, free base) on an FR5 schedule and associate an auditory/visual cue with each nicotine administration. Then, lever responding was extinguished by saline substitution of nicotine and omission of the cue. After rats reached an extinction criterion, reinstatement tests were conducted under five conditions: cue re-presentation, nicotine priming, stress, cue+priming, and cue+stress. Nicotine (0.25 mg/kg, s.c.) priming, stress (yohimbine, 2 mg/kg, i.p.), and response-contingent re-presentation of the cue significantly reinstated the extinguished nicotine-seeking behavior with cue producing the most robust effect. Combination of cue with either priming or stress did not produce additive effect. These results confirm the motivational effects of nicotine cue, priming, and stress in the present animal model of relapse and demonstrate the most robust ability of cue exposure to elicit nicotine-seeking after extinction. The present findings suggest that re-exposure to smoking-related environmental cues may play a critical role in the high recidivism rates of smoking and thereby lend support for the continued effort on cue management as a strategy for the treatment and prevention of smoking relapse.

Chapter 6 – A number of interventions can help people who smoke to quit. These include pharmacological treatments, such as nicotine replacement therapies, antidepressants and the lately developed nicotine receptor partial agonists. Behavioural approaches are also continiously tried, either delivered individually or in groups.

However, a significant proportion of initially successful quitters relapse over time and more commonly within the first two years after having stopped smoking. It is estimated that 50-80% of quitters relapse within the first year. The causes of relapse are beyond the scope of this chapter. The authors are rather focusing on the existing ways of preventing it.

Chapter 7 - In his insightful 2005 book *The World is Flat: A Brief History of the Twenty-First Century*, Thomas Friedman described how the digital age, transportation, political change, and economic influences have hastened "globalism" – an intermingling and unification of people from all countries and walks of life.

Tobacco companies are finding alternative means for profit – and countless lives are being lost as a result. Few public health problems are rooted in such a profit-hungry business model, and "Big Tobacco" must be stopped. We must no longer ignore the health of developing nations. We are connected to and dependent on their welfare as much as they are on ours. International efforts are clearly going to be necessary to reverse the pandemic-like spread of tobacco-related disease across other nations. Policy initiatives to prevent tobacco-related disease must occur globally, locally, and everywhere in between.

Chapter 8 - School-based cigarette smoking prevention has experienced a brief but active history, which was initiated shortly after the first Surgeon General's Report in 1964. This chapter highlights a sequence of events by which school-based tobacco use prevention research developed as an active science, and illustrates a pendulum effect, with confidence in tobacco use prevention increasing and decreasing at different points in time. Suggestions are offered to advance school-based smoking prevention research.

Chapter 9 - Smoking cessation reduces both the mortality and re-infarction rate amongst smokers who have experienced a myocardial infarction (MI). Smoking cessation programs have tended to be conducted with post-operative or seriously ill patients. In this study, the authors examined the efficacy of a relapse prevention program for hospital cardiovascular patients who did not require operative procedures or extensive hospitalization. A pre-post, two groups, control trial involving 208 patients (103 in the intervention group) recruited from three coronary care units in large metropolitan hospitals was used to assess the effect of the intervention. Smoking status of self-reported quitters were verified using CO concentrations in expired air. Complete follow-up was obtained from 129 (62.0%) of initial participants. At three months after discharge, the self-report quite rate in the intervention group was 19.4%, significantly higher than in the control group (7.6%) ($p = 0.046$). This difference persisted at nine months after discharge, when the self reported quit rate was 27.3% in the intervention group and 12.9% in the control group ($p = 0.043$). A behavior-based smoking cessation program was effective for less serious cardiovascular patients and the effect persisted for nine months after discharge.

In: Smoking Relapse: Causes, Prevention ... ISBN: 978-1-60876-580-5
Editors: J. Egger and M. Kalb

Chapter 1

SMOKING AS A RISK FACTOR FOR SUICIDE

***Maurizio Pompili*[1,2], *Marco Innamorati*[3], *Roberto Tatarelli*[1], *and David Lester*[4]**

[1]Department of Psychiatry, Sant'Andrea Hospital, Sapienza University of Rome, Italy.
[2]McLean Hospital – Harvard Medical School, USA.
[3]The Richard Stockton College of New Jersey, USA.
[4]Università Europea di Roma, Italy.

ABSTRACT

Cigarette smoking is associated with an increased risk for suicide (ideation, plans and actions). However, findings regarding this relationship are not yet consistent. Despite the fact that the prevalence of smoking is higher in suicidal individuals, it is not clear that smoking itself (or the effect of nicotine on brain function) is directly involved in suicidality or whether other factors associated with both suicide and smoking are implicated in this relationship. Indeed it has been found that several suicide risk factors are more common among current smokers than among those who have never smoked.

We identified the main hypotheses for explaining this association, focusing on the effect of nicotine exposure on the neurobiological system as a causal mechanism influencing suicidality in long-term smokers. Then we examined the association between tobacco and psychological problems (such as depression, alcohol use and schizophrenia) as possible determinants of an increased risk of suicide in smokers. Finally we reviewed the magnitude of smoking during adolescence.

Despite the large literature available, the findings are not yet consistent. Most likely, several factors contribute to the increased rate of suicidal behavior in current smokers. Future research is required to provide guidance in suicide prevention among smokers.

INTRODUCTION

The 2007 National Health Interview Survey indicates that approximately 19.8% (43.4 million) U.S. adults were current cigarette smokers in 2007 (CDC, 2007). Cigarette smoking is probably the leading preventable cause of premature death. It was estimated that, each year in USA, 443,000 people die prematurely as a result of smoking (CDC, 2008).

According to WHO data, approximately one million people died in 2008 by suicide (WHO, 2008), and suicide is now among the three leading causes of death among those aged 15-44 years for both sexes. An important branch of suicidology (defined as the discipline devoted to the scientific study of suicide and its prevention) is involved in identifying the predictors and the causes of suicidality. Unfortunately, it is often a difficult task because the causes of suicide are multifactorial with genetic and biologic vulnerability, environmental factors, psychological pain, mental and physical illnesses, substance abuse and personality disorders each playing a role (Mann, 1998). Therefore, it is not always easy to establish which variables independently contribute to the occurrence of suicidal behavior. However, several psychosocial, demographic and behavioral factors have been identified, including age, marital status, life events, social support, major depressive episodes, dysthymia, schizophrenia, alcohol use and smoking (Bernal, 2007; Casey, 2006).

Research has identified a strong relationship between tobacco smoking and suicidal behavior. In general, cigarette smoking is more frequent among people with suicidal ideation than among the general population (Malone, 2003; Kessler, 2007). More specifically, post-mortem studies of suicides has found that smokers are overrepresented (Angst, 1998). Moreover, suicides are more likely to have high blood and urine levels of nicotine and cotine in contrast to to those dying from other causes (Benwell, 1990; Kochi, 2005; Moriya, 2005, 2007).

A link between smoking and suicide has been reported in several studies, and smoking has been suggested as a possible risk factor for suicide, but the research findings are not completely consistent. Although the prevalence of smoking is higher in suicidal people, it is less clear that smoking itself (or the effect of nicotine on brain function) is directly involved in increasing the level of suicidality. Other factors associated with both suicide and smoking may be implicated in this relationship. For example, it has been found that several well-established risk factors for suicide, such as depressive moods, alcohol use and abuse, impulsivity, low emotional control, social isolation and schizophrenia, are more common among current than smokers than among those who have never smoked.

The main interpretations proposed to explain the association between smoking and suicide may be summarized in two opposed models. The first supports a causal influence of smoking on suicidality. It is based on evidence of the effect of nicotine exposure on human biochemistry. Nicotine has direct effects on the central nervous system, and these effects might be responsible for, or mediate, the link between smoking and suicidality in two different ways. The direct neurological effect of nicotine (or other tobacco components) may induce suicidal behavior or, alternatively, the central effect of nicotine may induce behavioral or mood alterations which in turn may act as mediators between smoking and suicide risk (see below).

An interesting and alternative approach endeavors to identify whether smoking habits precede (and so possibly cause) suicidal behavior or some of the possible suicide precursors (especially depression) (Choi, 1997; Breslau, 2004; Li-Tzy, 1999; Goodman, 2000). Related to this is the question of whether stopping smoking reduces the risk of suicide or suicide risk factors (Leistykow, 2003; Mino, 2000; Khaled, 2009). For example, Mino and colleagues evaluated mental status six months and one years after cessation of smoking and found a gradual improvement in physical health, perceived stress and family life satisfaction. An indirect confirmation of this first hypothesis is the finding that former smokers did not have higher rates of psychological disorders or suicidal behavior compared to non-smokers (Degenhardt, 2001). Only current smoking, and not previous smoking, is linked to increased suicidal behavior (Miller, 2000a, 2000b; Leistikow, 1999; Hemenway, 1993; Breslau, 2005).

The second possible interpretation stems from the observation that current smoking is correlated with many other risk factors for suicide. Various conditions (behavioral, psychiatric, and life events) and variables associated with smoking are also suicide risk factors, and they may act as potential mediators to produce the association between smoking and suicide (Boden, 2008; Kessler, 2008; Hintikka, 2009; Breslau, 1998). Therefore, the genetic, psychological, environmental and other risk factors for suicide may explain the association between smoking and suicide. In this view, cigarette smoking is independently correlated with traits predisposing to suicide, and smoking may be considered to be only an indicator, a useful marker, for an increased risk of suicidal behavior. Its effect on suicidality may not be direct and causal. Alternatively, specific psychological factors may produce an increased susceptibility to tobacco use, and they may act or contribute to the association between smoking and suicide.

Some authors also suggest that the association between smoking and suicide is the result of methodological artifacts and errors of interpretation of the data. For example, in some epidemiological studies, there are inadequate controls for psychological factors (Miller, 2000a; Kessler, 2007). Correcting for psychological variables (such as diagnosis, alcohol or drug use and abuse, experience of trauma, personality traits and poor emotional control) results in a reduction or elimination of the association between smoking and suicide (Boden, 2008; Hemmingsson, 2003; Patten, 2003; McGee, 2005).

Criticism regarding the possibility that the correlation between smoking and suicide implies causation was offered by Smith and colleagues (1992). They analyzed data from Multiple Risk Factor Intervention Trial (MRFIT), a study involving 361,662 men, with a 12-year follow-up. They found a strong dose-response association between smoking and completed suicide but also between smoking and homicide. They interpreted this as evidence against the biological plausibility of a causal interpretation of the smoking-suicide association.

The decreased risk of suicidal behavior may be a consequence of smoking cessation. There are two different situations associated with this. Stopping smoking may gradually reduce the level of depressive mood and may improve mental health and, as a side effect, decrease suicidality. However, research indicates that, in the first stages of smoking cessation, some individuals (especially those with a history of depression) may develop depressive symptoms and, occasionally, a major depressive episode (Covey, 1997; Glassman, 1988; Tsoh, 2000), along with increased suicidality. In additon, the emergence of depressive symptoms is associated with a failure in smoking cessation. The risk of developing a major depressive episode (and consequently an increase in suicidality) during the first months without cigarettes is partly due to suspension symptoms. In nicotine dependent people, a sudden interruption or reduction in nicotine intake may bring about withdrawal symptoms, including insomnia, irritability, anger, difficulty in concentration and restlessness, as well as dysphoria, depression and anxiety (APA, 2000). The emergence of depressive symptoms may extend beyond the usual withdrawal period (2-4 weeks) (Covey, 1997). Second, there is evidence about that two products used in smoking cessation programs may enhance depression and cause suicidality. The US Food and Drug Administration (FDA) has issued warnings about the possibility that depressed mood, suicidal ideation and suicidal behavior can occur in patients, with and without a psychiatric history, who attempt to quit smoking using Verenicline or Bupropion (FDA, 2005, 2008).

Studies of adolescents are important. The onset of daily smoking rarely occurs after the age of 25 (Breslau, 2001). Those who start smoking before the age of 16 are 1.6 times more likely to become nicotine dependent than those who start smoking at an older age (Breslau, 1993; Martinez-Ortega, 2008). Adolescence is considered to be a time of high risk for both suicide and smoking. Adolescents are more vulnerable to emotional perturbations and distress and, therefore, are at an increased risk of suicide. Among adolescents suicide is the third leading cause of death.

Menti and coworkers (2007) found that smoking was 10-times more frequent among young suicide attempters (age 9-20) than among controls. According to The Youth Risk Behavior Surveillance, 14.5% of the students had seriously considered attempting suicide, 11.3% of students had made a plan about how they would attempt suicide and 6.9% of students had attempted suicide one or more times during the 12 months before the survey (Eaton, 2008).

Around 20.0% of students currently smoke (Eaton, 2008). Initially, smoking during youth is limited to social situations. Gradually a dependence is established and, at the same time, the number of cigarettes smoked increases (Patton, 1998). In this context, depression seems to be a predictor for smoking initiation (Patton, 1998). On the other hand, other research demonstrates that, during adolescence, tobacco smoking is associated with an increased risk for the subsequent onset of depressed mood (Li-Tzy, 1999). Brown and colleagues (1996) conducted a prospective study to establish whether adolescent smokers are more likely to develop a major depressive episode in the follow-up period (12 months) or whether those with previous psychiatric disorders, such as depression, are more likely to develop a smoking habit in the following year. Their findings indicated that the presence of a major depressive disorder (but not other psychiatric disorders) was a risk factor for beginning cigarette smoking, while smoking at the onset of the study was a predictor for the development of depression. This bidirectionality between smoking and depression may support the above-mentioned hypothesis of a common vulnerability to both, or it may support the self-medication hypothesis and the possibility that same psychosocial problems associated with smoking risk are also associated with an increased susceptibility to depressive mood.

In this chapter, we review the effects of nicotine exposure on the neurobiological system and research on the association between nicotine consumption and different psychiatric disorders. In addition, we evaluate the possible implication of smoking cessation on the neurobiological system and on suicide.

1. Nicotine Biochemical Interactions And Suicide

Nicotine is a potent psychoactive drug with both acute and chronic central nervous system effects, including influences on mood. In particular, the interaction between nicotine and the serotonergic system is of particular clinical importance given the central role of these receptors in anxiety and depression-related illness. In this biochemical context, the difficulty in determining what is the real role of tobacco on suicidality is due to the fact that nicotine has a double effect in regulating the serotonergic system. Specifically, the acute administration of nicotine induces the release of 5-HT (Ribeiro, 1993; Kenny, 2001), while chronic smoking reduces 5-HT1A receptor gene expression and the sensitivity of serotonin receptors in the frontal cortex (Kenny, 2001), reduces serotonin reuptake (Benwell, 1990), and ultimately diminishes serotonergic transmission. The immediate antidepressant-like effect of nicotine may relieve feelings of stress, depression, anger and dysphoria. This effect is, therefore, ill-suited to explain a direct relationship between smoking and suicide. The use of nicotine as a form of self-medication may, however, explain the association between depression and smoking.

On the other hand, long-term smoking may cause lower brain serotonin function that, in turn, is associated with an increased susceptibility to suicide. The increased anxiety and negative affect observed in smokers may also be relevant. Consistent with these results, research has identified differences between suicides and control groups in markers of central nervous system serotonin function such as lower central 5-HT activity (Mann, 2002, 2003; Kamali, 2001). Lower platelet 5-HT (blood platelets are often used as a limited peripheral model for central 5-HT neural function) has been associated with suicidal behavior in psychotic and non-psychotic depressed patients (Muck-Seler et al, 1996; Pivac et al, 1997) and in patients with first episode of psychosis (Marcinko et al, 2007). Another relelvant biochemical aspect is monoamine oxidase (MAO) activity. The influence of smoking on MAO may play a role in the psychopathology of depression and suicide in smokers (Whitfield, 2000). MAO activity seems to be lower in current smokers than former smokers and those who have never smoked (Merlin, 1995; Berlin, 1995). MAO activity has been shown to be inversely associated with impulsive behavior, and it is also lower in suicidal patients as compared to nonsuicidal depressed patients and healthy controls (Roggenbach, 2006; Stålenheim, 2001; Verkes, 1998).

McGee and coworkers (2005) found that tobacco smoking does not appear to elevate the risk of later suicidal ideation in adolescents. However, they did not take into account the level of nicotine dependence. Heatherton et al. (1989) found that those individuals who smoke soon after waking up are highly nicotine-dependent. The likelihood of suicidality is known to be correlated with the amount of smoking via lowered serotonergic function. When measuring levels of CSF 5-HIAA (5-hydroxyindoleacetic acid concentrations in the cerebrospinal fluid) in depressed subjects, Malone and colleagues (2003) found that CSF 5-HIAA levels were negatively correlated with the amount of cigarette smoking, but were not related to suicide attempter status. Furthermore, the number of cigarettes smoked correlated positively with aggression scores. Thus, according to Malone et al., nicotine may have both biological and behavioral effects in the brain that increase the probability of suicidal behaviour in depressed patients. As also shown in previous studies (Breslau et al, 2005), early morning smoking and a high number of cigarettes smoked per day, as opposed to moderate smoking, are valid indicators of nicotine dependence. Therefore, nicotine dependence might explain the finding of an increased risk for suicidal attempts, but not suicidal ideation, in adolescent heavy daily smoking.

Audrain and coworkers (2004) followed 15-year-old students enrolled in public schools in northern Virginia and provided the first evidence for an association of the DRD2 A1 allele with smoking progression among adolescents and a relationship between the adolescents' response to their first exposure to nicotine and their subsequent risk for nicotine dependence. (The SLC6A3 polymorphism was not associated with smoking progression.)

2. COMORBIDITY

Research investigating the association between nicotine consumption and various psychiatric disorders has shown that nicotine dependence is much more prevalent among psychiatric patients than in the general population. People with mental illness are about twice as likely to smoke (Lasser, 2000; Poirier, 2002; Kessler, 2007; Grant, 2004). Although the mechanisms that influence this association are unclear, this could account for the high rate of suicidal behavior among smokers. Several possible explanations have been considered for the association between psychiatric disorders and smoking. Nicotine may have a direct deleterious effect on mental health status (i.e., a nicotine central effect) and generate depression. Alternatively, pre-existing mental health problems may lead to smoking, or there may be a shared, possibly genetic, etiology. Whatever the cause, the relationship between tobacco and problems such as depression, schizophrenia, and alcohol and substance use have to be considered in the association of an increased risk of suicide in smokers.

Research suggests that smokers are more likely to be depressed than nonsmokers (Pedersen, 2009; Murphy, 2003), and this association between smoking and depression may be particularly important in the genesis of suicidal pathways in smokers. Regarding the possibility that major depression and psychotic disorders may play a causal role in beginning smoking, this may reflect the use of smoking for self-medication. The acute chemical impact of nicotine may improve mood and reduce psychological symptoms such as dysphoria, anxiety, stress and anger and enhance attention and improve cognitive performance (Glassman, 1990; Xu, 2007; Kassel, 1997; Balfour, 2000). Moreover, the antidepressant effect of tobacco components may explain why depressed and other psychiatric patients find it more difficult to stop smoking and why there are an increase likelihood that they become heavy smokers (Murphy et al, 2003), and why some (but not all) studies report that depressive symptoms predict the development of smoking onset (Hemmingsson, 2003; Breslau, 1998; Goodman, 2000; Murphy et al, 2003), or that smoking at baseline does not predict following depression (Murphy et al, 2003). Murphy and coworkers (2003) studied the incidence of depression in cohorts of smokers and non-smokers over a 40-year period (1952-1970, 1970-1992). Over the years, the proportion of smokers declined, and the association between smoking and depressive mood was lower in 1952 and 1970, but strong in 1992. It seems that the increased awareness of the unhealthy effect of tobacco had resulted in reducing the number of smokers but, on the other hand, it selected a group of new smokers and those who persisted in smoking. This generational change suggests a psychopathologic origin (or component) in smoking initiation and continuation (Breslau, 2001). A similar observation can be made regarding the prominent abuse of cigarettes in schizophrenic patients (de Leon & Diaz, 2005).

Through dopamine release and raising dopamine levels in the prefrontal cortex and the nucleus accumbens (Dalack, 1998), nicotine may be used to manage negative symptoms (Smith, 2002). Nicotine helps reduce the extrapyramidal side effects of neuroleptics (Poirier, 2002; Yang, 2002; Goff, 1992) and reduce cognitive deficits (Adler, 1998). It is possible that genetic factors influence the genesis of both smoking and depression, and a genetic susceptibility/component to both smoking (Li, 2003; Lerman, 2003) and depression (Sullivan, 2000) has been demonstrated. Several researchers have propose that common factors, probably genetic, may predispose people to the development of both nicotine dependence and major depression (Kenneth, 1993; Breslaw, 1993; Kendler, 1993). Furthemore, it has been found that genetic subgroups of depressed patients with a specific variation in dopamine receptor genes are also more predisposed to begin smoking (Lerman, 1998), suggesting a genetic overlap between smoking and depression. On the other hand, depression may simply reinforce the effect of DRD2 A1 allelic variants (which induce lower endogenous dopamine activity) on smoking progression (Audrian-Mcgoven, 2004).

Alcohol abuse and smoking are also associated, and there is a general smoking and substance use/abuse comorbidity. Alcohol use is more frequent in smokers than in non-smokers (Degenhardt, 2001; Harrison, 2008; Leon, 2007; John, 2003; Miller, 2000b), and alsohol use and misuse is positively associated with suicidal ideation and deliberate self-harm (McCloud, 2004; Sher, 2006a; Cherpitel, 2004). Incidentally, alcohol abuse influences serotonergic metabolism and increases impulsivity and aggressive behavior (Sher, 2006b). Thus, its effect on suicidality in smokers may be a result of synergic effects.

Regarding the possibility that a positive association between alcohol and smoking alone may explain the link between smoking and suicide, Hemmingsson and Kriebel (2003) examined a longitudinal cohort study of 49,323 Swedish men to establish whether smoking at age 18–20 was related to suicide mortality during 26 years of follow-up and whether this relationship was attributable to an increased prevalence of indicators of poor mental well-being and alcohol use among the smokers. The suicides occurring during the 26-year follow-up period were linked with previous/early smoking status but, when the suicide risk was adjusted for the set of risk factors measured at age 18-20 and for a diagnosis of alcoholism during the follow-up, very little evidence of elevated suicide risk among the smokers remained. Hemmingsson and Kriebel concluded that the increased risk of suicide among smokers was almost entirely explained by the increased prevalence of heavy alcohol consumption and low mental well-being among smokers.

3. Personality, Smoking and Suicide

As mentioned above, it is not clear whether cigarette smoking *per se* increases suicidality or whether other smoking-associated factors intervene. One possibility is that the personality of the smoker makes the individual prone to suicidal behavior. The impulsivity and increased distressed behavior among smokers reported in the literature may partly account for their proneness to engage in suicidal behavior. In this view, smoking, heavy drinking, drug use, and other risky behavior represent what Shneidman called *subintentioned suicide* (Shneidman, 1985), perhaps resulting from an unconscious death wish. Ellis and Trumpower (2008) found that people reporting suicidal ideation were more likely to report risky health-related behavior (especially cigarette smoking, drinking and other substance-related involvement). This association was found even after controlling for depression.

Smokers are also more likely to have higher levels of impulsivity and aggressive behavior (Angst, 1998; Tanskanen, 1998). This may be due to the effect of nicotine on serotonergic activity that could predispose susceptible individuals to impulsive and aggressive behavior and, in turn, to suicide attempts (Horesh, 1997). Whatever the genesis, impulsive/aggressive traits are correlated with suicide attempts independently of psychiatric diagnosis. Across diagnostic categories, patients who attempted suicide have an elevated lifetime trait of aggression and impulsivity (Mann, 1999; Oquedo, 2004), and impulsivity contributes to the long-term risk for suicide (Maser, 2002).

4. Smoking and Suicide: Is Smoking a Causal or a Casual Associated Factor?

a. Studies that have Investigated a Direct Relationship between Smoking and Suicide

Tanskanen et al. (1998) studied a sample of 1,217 psychiatric patients (56% female and 44% male) in whom schizophrenia was the most common psychiatric diagnosis (33%) followed by affective disorder (29%), personality disorder (11%), dysthymia (8%) and anxiety disorder (8%). Twenty-four percent of the men and 26% of the women had attempted suicide at least once. Current smokers were defined as those who smoked at least one cigarette per day. The results showed that the rate of previous suicide attempts was significantly higher for current smokers than for nonsmokers, both for men and women.

They performed two multiple logistic regression analyses to estimate the adjusted odds ratios with 95% confidence intervals for current smoking and other possible predictors: sex, age, marital status, education, income level, employment status, psychiatric diagnosis (involving five dummy variables), alcohol drinking habits, and level of depression. In the first regression, severe depression, current smoking, male gender and anxiety disorder were associated with previous suicide attempts and entered the model in this order as significant predictors. In the second regression, severe depression, schizophrenia, female gender, current smoking and major affective disorder were associated with suicidal ideation. The authors suggested that depression could be the "third factor" linking smoking to suicidal behavior. It is known that nicotine use can provoke depression (Glassman, 1993) but, on the other hand, people with depressive symptoms find nicotine to be an effective self-medication and, in some individuals, nicotine may act as an antidepressant (Salin-Pascual et al, 1996).

• Two studies with a large sample

Two large-scale studies published in 2000, tried to clarify the association between smoking and suicide (Miller, Hemenway, & Rimm, 2000; Miller et al., 2000). A prospective study of 50,000 American men, followed up prospectively for 8 years, found a dose-response relationship between smoking and suicide (Miller, Hemenway, & Rimm, 2000). Men were characterized according to their smoking status as never smokers, current smokers or former smokers. Current smokers were characterized as smoking 1 to 14 or 15 or more cigarettes per day. Eighty-two members of the cohort committed suicide in the 8-year period. Smokers were more likely than nonsmokers to be unmarried, to be less physically active, to drink alcohol and drink heavily, to consume coffee, and to develop cancer. These tendencies were most pronounced in heavy smokers and least pronounced in former smokers. Compared with never-smokers, heavy smokers were at increased risk for suicide. The risk of suicide increased with the number of cigarettes smoked daily: current smokers of 15 or more cigarettes per day had more than 4 times the risk of suicide compared with never-smokers. The suicide risk among former smokers was intermediate between the risks among never and current smokers.

One possible interpretation of these results is that smokers and nonsmokers differ on many characteristics related to the risk of suicide. Depression (Kendler et al., 1993), schizophrenia (Lohr & Flynn, 1992; De Leon et al., 1995), alcohol and illicit drug use (Istavan & Matarazzo, 1984), suicidal ideation and suicide attempts (Tanskanen et al., 1998), developing cancer, not being married, and otherwise being socially isolated are all risk factors for suicide that are more common among smokers than among nonsmokers. Compared with nonsmokers, smokers also tend to act out hostility and have obsessional traits and anxiety (Chiles, Benjamin & Cahn, 1990).

Four possible explanations for the smoking-suicide connection have been proposed: (1) depression is a common antecedent of suicide and a condition that leads to smoking as a form of self-medication; (2) smoking alters brain chemistry, leading to depression, which increases the risk of suicide; (3) smoking leads to malignant disease, such as cancer, which increases the risk of suicide; and (4) smoking is associated with other characteristics that predispose individuals to suicide, such as low self-esteem.

Miller et al. (2000) examined the relation between cigarette smoking and suicide in a cohort study of 300,000 male American soldiers. The authors took into account a number of potential confounders, including age, race, alcohol intake, marital status, education, military rank, and physical activity. During the follow-up period, there were 113 suicides in the cohort. Miller et al. found that smokers were more likely than nonsmokers to be white, drink heavily, be married, be less educated, be of enlisted rank, and exercise less often. Except for marital status, these tendencies were more extreme in heavy smokers than in light smokers. The suicide rate increased with an increasing number of cigarettes smoked daily.

Multivariable-adjusted analyses showed that, compared with never-smokers, the relative risks of suicide were 1.2 for smokers of 10 or fewer cigarettes a day, 1.8 for smokers of 11-20 cigarettes a day, and 2.3 for smokers of more than 20 cigarettes a day. The relative risk of suicide for former smokers was 1.3. As in the general population, smokers in the cohort were more likely to have established risk factors for depression, such as being white, drinking heavily, not attending college and not exercising. After controlling for these factors, they found a strong, positive, and dose-related association between smoking and completed suicide. In other words, their findings indicated that the smoking-suicide connection was not explained by the greater tendency of smokers to be white, drink heavily, have less education, be of enlisted rank, and exercise less often. A limitation of this study was a lack information about some risk factors for suicide, including mental illness.

- ***Smoking, alcohol and coffee: the "everyday substance abuse disorder"***

Some authors have suggested that smoking cigarettes increases the risk of suicide if it is associated with heavy use of alcohol and coffee. Tanskanen et al. (2000) followed up 36,689 subjects in whom smoking was assessed using a standard set of questions. The amount of coffee drinking was determined with an open-ended question: "How many cups of coffee do you usually drink daily?" Alcohol intake was measured as the amount of pure alcohol used per week. In this sample, 138 suicides occurred among the men (55.0 per 100,000 per year) and 31 suicides among the women. The most common suicide methods were hanging (n =74), firearm (n= 39) and drug overdose (n=30). The results showed that the adjusted relative risk of suicide increased linearly with increasing level of joint heavy use of alcohol, cigarettes and coffee. According to the stress-diathesis model of the neurobiology of suicide (Mann, 1998), the authors suggested that alcohol and smoking are involved in serotonergic dysfunction, and caffeine can activate the noradrenaline neurons. Another hypothesis (Markou et al, 1998) suggests that people with mental health problems could self-medicate with alcohol, cigarettes and coffee in an attempt to obtain relief from the symptoms. However, in some circumstances, this self-medication may lead to substance abuse, which worsens the problem, eventually leading to suicidal behavior.

Iwasaki and coworkers (2005) examined a sample of 45,209 middle-aged Japanese men to investigate the following issues: (1) the effect of smoking status and the dose–response relationship, such as pack-years or number of cigarettes smoked per day; (2) the effect of smoking cessation; and (3) the effect of age at the start of smoking. The data came from from the Japan Public Health Center-based Prospective Study on Cancer and Cardiovascular Disease (JPHC Study), which began in 1990 for Cohort I and in 1993 for Cohort II. The study population was defined as all residents aged 40 to 59 years in Cohort I and 40 to 69 years in Cohort II. A self-administered questionnaire was distributed by hand or mail to the JPHC study subjects in 1990 (Cohort I) and in 1993 and 1994 (Cohort II). Among the eligible subjects, 45,452 men returned the questionnaire. The subjects were asked about their personal and family medical histories, anthropometric factors, smoking history, habitual intake of foods and beverages (including alcohol), physical activity, and other lifestyle factors. Questions concerning current or former smoking status, age at the start of smoking, number of cigarettes consumed per day, and age at the cessation of smoking were included in questionnaires. All registered subjects were followed from January 1 of the year of the baseline questionnaire survey until December 31, 1999 (Cohort I), and December 31, 2000 (Cohort II). During the follow-up period, 173 suicides occurred.

The results showed that current smokers with more than 60 pack-years of cigarettes had a significantly higher risk of suicide than that of never-smokers. Among current smokers, the suicide risk increased as the number of cigarettes smoked per day at baseline increased. This association was statistically significant even after adjusting for potential confounders such as the duration of smoking. The duration of smoking was not significantly associated with the suicide risk. The results indicated that heavy smokers, rather than long-term smokers, have a significantly increased risk of suicide. Additionally, since nicotine dependence has been associated with the risk of major depression (Breslau et al, 1993), the number of cigarettes smoked per day, rather than the duration of smoking, might be more strongly correlated with mental disorders, such as depression or one or more of the factors predisposing the subject to mental disorders that increase the risk of suicide (Harris & Barraclough, 1997). Another interesting result showed that the associations between subsequent suicide and the pack-years of cigarette smoking and the number of cigarettes smoked per day were somewhat attenuated, and the statistical significance disappeared, when the suicides which occurred during the first 2 years of the follow-up period were excluded. The statistical significance was preserved when subjects with a past history of chronic diseases were excluded. The lack of statistical significance might reflect the reduction in the number of cases or a lack of statistical power. Alternatively, the exclusion of the suicides that occurred during the first 2 years of the follow-up period, may have served as a control for the effects of mental illness on the risk of suicide to some extent.

- ***Studies in the psychiatric population***

Regarding mental health status, one study (Statham et al., 1998) investigated the clinical predictors of suicidal behavior after a major depressive episode in patients with a major depressive disorder or a bipolar disorder. The results supported a stress-diathesis model for suicidal behavior with stressors as precipitants for suicidal acts and a tendency toward pessimism and a propensity for aggression/impulsivity as the diathesis.

The authors studied a total of 308 patients, aged 18–75 years, with a DSM-III-R major mood disorder (79% with major depressive disorder and 21% with bipolar disorder) based on the Structured Clinical Interview for DSMIII-R (SCID). Exclusion criteria were current substance or alcohol abuse, neurological illness, or active medical conditions that could confound diagnosis and the clinical characterization of psychopathology. Patients were evaluated after 3 months, 1 year and 2 years. A multivariate Cox proportional hazards analysis, that included all correlates of past suicide attempts and additional risk factors identified from the literature, showed that a history of suicide attempt, a higher subjective rating of depression severity (using the Beck Depression Inventory), and cigarette smoking were the three strongest predictors. The effect of these predictors on the risk of suicidal acts in the follow-up period, was additive. In this study, smoking was associated with alcohol or other substance use disorder, and substance use disorders have been reported to increase the risk for eventual suicidal behavior (Statham et al., 1998).

This effect may be mediated through pharmacologically-induced disinhibition, depletion of monoamines, a common diathesis, or an association with relevant psychopathology such as aggression/ impulsivity. Perhaps some of the predictive power of cigarette smoking stems from its association with these other risk factors. Indeed, cigarette smokers have been found to have lower serotonergic functioning than nonsmokers (Malone et al., 2003) and more aggressive/impulsive traits (Meulemans et al., 1992; Tanskanen et al., 1998).

Iancu et al. (2006) studied the risk factors for suicidal behavior, using the suicide risk scale (SRS), in medicated smoking and medicated nonsmoking schizophrenic patients. In a small sample of 61 persons, they found a higher suicide risk in smoking patients and a trend for higher impulsivity. The small sample is a limitation of this study.

Recently Schneider and colleagues (2009) investigated the association between smoking and suicide among patients with personality disorders and affective disorders, with two hypotheses:

(1) The association between psychiatric disorders, sociodemographic variables and suicide is modified by smoking status (never smokers, former smokers, and current smokers);
(2) Adjustment for social factors and life events might alter the association between suicide, smoking status and psychiatric disorders.

In a sample of 263 suicides, the authors found that affective disorders predicted increased suicide risk in smokers, non-smokers, and former smokers, with the highest increased risk in never smokers. Suicide risk associated with substance use disorders was elevated by current smoking. No professional training and at least one significant life event during the last three months led to a higher increased suicide risk in smokers than in never and former smokers.

- ***Three longitudinal studies***

Breslau et al. (2005) studied a sample of 1,200 persons interviewed initially in 1989, with repeated assessments over a 10-year follow-up. The authors controlled for potential confounders, including major depression and substance abuse disorder. The results indicated an increased risk for subsequent suicidal thoughts or attempts associated with current daily smoking. A history of past daily smoking did not significantly predict subsequent suicidal thoughts or attempts.

The estimated risk for subsequent suicidal thoughts or attempts associated with current daily smoking was reduced somewhat when it was adjusted for major depression but remained significant. The estimated risk was further reduced when adjusted additionally for alcohol and drug use disorders but remained significant. The adjusted estimates of suicidal thoughts and attempts associated with current daily smoking were significantly higher than the estimates associated with past daily smoking. In other words, compared with never daily smokers, current daily smokers had an increased risk of subsequent suicidal thoughts or attempts. The limitations of the study were that there were no data on completed suicide and that the number of suicide attempts was small and was, therefore, combined with suicidal thoughts.

Kaisa et al. (2009) found that longitudinal smoking habits were a risk for early onset and repetitive suicide attempts in a cohort study of 12,058 persons.

In this prospective longitudinal study, they found that the prevalence of hospital-treated suicide attempters was greater among prolonged smokers compared with ex-smokers and infrequent smokers in both sexes. During the follow-up period, up to the age of 39 years, female cohort members with prolonged or adult-onset smoking were found to be at increased risk for early-onset suicide attempts. Among men, a corresponding association was found only among adult smokers. A novel finding was that female cohort members with adult/prolonged smoking repeated suicidal acts more often than male cohort members.

Boden, Fergusson and Horwood (2007) found different results. In their 25-year longitudinal study, they found that the associations between the frequency of cigarette smoking and suicidal behavior may be explained largely by non-observed background factors and life circumstances that are associated with both cigarette smoking and suicidal behavior. In this study a birth cohort of 1,265 children (635 males, 630 females) born in the Christchurch (New Zealand) urban region in mid-1977 was studied at birth, 4 months, 1 year and annually to age 16, and again at ages 18, 21 and 25. The cohort was recruited by contacting all mothers giving birth in all Christchurch maternity hospitals during a 4-month period in mid-1977. The study has collected information from a variety of sources including parental interviews, teacher reports, self-reports, psychometric assessments, and medical and other records. The data were collected by trained interviewers via face-to-face or telephone interviews. A statistical analysis, conducted in three stages, has shown an evidence of clear and significant tendencies for increasing frequency of smoking to be associated with increasing levels of suicidal ideation and increasing rates of suicide attempts. After adjustment for fixed effects, there remained a modest, but statistically non-significant association between cigarette smoking and suicide attempts, suggesting that cigarette smoking does not play a causal role *per se* in increasing the risk of suicidal behavior and that these associations largely reflected the effects of non-observed background factors and adverse life experiences that are correlated with cigarette smoking and both suicidal ideation and suicide attempts.

b. Studies that Found an Indirect Relationship between Smoking and Suicide

Beratis et al. (1997) studied the positive association between smoking and suicide to see if this correlation could be secondary to existing psychological factors (see Doll & Peto, 1976). In this study, the authors started from the research that smokers have particular personality characteristics. For example, smokers have been described as more extraverted, (Eysenck et al., 1960) more psychopathic (McManus & Weeks, 1982) and more impulsive, with more risk-taking, danger-loving and belligerent behavior toward authority (Royal College of Physicians, 1977). In addition, smokers have been reported to be more disagreeable than nonsmokers (Smith, 1969), more spontaneous, more likely to seek stimuli, and more sensitive to feeling distressed. The sample was 100 consecutive suicide attempters admitted to a Greek General University Hospital from January 1992 to July 1995. Fifty-seven of these suicide attempters were female and 43 were male.

A semistructured interview was used to determine the residence, education, profession, marital status, previous suicidal behavior, psychopathology, tobacco smoking, age of initiation of smoking, and alcohol and illicit drug use. One hundred normal subjects matched for age, sex, socioeconomic and marital status, level of education, and place of residence (urban or rural) were used as controls. A second control group consisted of patients with psychiatric disorders matched with the suicide attempters for the parameters already mentioned and for the DSM-III-R diagnosis, age at onset, and approximate number of hospitalizations (designated psychiatric controls). The findings showed that those who smoke, particularly females and heavy smokers of both sexes, were at a greater risk for attempting suicide than those who did not smoke. This association might be either noncausal, resulting from the influence of factors predisposing to both smoking and suicidal behavior, or causal, resulting from a direct nicotine effect on brain function. Dysphoria, a pharmacological effect of nicotine ingested via smoking (Henningfield et al., 1985), could predispose susceptible individuals to impulsive behavior and suicide attempts. On the other hand, the observation that female suicide attempters had initiated smoking 3.3 years earlier than control subjects suggests that both cigarette smoking and suicide attempts are components of the same personality structure.

Kessler and coworkers (2008) studied the role of mental disorders in the consistently documented association between smoking and suicidal behavior. The data for the study derived from the National Comorbidity Survey Replication (NCS-R), a psychiatric epidemiological survey carried out in a multi-stage clustered area probability sample of the American household population between February 2001 and April 2003. The NCS-R interview was administered in two parts and included questions about suicidal behavior and smoking habits. DSM-IV psychiatric disorders were included as control variables in order to determine whether they statistically explained the association between smoking and suicidal behaviors. Both lifetime and past year disorders were assessed. All logistic regression analyses included controls for age, sex, race, ethnicity, marital status, employment status and family income, in order to control for the effects of ascribed status (i.e., age, sex, race-ethnicity), achieved status (i.e., marital status, employment status), and social statuses and socio-economic status (indicated by family income) that could be associated both with different norms regarding smoking and with differential risk for stressful experiences that predispose people to suicidal behaviors. The results demonstrated that statistically significant odds-ratios (2.9-3.1) were found between 12-month smoking and 12-month suicidal behaviors. However, the associations of smoking with the outcomes became nonsignificant after controls for DSM-IV psychiatric disorders. These findings are consistent with an interpretation that psychiatric disorders, or some causal factors of which psychiatric disorders are markers, cause both smoking and suicidal behaviors.

5. Smoking Cessation and Suicide Risk: Epidemiological Data

Smoking is an acknowledged to be an immense, increasing, modifiable risk factor for certain injuries, injury precursors and illnesses. Research indicates that smoking causes a physical dependence on nicotine, and this results in a withdrawal syndrome that includes worsened mood and other behaviors that would increase the risk of aggressive behavior and suicide attempts (Hughes, 2007a, 2007b). Many studies have found that negative affect symptoms are the most common symptoms of tobacco withdrawal, and several studies suggest that smoking cessation can precipitate a clinical depression in a subset of smokers (Hughes, 2006). Thus, increased suicidal behavior early after nicotine withdrawal is plausible. In contrast, most data indicate that prolonged abstinence for months or even years is associated with less, not more, depressed mood (US Department of Health and Human Services, 1990a).

Only one study has clearly quantified suicidal ideation early after smoking cessation. In this study, among 304 women who tried to stop smoking, 21 (7%) reported suicidal ideation during the 6 months post-cessation (Tsoh et al., 2000). Although this study lacked a control group, the rate of suicidal ideation is substantially elevated compared to epidemiological studies of smokers not trying to quit. A recent meta-analysis provided significant findings on whether cessation might change suicidal behavior (Leistikow & Shipley, 1999). This analysis searched for smoking cessation trials in which the rates of smoking cessation were ≥10% greater in the active versus the control condition and had a sufficient sample size to detect suicides. The study located three large randomized controlled trials in which the quit rates were 21%–24% greater in the active condition. The pooled rate of suicide in the control conditions in these studies was 0.22%. In the active conditions (in which much more smoking cessation occurred), it was 0.11%. This trend for fewer, not more, suicides in the group who had more abstinence was not statistically significant but certainly contradicts the hypothesis that cessation of smoking increases suicidal behaviors.

a. Association of Suicide and the Use of Smoking Cessation Medications

Two of the major medications for smoking cessation are full agonist nicotine replacement therapies (nicotine gum, patch, inhaler, lozenge/microtab and nasal spray) and the partial nicotine agonist varenicline (®Champix in England, French, Italy). Since full agonist nicotine replacement therapy (West & Shiffman, 2001) and partial agonist therapy (Fagerstrom & Hughes, 2008) both reduce nicotine withdrawal, including depression, this should reduce the appearance of suicidal behavior initially after cessation. On the other hand, since these medications are nicotine agents, the same arguments stated above – (a) nicotine is a psychological toxin and (b) since nicotine is an antidepressant, it might cause suicide – might apply. It could be argued that since varenicline is a partial agonist, its antidepressant effects should be less than that of full agonists and, therefore, the suicide risk should be less. On the other hand, varenicline does have antagonist effects, and nicotine antagonists appear to have antidepressant actions and, therefore, might have the potential to induce suicide (Rabenstein et al., 2006). Because of its potential effects on behavior, varenicline's influence on the mental functioning of the user should be considered in cases of suicide. Therefore, in cases of fatal outcome of patients under therapy with varenicline, a specific analysis for the drug should be performed.

There are two proven non-nicotine smoking cessation medications: antidepressants (McEwen et al., 2006; Hughes et al., 2007) and clonidine (Gourlay et al., 1999). The proven antidepressants are bupropion, an atypical antidepressant, and nortriptyline, a tricyclic antidepressant. The US Food and Drug Administration issued a warning that antidepressants could cause suicide

(Gibbons et al., 2005). This warning was based on data from selective serotonin reuptake inhibitors (which are not effective for smoking cessation), but it has been extended to all antidepressants, including bupropion and nortriptyline (US Food and Drug Administration, 2007a). On the other hand, given that the biological or psychological mechanism of how antidepressants might increase the risk of suicide is unclear, it is unclear whether to expect an increased risk of suicide to occur also with nortriptyline and bupropion. Although there are no reports about suicide during the use of clonidine, an infrequent adverse event from clonidine is depressive symptoms which might lead to suicidal behavior. Rimonabant, a cannabinoid antagonist, is another nonnicotine medication being developed both as a treatment for obesity and for smoking cessation. In two post-mortem studies, completed suicides had higher levels of cannabinoid receptor activation than non-suicides (Vinod & Hungund, 2006). In addition, rimonabant acts similarly to SSRIs in its effects on neurotransmitters and in animal tests of antidepressant activity. Therefore, the antidepressant effects of rimonabant could cause it to increase suicidal behavior (Vinod & Hungund, 2006).

The main nicotine replacement therapies (NRT) are nicotine gum, inhaler, lozenge, microtab, nasal spray and patch (Fiore et al., 2008). Over 20,000 smokers have been exposed to full nicotine agonists via nicotine replacement therapy in published trials (Silagy et al., 2004). Meta-analyses and reviews of adverse events (AEs) from full nicotine agonists do not report increased suicidal behavior or worsened mood as plausible AEs from nicotine replacement (Silagy et al., 2004). The best test of the association of use of nicotine replacement and suicide comes from an analysis from the Lung Health Study, which randomly assigned smokers to nicotine gum or no medication. Over the 5 years of the study, the incidence of suicide was not greater in the nicotine gum versus the control group. If anything, suicides appeared to be less common in the nicotine gum group (0.05%) than in in the control group (0.25%). The only other data come from case reports of intentional overdoses of nicotine replacement therapy or bupropion. Interestingly, none of these attempts occurred in the context of using the medication to stop smoking. All appeared to be due to a pre-existing psychological or psychiatric problem.

b. Which Drug to be Used in Smoking Cessation?

From a review of recent literature, it could be recommended that the first agents to be used in smoking cessation treatment should be NRTs as they are the best documented product with mild side effects. It might be optimal to combine the patch with either gum, inhaler, sublingual tablets or nasal spray. In subjects that have failed with NRTs, varinicline should be the choice. Bupropion is preferred only for subjects with depression or smokers who have failed with the previous two agents, due to the many contra-indications and side effects of bupropion.

Nicotine vaccination is one promising new therapy under development that may have an effect on relapse. The principle is to induce nicotine antibodies into the blood so that inhaled nicotine from cigarette is prevented from reaching the CNS and, in that way, the pleasure from smoking is decreased.

6. Smoking and Suicide in Adolescence

Cigarette smoking among American adults has declined during the past 30 years but, among adolescents, smoking has increased more than 32% (National Center for Health Statistics, 1998). Daily smoking rates among high school seniors decreased between 1976 and 1984 from 28.8% to 18.7% but increased again to 24.6% by 1997 (Johnston, 1998). Despite public education about the dangers of tobacco use, adolescent smoking rates have decreased just slightly to 22.4% in 1998 from 24.6% reported in 1997 (Johnston, 1998). In 1998, the Centers for Disease Control and Prevention (CDC) reported current and frequent tobacco use among adolescents as risk behaviors that increased from 1991 to 1997 (CDC, 1998). Approximately 90% of adult smokers begin smoking as adolescents (Gorin & Arnold, 1998). The mean age of first-time use of tobacco is 14.5 years, and approximately 89% of daily smokers tried cigarettes by age 18 (Smith & Fiore, 1999). Data obtained from the 1997 Youth Risk Behavior Surveillance Survey (YRBSS) indicate that, of the 70.2% high school students who had tried cigarettes, 36.4% became current smokers and 16.7% became frequent smokers (CDC, 1998).

Suicidal behaviors have been associated with other problem behaviors that increase with age, including gun carrying, tobacco use, lack of seatbelt use, and condom nonuse (Brent et al., 1999; Brooks, Harris, Thrall, & Woods,

2002; Woods et al., 1997).The relative contribution of risk factors throughout the adolescent period, however, has yet to be examined thoroughly.

In the United States (Eaton et al., 2006), 71% of all deaths among youth and young adults aged 10-24 years result from four causes: motor vehicle crashes (31%), other unintentional injuries (14%), homicide (15%), and suicide (11%) (CDC, NCHS, 2006). Adolescent suicide and suicidal behaviors have caused great concern within the medical and public health community. Although the incidence of youth suicide has declined over the last decade, suicide remains one of the leading causes of adolescent mortality in the United States (Gould, Greenberg, Velting & Shaffer, 2003). While current annual rates for suicide are low (1.5 per 100,000 for 10–14 year olds and 8.2 per 100,000 for 15–19 year olds), rates of suicidal behaviors in community samples are much higher (De Man & Leduc, 1994; Lewinsohn, Rohde & Seeley, 1994; Reynolds, 1999). The 2001 Youth Risk Behavior Surveillance Survey (YRBS) conducted by the Centers for Disease Control and Prevention (CDC) found that 8.8% of youth had attempted suicide in the prior 12 months (CDC, 2003). Other epidemiological studies suggest that the lifetime rate of suicide attempts ranges from 3% to 15% (Lewinsohn, Rohde, Seeley & Baldwin, 2001).

Suicidal ideation is generally more common in young populations, suggesting important developmental issues (McAuliffe, 2002). In international comparisons of high school students, the prevalence of lifetime suicidal ideation was reported to vary from 19% to 44% (Tomori et al., 2001; Dervic et al., 2005; Liu, Tein, Zhao & Sandler, 2005; Miller & Taylor, 2005; Payci et al., 2005). The assessment of lifetime suicidal ideation is important because it may indicate tolerance of suicidal behavior as a potential coping option (McAuliffe, 2002). Indeed, it has been reported that attitudes exert a distal influence on behavior (Schuman & Johnson, 1976). For example, seeing suicide as a solution to problems might make an individual more prone to suicidal behavior in a crisis situation. Therefore, in addition to current suicidal thoughts, an individual's lifetime suicidal ideation should also be considered relevant in an assessment of suicide risk (McAuliffe, 2002).

Epidemiological studies indicate that the lifetime prevalence of suicide attempts among high school students ranges from 3% to 15% (Lewinsohn, Rohde, Seeley & Baldwin, (2001), with the rates being even higher among indigenous adolescents (up to 30%) (Kirmayer, Brass & Tait, 2000). Affective, disruptive, psychotic and substance abuse disorders are well-known risk predictors related to suicidal behavior in adolescence (Brent, 1995), and female gender is one of the strongest predictors of suicide ideation and attempts (Canetto & Sakinofsky, 1998).

Several explanations for the female predominance in nonfatal suicidal behavior exist and include lethality of methods, differential risk factors and differential socialization (Canetto & Sakinofsky, 1998). Among these, the differential risk factor explanation seems to be a valid potential explanation for the gender difference (Wichstrøm & Rossow, 2002). Adolescent females are found to be significantly more likely to report cigarette use in the past 30 days than are adolescent males (Aaron et al., 1995). Smoking among adolescent females has potential risks for their own future health and also for the infants born to adolescent mothers. Smoking during pregnancy has been implicated in small-for-gestational-age babies, perinatal loss, and premature rupture of membranes (American College of Obstetricians and Gynecologists, 1997). Adolescents engaging in risky behavior, such as drinking, smoking and/or sexual activity, are in increased odds for depression, suicidal ideation, and suicide attempts (Hallfors et al., 2004).

The influence of psychosocial risk factors on children's development and mental health is and has for a long time been a critical issue. Much effort has been made to identify risk factors as well as protective factors and to determine under which circumstances these factors operate (Rutter, 2000). Rohde et al. (2003), for example, included risk factors from 6 categories presumed to contribute to suicide-prone action, thoughts, and feelings for adolescents: demographic factors, suicide/depression, problem behavior factors, personality factors, parent/family factors, and peer factors. Beautrais (2000) noted that the risk factors related to youth suicidal behavior could be categorized into several domains including social and educational disadvantages, childhood and family adversity, psychopathology, individual and personal vulnerabilities, exposure to stressful life events and circumstances, and social, cultural, and contextual factors.

a. Predictors of Suicide in Adolescence

Adolescence has been conceptualized as a period in the lifespan characterized by numerous developmental challenges (e.g., identity formation and individuation from parents) and changes (e.g., puberty), and by the potential for high levels of associated stressful life events (Newcomb, Huba & Bentler, 1981; Windle, 1992). In this regard, research has consistently indicated higher levels of stressors among adolescent suicide attempters (de

Wilde, Kienhorst, Diekstra & Wolters, 1992; Wilson et al., 1995) and completers (Brent, 1995) relative to nonsuicidal controls. Rickelman and Houfek (1995) reviewed research that indicated deficits in problem-solving abilities (e.g., dichotomous thinking and cognitive rigidity) among suicide attempters relative to nonsuicidal individuals. Kotila and Lonnqvist (1988) investigated the suicidal motives among a sample of 15-19 year-old hospitalized suicide attempters and found that an "escape or solution" motive was the one most frequently endorsed by the study's participants (by 35% of boys and 33% of girls). Psychological theories related to sex differences in coping styles and socialization processes offer explanations for these findings. Nolen-Hoeksema (1994) suggested that girls' coping styles are less action-oriented relative to boys' coping styles, and that adolescent girls are more likely to focus on and ruminate about their negative emotions than are boys. She further suggested that the interaction between a ruminative style of coping and higher levels of life stressors among girls accounts for their greater susceptibility to depression. Additionally, the gender intensification hypothesis (Hill & Lynch, 1983) suggests that the developmental period of adolescence is perceived by girls as a more stressful time due to socialization pressures, imposed by peers, parents and society, for girls to conform to traditional gender-specific behaviors (e.g., more interpersonal orientation, greater conformity and less achievement orientation). Whatever the mechanisms that account for sex differences during adolescence, research has been consistent in showing that adolescent girls experience higher levels of depressive symptoms, stressful life events, self-consciousness and social anxiety, and lower levels of self-esteem (Allgood-Merten, Lewinsohn, & Hops, 1990; Hill & Lynch, 1983).

Hemmingsson and Kriebel (2003) found that smoking at 18–20 years of age was associated with suicide during a follow-up period of 26 years. The trend of increasing suicide risk with increasing smoking that was observed is remarkably similar in magnitude to that reported for several other populations (Davey Smith, Phillips & Neaton, 1992; Miller, Hemenway & Rimm, 2000; Tanskanen et al., 2000; Leistikow, Martin & Samuels, 2000). However, unlike many previous studies, a number of indicators of mental well-being, substance abuse, and early life stresses were available for their analysis. When these factors were taken into consideration, there was little evidence for a smoking–suicide association among these young Swedish men. The increased risk of suicide among smokers in early adulthood was almost entirely explained by increased prevalence of people with low mental well-being and by substance abuse among smokers (Hemmingsson & Kriebel, 2003).

Smoking among youths is higher when parents, siblings, or peers smoke (Taylor et al., 2004; Johnson, Myers, Webber & Boris, 2004; Spijkerman, van den Eijnden, Vitale & Engels, 2004). Conduct disorder and parental smoking predicted earlier onset of daily cigarette smoking (Clark & Cornelius, 2004). In a survey of adolescent juvenile offenders, Helstrom et al. (2004) found that parental reports of externalizing problems were significantly related to self-reported tobacco use. Smoking is also higher in youths with histories of early conduct problems, drinking and illegal drug use, depression and suicidal behaviors. Among young people, early conduct problems and associated early onset of daily smoking predict a greater likelihood of becoming nicotine dependent.

Woods et al. (1997) studied 3,054 9th-12th grade adolescents to determine whether suicide attempts were associated with other risk and problem behaviors. Using stepwise logistic regression analysis, Woods found that significant predictors of attempted suicide by adolescents included (a) having had a physical fight (within the past 30 days), (b) regular cigarette use (within the past 30 days), (c) female gender, (d) alcohol (or other drug) use before the most recent sexual activity, (e) lifetime drug use, and (f) being Native American or other races or ethnicities. (Other races and ethnicities were defined as those other than White, Black, Hispanic, and Asian.)

Early use of tobacco and early initiation of sexual intercourse are thought to be related. In a large study of 2,439 9th-12th grade public school students, the investigators found that the behavior most consistently associated with early initiation of sexual intercourse across all racial and gender groups included trying cigarettes and regular cigarette use before the age of 13 (Parillo, Felts & Mikow-Porto, 1997). Regular cigarette use before the age of 13 years was also significantly associated with early sexual intercourse initiation across all gender and racial groups except Black males.

Early cigarette initiation age often results in adult nicotine dependency (Chassin, Presson, Sherman & Edwards, 1990; Giovino et al., 1995). In a longitudinal study of 4,156 adults, researchers found a significant main effect of the school grade at which initiation of smoking occurred. The earlier the school grade of smoking onset, the greater risk of regular adult smoking (Chassin, Presson, Sherman, & Edwards, 1990) and an increase in smoking prevalence (tried cigarette smoking, used cigarettes frequently, and used cigarettes regularly) among students in higher grades (Kann et al., 1995). Parillo et al.'s (1997) research identified a relationship between cigarette smoking and early sexual initiation. According to the CDC (1994), the average

age of first- time sexual experience is 17 years in females and 15 to 16 years in males.

Factors positively associated with a history of suicidal ideation are female gender, being a victim of bullying, lack of parental supervision, loneliness, age, current cigarette smoking, and alcohol use. Persistently high levels of problem drinking and depressive symptoms are associated with higher levels of suicidal thoughts and attempts. Higher levels of depressive symptoms and greater cigarette and illicit drug use distinguish suicidal ideators from attempters. Adolescents attempting suicide report lower levels of family social support, a greater use of substances to cope with stressors, and a higher density of substance-using peers (Windle & Windle, 1997). Moreover, Dong and colleagues (2005) found a graded relationship between the frequency of childhood residential moves and deleterious health outcomes throughout the lifespan, including early sexual initiation, teenage pregnancy, depressed affect, attempted suicide, smoking and alcoholism. Similarly, as the number of ACEs (Adverse Childhood Experiences) increased, the risk of these outcomes also increased. Thus, the apparent relationship between childhood residential mobility and negative health and social outcomes is mostly, if not solely, due to the effects of underlying ACEs that occur with high frequency in extremely mobile families. Children in these situations are likely coping with ACEs that have their own direct effects on childhood development and that may also exacerbate the vulnerabilities that accompany changes in residences, schools, and various social attachments.

All of these factors have been described as being associated with suicidal ideation in other studies (Lam et al., 2004; Borges, Walters & Kessler, 2000; McKeown et al., 1998; Parks, Schepp, Jang & Koo, 2006; Ali & Maharajh, 2005). It is also important to recognize that not all suicidal ideation will result in later suicide attempts or suicide (American Academy of Child and Adolescent Psychiatry Association, 2000). In line with the findings of previous longitudinal studies and reviews, a history of a suicidal act was found to be a significant predictor (Fergusson, Horwood, Ridder & Beautrais, 2005; Apter & King, 2006) irrespective of age, that is, it was a predictor across the entire period of adolescence (Lewinsohn, Rohde, Seeley & Baldwin, 2001; Lewinsohn, Rohde & Seeley, 1994; Fergusson, Beautrais & Horwood, 2003; Bridge, Goldstein & Brent, 2006; Foley, Goldston, Costello & Angold, 2006), while not living with both biological parents was a predictor relevant to middle adolescence (Wichstrøm, 2000) and a diagnosis of any depressive disorder was a predictor relevant to late adolescence/late adulthood (Lewinsohn, Rohde, Seeley & Baldwin, 2001; Bridge, Goldstein & Brent, 2006; Foley,

Goldston, Costello & Angold, 2006), even when adjusted for familial, peer and individual factors. Nrugham and colleagues (2008) found that the quality of the relationship with parents and the use of stimulants, intoxicants and narcotics, although significant, differed according to age and the point in time in their importance as significant independent predictors of suicidal acts. Early indulgence in high risk behaviors such as use of alcohol or narcotics is significant in bivariate analyses (Lewinsohn, Rohde & Seeley, 1994), and daily smoking is significant as a bivariate predictor of suicidal acts performed up to early adulthood, indicating these as high risk factors across the entire period of adolescence.

In order to identify differences in risk factors for suicide attempts throughout adolescence, Hacker and colleagues (2006) conducted a school-based survey of ninth and eleventh graders. Suicide attempts were associated with cigarette and alcohol use, family violence, and depression for ninth graders and with illicit drug use, school violence, and sexual abuse for eleventh graders, while having friends was protective for both groups. Additionally, having more than one risk factor imparted an exponential risk for suicide attempts. There were important differences in the risk factors for ninth and eleventh graders consistent with the developmental changes of adolescence. "Worry about depression" was a predictor of suicide attempts for both groups. The risk of suicide attempts for ninth graders who were worried about depression was almost double that for eleventh graders. The relationship between depression and suicide attempts was not.

Lewinsohn et al. (2001) found that suicide attempts decreased with age more significantly than major depression did. While developmental maturation and decreasing impulsivity may be partly responsible for this change, it is also likely that psychopathology plays a more important role with age. This may be particularly true of substance abuse, which peaks in later adolescence. Brent et al.'s (1999) psychological autopsy study found that older adolescent suicides were more likely to be substance abusers and have conduct and mood disorders than younger suicides. Hacker and colleagues (2006) found that substance use increased the risk for suicide attempts for students in both grades. For ninth graders, alcohol and cigarette use made it into the final model, while for eleventh graders, other drugs played a more significant role.

The typical sequence of drug use in adolescence begins with cigarettes and alcohol and progresses to illicit substances (Kandel, Yamaguchi & Chen, 1992). While individual risk factors are significant predictors of suicide attempts, having multiple risk factors increases the risk for suicide attempts exponentially in both grades. The cumulative risk of exposure to violence, substance use and depression is of particular concern. Although true for both grades, this cumulative effect was particularly strong for ninth graders, suggesting that the impact of cumulative risk on younger adolescents may be greater. Risk behaviors are less frequent in ninth grade and their presence, therefore, is even more indicative of major problems. Identifying these students early and connecting them to services is an important step in prevention.

In another study based on students at the secondary grammar school Dervic et al. (2007) reported a comparatively greater prevalence of lifetime suicidal ideation and depression. In this context, a number of factors such as school stress, class, well-being, teacher support and grades/achievement have been reported to be associated with adolescent depression (Undheim & Sund, 2005) and suicidal ideation (De Man & Leduc, 1995). Given that school problems are a risk factor in youth suicidal behavior (Gould et al., 1996), the relationship between school-associated factors and adolescent suicidal ideation/behavior warrants further study in adolescents. Dervic et al. found that adolescent lifetime suicidal ideation was associated with substance problems and cigarette smoking. Substance problems are often reported as a risk factor in adolescent suicidal ideation and behavior (De Man & Leduc, 1995; Wu et al., 2004; Shaffer et al., 1996), and school pupils requiring the attention of health professionals for suicidal ideation or behavior should be asked about substance use and directed to appropriate treatment if necessary (Brener, Hassan & Barrios, 1999). Consistent with previous reports (King et al., 2001; Tomori et al., 2001; Takakura, Ueji & Sakihara, 2001; Hallfors et al., 2004), cigarette smoking was associated with suicidal ideation, even after adjusting for the presence of a mood disorder.

A study based on a community sample of urban high school students (Cho, Hallfors & Iritani, 2007) extended previous research by demonstrating that the association between onset of substance use and suicide risk indicators varies both by type of substance and by gender. Controlling for current substance use, it was found that, for boys, earlier initiation of hard drug use was significantly associated with all of the suicide risk factors, while early cigarette use was associated with suicide ideation. For girls, early onset of cigarette smoking was associated with suicide ideation, suicide ideation combined with alcohol and/or drug use, and endorsement of suicide. For girls, early onset of getting drunk was associated with depressive symptoms, and early onset of hard drug use was associated with suicide ideation combined with alcohol and/or drug use. Early onset of substance use is known to be a marker for co-occurring problem behaviors among adolescents. Thus, both early onset and current use of substances are related to suicide risk, and there are significant differences by gender as well as by type of substance use in these associations, especially in males. Males who are involved in behaviors such as smoking, drinking and using drugs, who are victims of bullying, and who have a homosexual orientation or bisexual orientation should be observed closely because they may have the potential for developing suicidal behavior (Parks, Schepp, Jang & Koo, 2006). Males who reported smoking were 2.6 times more likely to report suicidal ideation than males who did not report smoking. This may be related to the relationship of smoking and depression for males (Hurford, Smith & Cole, 2003; Weiss et al., 2005). Therefore, boys who have early onset of hard drug use should be screened for suicide risk and should be counseled to reduce or quit hard drug use. g Girls who had an early onset of smoking or alcohol use should similarly be screened.

Smoking is not only associated with suicide attempts, but also with self-mutilation behavior (Makikyro et al., 2004). However, the direction of the causality between smoking, attempted suicide, and self-mutilation remains unclear. Smoking adolescents who attempt suicide or mutilate themselves may have impaired catecholaminergic and 5-HT function in the CNS, leading to more impulsive and aggressive behavior than adolescents who have suicidal ideation alone (Linnoila & Virkkunen, 1992). Exposure to nicotine during adolescence causes changes in the CNS noradrenergic, dopaminergic, and serotonergic (5HT) function (Trauth et al., 2001; Xu et al., 2002). Thus, it is tempting to speculate that adolescents who smoke may be attempting to "self-medicate" their feelings of depression, despair, impulsivity and suicidality.

In conclusion, school health personnel and clinicians assessing suicidal risk among adolescents should be alerted to the importance of a history of a suicidal act, a diagnosis of any depressive disorder and not living with both biological parents as powerful potential predictors of suicidal acts from early adolescence to early adulthood.

b. Protective Factors

Protective factors for suicide in adolescence include family cohesion and stability, coping and problem solving skills, positive self-worth and impulse control, positive connections to school and extracurricular participation, academic success, good relationships with other youths, seeking adult help when needed, lack of access to suicidal means, access to mental health care, religiosity, and sports.

The protective role of youth involvement in sports and the lesser opportunity to smoke among youths involved in religious practice has also been reported. Chen and colleagues (2004) reported that the degree of religious practice is inversely related to the earliest stages of smoking (i.e., the first chance to try a cigarette and the first actual use). With increased religious practice, there was a reduced likelihood of smoking. The occurrence of the first actual use of tobacco was not associated with religious practice among youths who had already been exposed to the opportunity to try a cigarette. In a survey of Hungarian adolescents, Piko et al. (2004), reported that religiosity was inversely related to tobacco use. Those investigators also reported that membership of a sports club was inversely related to smoking.

c. Smoking, Suicide and Psychiatric Disorders in Adolescents

The association between smoking and suicidality has been studied among adult psychiatric patients (Mann et al., 1999; Tanskanen et al., 1998), but no previous studies have focused on adolescent psychiatric inpatients.

In a recent study (Riala, Viilo, Hakko & Rasanen, 2007), it was found that adolescents who are heavy daily smokers are at increased risk for suicidal attempts compared to non-smoking adolescents undergoing inpatient psychiatric hospitalization. This association was positive even after adjusting for the presence of psychiatric disorders. No association was observed between the heaviness of smoking and suicidal ideation. Among adolescents with severe psychiatric illnesses, heavy daily smoking may increase the risk of suicidal behavior independently of current psychiatric diagnosis. The degree of nicotine dependence of an adolescent should, therefore, be carefully assessed as part of a psychiatric evaluation.

Compared with current smokers, former smokers reported lower levels of delinquency, less coping through taking drugs, lesser availability of cigarettes, and less alcohol and marijuana use. Huebner and colleagues (2005) reported less depression, fewer suicidal thoughts, and fewer suicide attempts in former smokers than in current smokers. Makikyro et al. (2004), analyzed data from 157 patients (age 12–17 years) admitted to a psychiatric hospital in Oulu, Finland. They found that daily smoking was associated with suicide attempts after controlling for depression. In addition, adolescent smokers had three times greater risk for frequent self-mutilation. Hallfords et al. (2004), in a survey of 15–19-year-olds from the National Longitudinal Study of Adolescent Health, showed that smoking was associated with significantly increased odds of depression, suicidal ideation, and suicide attempts. The associations with suicidal ideation and attempt remained after statistical adjustment for depression. Toros et al. (2004) surveyed 4,256 Turkish adolescents (age 10–20 years) and found that regular smoking was associated with suicide attempts after controlling for depression.

As reported for both adults (Beratis, Lekka & Gabriel, 1997) and adolescents (Andrews et al., 2004; D'Eramo et al., 2004; Mäkikyrö et al., 2004), there is an increased frequency of psychiatric disorders among those who attempt suicide. Cigarette smoking has been reported to be more common among psychiatric patients with major depression (Hughes, Hatsukami, Michell & Dahlgren, 1986; Kendler et al., 1993), schizophrenia (Lohr & Flynn, 1992; Goff, Henderson & Amico , 1992; De Leon et al., 1995), and anxiety disorders (Breslau, Kilbey & Andreski, 1991; Glassman, 1993).

Smoking among adolescents with depressed mood or with a diagnosis of depression was not associated with a greater risk of suicidal ideation. Furthermore, despite reports to the contrary (Upadhyaya, Deas, Brady & Kruesi, 2002), tobacco smoking at age 15 was not predictive of later depressive disorder. A recent study (Fergusson, Goodwin & Horwood, 2003), suggested a small but significant association between depression and tobacco smoking and argued for a self-medication hypothesis whereby depressed individuals smoke to reduce their symptoms of depression. There are strong associations between anxiety and depression among young people (Fergusson, Goodwin & Horwood, 2003; McGee et al., 1990) and between smoking and anxiety disorders such as panic disorder (Breslau & Klein, 1999).

Previous studies have consistently reported that the prevalence of cigarette smoking among schizophrenic patients is higher than in the general population (Hughes, Hatsukami, Mitchell & Dahlgren, 1986; de Leon et al., 1995), a finding that has been interpreted as a reflection of self-medication for either symptoms of the disease or the adverse side effects of treatment. Weiser et al. (2004) reported that smokers were at higher risk for later onset of schizophrenia. Compared with nonsmokers, male adolescents who smoked one to nine cigarettes per day were 1.4 times more likely to be hospitalized for schizophrenia during the follow-up period, and adolescents who smoked 10 or more cigarettes per day were at 2.3 times greater risk. The latter difference remained statistically significant after controlling for cognitive performance, social adjustment, presence of non-psychotic mental illness, and socio-economic status. The authors noted the limitation due to the lack of data on use of cannabis (previously found to be associated with an elevated risk for schizophrenia) in this sample.

The significantly increased frequency of psychiatric disorders in the suicide attempters persisted after correction for several confounding factors including smoking (Menti et al., 2007). The independent effect of smoking on suicidal behavior from that caused by the presence of psychiatric disorders was also shown by the significantly greater frequency of smoking in the suicide attempters with psychiatric disorders than in non-suicidal control subjects matched for psychiatric disorder.

The significance of the smoking habits of adolescent psychiatric patients is often obscured by their severe other problems which may preclude attention to smoking. Smoking cessation should be supported because it may play a role in recovery from suicidality (Hintikka et al., 2001).

A surprisingly high proportion of the girls who smoked reported self-mutilation behavior. Suicidality among individuals with self-mutilation behaviors has often been underestimated and interpreted as manipulative or attention-seeking behavior. A recent study by Stanley et al. (2001) indicated that the number of suicide attempts or the lethality of the attempts did not differ between patients with and without a history of self-mutilation. Self-mutilators commonly underestimate the lethality of their suicidal behavior and view death with less finality. Depression, anxiety, disruptive disorders, and substance abuse/dependence have been found to be risk factors for attempted and completed suicides among teenagers (Gould et al., 1998; Marttunen et al., 1991; Shaffer et al., 1996). Many authors have noted that young women engage in more suicidal gestures, whereas young men have more completed suicides (Husain, 1990; King et al., 1993; Woods et al., 1997). Individuals with depression are also at a higher risk for attempting suicide and self-mutilation. According to some previous studies (King et al., 2002; Mann et al., 1999), smoking is independently associated with suicidality even after controlling for psychiatric diagnoses (Makikyro et al., 2004).

Two additional predictor variables have been found to contribute significantly to suicide attempts. These contributing factors exert an independent effect on suicidal behavior, including the effect of both smoking and presence of psychiatric disorders. Parent-child relational problems are by far the most frequent of the other conditions that may be a focus of clinical attention observed in slightly less than half of the attempted suicides, followed by relational problems. Of the psychosocial and environmental problems, health problems in family, parental overprotection, death of a family member, and parental divorce are the most frequent problems observed. It should be mentioned, however, that becoming drunk or any drinking, including alcohol and coffee, has been associated with suicidal ideation and suicide attempts

(Hallfors et al., 2004; King et al., 2001). Other possible risk factors, such as the maternal and paternal smoking status does not contribute to attempting suicide. Hashish, a well-known risk factor (Breslau, Kilbey & Andreski, 1991; Glassman, 1993; Tomori et al., 2001) was the illicit substance used by only 3 attempters and 1 of the psychiatric control subjects. These findings indicate the relative importance of the risk factors that lead young people to make suicide attempts.

Menti et al. (2007), argued that the association between smoking and suicide attempts was related to personality characteristics of the smokers rather than to a direct effect of nicotine. Smokers are characterized by impulsivity, excitement seeking, low self-discipline, lack of careful consideration of the consequences of their actions, risk taking, thrill and danger seeking, emotional lability, rebelliousness, novelty seeking, and inattention (Tercyak & Audrain-McGovern, 2003; Terracciano & Costa, 2004; Dinn, Aycicegi & Harris, 2004; File, Dinnis, Heard & Irvine, 2002; Jacobs et al., 1966)

d. Children of Mothers at Psychosocial Risk

Life events of different types cause turmoil in the lives of children in a negative way. This exposure to negative life events may continue to affect the next generation.

Wadsby and colleagues (2007) showed that children, especially boys, of mothers who are exposed to psychosocial risks during pregnancy, particularly of those mothers with alcohol/drug problems, mental ill-health, poor self-image, negative life events and lack of confidence for their futures, reported more symptoms of poor mental health than children of non-risk mothers. It seems that there is a socially disadvantageous inheritance passed on from mothers at psychosocial risk to their children, and this affects the children and their functioning even when they have reached the age of 16. They have a more negative self-image, have experienced more life events of negative character that have been difficult to adjust to, and they more often have not successfully completed compulsory schooling. They have more often been placed in foster-care, are less satisfied with their school situation, and have a less positive opinion about their ability to direct their own future. Habitual smoking is more common among these teenagers. The girls in the index group more often had serious thoughts about committing suicide. In summary, this 16-year follow-up confirmed that children, especially boys, of psychosocial risk mothers are in many aspects worse off than children of non-risk mothers.

In this respect, the outcome of the study was in line with the outcome of other longitudinal studies (Laucht et al., 2000a, 2000b, 2002), with the reservation that these later studies did not necessarily show differences related to gender.

e. Implications for Pediatric and Adolescent Nursing

School nurses, pediatric nurse practitioners, and others who work with adolescents should be aware of the interrelated nature of risk behaviors The identification of adolescents who are current smokers should alert health care providers to assess their clients for other problem behaviors. Early education, prevention, and intervention related to health risk behavior is essential in reducing levels of risk and should be initiated with school-aged and early adolescents in order to be effective in preventing negative outcomes. Other risky behaviors such as sexual activity, substance abuse, and fighting may prove more sensitive for adolescents than does smoking.

Parents and their children need education related to smoking and nicotine addiction beginning as early as elementary school. Parents should be aware that the early initiation of cigarette use increases the risk of addiction in later years and may be an indicator for other risk behaviors. School nurses have the potential for making an impact on the prevention of smoking among grade school children by educating parents about multiple-risk behaviors in early smokers.

f. Prevention

The continued high rates of suicide among adolescents (i.e., persons aged 15–19 years) and young adults (persons aged 20–24 years) have heightened the need for allocation of prevention resources. To better focus these resources, CDC's National Center for Injury Prevention and Control recently published *Youth Suicide Prevention Programs: A Resource Guide*. The guide describes the rationale and evidence for the effectiveness of various suicide prevention strategies and identifies model programs that incorporate these strategies. It is intended as an aid for communities interested in developing or augmenting suicide prevention programs targeted toward adolescents and young adults. There are eight prevention strategies described in the Resource Guide.

School gatekeeper training. This type of program is designed to help school staff (e.g., teachers, counselors, and coaches) identify and refer students at risk for suicide. These programs also teach staff how to respond to suicide or other crises in the school.

Community gatekeeper training. These programs train community members (e.g., clergy, police, merchants, and recreation staff) and clinical health-care providers who see adolescent and young adult patients (e.g., physicians and nurses) to identify and refer persons in this age group who are at risk for suicide.

General suicide education. Students learn about suicide, its warning signs, and how to seek help for themselves or others. These programs often incorporate a variety of activities that develop self-esteem and social competency.

Screening programs. A questionnaire or other screening instrument is used to identify high-risk adolescents and young adults and provide further assessment and treatment. Repeated assessment can be used to measure changes in attitudes or behaviors over time, to test the effectiveness of a prevention strategy, and to detect potential suicidal behavior.

Peer support programs. These programs, which can be conducted in or outside of school, are designed to foster peer relationships and competency in social skills among high-risk adolescents and young adults.

Crisis centers and hotlines. Trained volunteers and paid staff provide telephone counseling and other services for suicidal persons. Such programs also may offer a "drop-in" crisis center and referral to mental health services.

Restriction of access to lethal means. Activities are designed to restrict access to handguns, drugs, and other common means of suicide.

Intervention after a suicide. These programs focus on friends and relatives of persons who have committed suicide. They are designed to help prevent or contain suicide clusters and to help adolescents and young adults cope effectively with the feelings of loss that follow the sudden death or suicide of a peer.

Integrated prevention strategies that address multiple associated factors (e.g., substance abuse prevention, family and peer support, and access to health services) are likely to be more effective in reducing suicidal behavior than programs that focus on a single risk factor (Anderson et al., 2004).

7. Conclusions

Despite the large literature available about smoking as direct risk factor for suicide, the findings are not yet consistent. It is clear that the prevalence of smoking is higher in suicidal people, but it is less certain that smoking itself (or the nicotine effect on brain function) is directly involved in suicidality. Other elements associated with both suicide and smoking may be implicated in this relationship. Inclusion of data on important confounds (i.e., the presence of debilitating smoking-related illness, psychiatric disorder, withdrawal symptoms and patterns of medication use) is necessary. Most likely, several factors contribute to an increased rate of suicidal behavior in current smokers. The three most plausible (but relatively untested) explanations for the association are (1) that smokers have preexisting conditions that increase their risk for suicide, (2) smoking causes painful and debilitating conditions that might lead to suicide, and (3) smoking decreases serotonin and monoamine oxidase levels. Stopping smoking appears to lead to major depression in some smokers and, therefore, it could induce suicide. However, smoking cessation has not been associated with suicide in the few studies conducted. Regulatory agencies have stated that bupropion, rimonabant and varenicline appear to be associated with suicide, but the data for these statements have not been presented in sufficient detail to assess their validity.

The present review indicates that there are important gender differences in the association between substance use and suicide risk. The review also underscores the importance of preventing the early onset of substance use to alleviate mental health problems related to suicide.

Further research is needed to explore the causal mechanisms of gender-specific substance use behavior and suicide risk factors. As Fergusson and Lynskey (1995) suggested, the value of identifying variables that successfully distinguish suicide attempters from ideators relates to our increased ability to identify those adolescents who are at greatest risk for attempting suicide based on their "burden" of psychosocial and behavioral risk indicators.

REFERENCES

Aaron D. J., Dearwater, S. R., Anderson, R., et al. (1995). Physical activity and the initiation of high-risk health behaviors in adolescents. *Med Sci Sports Exerc, 27 (12)*: 1639-1645.

Adler, L. E., Olincy, A., Waldo, M., et al. (1998). Schizophrenia, sensory gating, and nicotinic receptors. *Schizophr Bull, 24 (2)*: 189-202.

Ali, A. & Maharajh, H. D. (2005). Social predictors of suicidal behaviour in Trinidad and Tobago. *Soc Psychiatry Psychiatric Epidemiol 40*, 186-91.

Allgood-Merten, B., Lewinsohn, P. M. & Hops, H. (1990). Sex differences and adolescent depression. *J Abnorm Psychol, 99*, 55-63.

American Academy of Child and Adolescent Psychiatry Association, (2000). Practice Parameters for the assessment and treatment of children and adolescents with suicidal behaviours. [http://www.aacap.org/galleries/PracticeParameters/Suicide.pdf].

American College of Obstetricians and Gynecologists, (1997). Smoking and women's health. *ACOG Educational Bulletin. No. 240*. Washington, DC: Author.

American Psychiatric Association (APA), (2000). *Diagnostic and statistical manual for mental disorders 4th edition, Text Revision*. Washington, DC: Author.

Anderson, R. N., Minino, A. M., Fingerhut, L. A., et al. (2004). Deaths: injuries, 2001. *Natl Vital Stat Rep, 52*, 1–86.

Andrews, J. A. & Lewinsohn, P. M. (1992). Suicidal attempts among older adolescents: prevalence and co-occurrence with psychiatric disorders. *J Am Acad Child Adolesc Psychiatry, 31*, 655-62.

Angst, J. & Clayton, P. J. (1998). Personality, smoking and suicide: a prospective study. *J Affect Disord, 51 (1)*, 55-62.

Apter, A. & King, R. A. (2006). Management of the depressed suicidal child or adolescent. *Child Adolesc Psychiatr Clin N Am, 15 (4)*, 999–1013.

Audrain-McGovern, J., Lerman, C., Wileyto., E. P., et al. (2004). Interacting effects of genetic predisposition and depression on adolescent smoking progression. *Am J Psychiatry, 161*, 1224–1230.

Balfour, D. J. & Ridley, D. L. (2000). The effects of nicotine on neural pathways implicated in depression: a factor in nicotine addiction? *Pharmacol Biochem Behav, 66 (1*), 79-85.

Beautrais, A. L. (2000). Risk factors for suicide and attempted suicide among young people. *Aust N Z J Psychiatry, 34*, 420–436.

Benwell, M., Balfour, D & Anderson, J. (1990). Smoking-associated changes in the serotonergic systems of discrete regions of human brain. *Psychopharmacology 102*, 68-72.

Beratis, S., Lekka., N. P. & Gabriel, J. (1997). Smoking among suicide attempters. *Compr Psychiatry, 38*, 74-9.

Berlin, I., Said, S., Spreux-Varoquaux, O., et al. (1995). Monoamine oxidase A and B activities in heavy smokers. *Biol Psychiatry, 38*, 756-761.

Bernal, M., Haro, J. M., Bernert, S., et al., the ESEMED/MHEDEA Investigators, (2007) Risk factors for suicidality in Europe: results from the ESEMED study. *J Affect Dis, 101*, 27–34.

Boden, J. M., Fergusson, D. M. & Horwood, L. J. (2008). Cigarette smoking and suicidal behaviour: results from a 25-year longitudinal study. *Psychol Med, 38*, 433–439.

Borges, G., Walters, E. E. & Kessler, R. C. (2000). Associations of substance use, abuse, and dependence with subsequent suicidal behavior. *Am J Epidemiol, 151*, 781-9.

Brener, N. D., Hassan, S. S. & Barrios, L. C. (1999). Suicidal ideation among college students in the United States. *J Consult Clin Psychol, 67*, 1004–1008.

Brent, D. A., (1995). Risk factors for adolescent suicide and suicidal behaviour: Mental and substance abuse disorders, family environmental factors, and life stress. *Suicide Life Threat Behav, 25*, 52–63.

Brent, D. A., Baugher, M., Bridge, J., et al., (1999). Age- and sex-related risk factors for adolescent suicide. *J Am Acad Child Adolesc Psychiatry, 38*, 1497–1505.

Breslau, N., Fenn, N. & Peterson, E. L. (1993c). Early smoking initiation and nicotine dependence in a cohort of young adults. *Drug Alcohol Depend, 33*, 129–37.

Breslau, N., Johnson, E. O., Hiripi, E. & Kessler, R. (2001). Nicotine dependence in the United States: prevalence, trends, and smoking persistence. *Arch Gen Psychiatry, 58 (9)*, 810–816.

Breslau, N. & Klein, D. F. (1999). Smoking and panic attacks: an epidemiologic investigation. *Arch Gen Psychiatry, 56*, 1141–1147.

Breslau, N., Kilbey, M. M. & Andreski, P. (1991). Nicotine dependence, major depression, and anxiety in young adults. *Arch Gen Psychiatry, 8*, 1069-74.

Breslau, N., Kilbey, M. M. & Andreski, P. (1993). Nicotine dependence and major depression. New evidence from a prospective investigation. *Arch Gen Psychiatry, 50 (1)*, 31-5.

Breslau, N., Novak, P. & Kessler., R. C., (2004). Daily smoking and the subsequent onset of psychiatric disorder. *Psychol Med, 34*, 323–33.

Breslau, N, Peterson, E. L., Schultz, L. R., et al. (1998). Major depression and stages of smoking. A longitudinal investigation. *Arch Gen Psychiatry, 55 (2)*, 161-6.

Breslau, N., Schultz, L. R., Johnson, E. O., et al. (2005). Smoking and the risk of suicidal behavior: a prospective study of a community sample. *Arch Gen Psychiatry, 62*, 328-334.

Bridge, J. A., Goldstein, T. R. & Brent, D. A. (2006). Adolescent suicide and suicidal behaviour. *J Child Psychol Psychiatry, 47 (3/4)*, 372–394.

Brooks, T. L., Harris, S. K., Thrall, J. S. & Woods, E. R., (2002). Association of adolescent risk behaviors with mental health symptoms in high school students. *J Adolesc Health, 31*, 240–246.

Brown, R. A., Lewinsohn, P. M., Seeley, J. R. & Wagner, E. F. (1996). Cigarette smoking, major depression, and other psychiatric disorders among adolescents. *J Am Acad Child Adolesc Psychiatry, 35 (12),* 1602-10.

Canetto, S. S. & Sakinofsky, I. (1998). The gender paradox in suicide. *Suicide Life Threat Behav*, *28 (1*), 1–23.

Casey, P. R., Dunn, G., Kelly, B. D., et al. on behalf of the ODIN group, (2006). Factors associated with suicidal ideation in the general population. Five-centre analysis from the ODIN study. *Br J Psychiatry*, 189, 410–415.

CDC, (1992) . *Youth suicide prevention programs: a resource guide*. Atlanta: US Department of Health and Human Services, Public Health Service.

CDC, (2008). Annual smoking-attributable mortality. Cigarette Smoking Among Adults-United States. *MMWR Morb Mortal Wkly Rep*, *45*, 1226–1228.

CDC, NCHS, (2006). *Public Use Data File and Documentation: Multiple Cause of Death for ICD-10 2003 Data*. Hyattsville, Md: National Center of Health Statistics.

Centers for Disease Control & Prevention, (1994). Medical care expenditures attributable to cigarette smoking—United States, 1993. *MMWR Morb Mortal Wkly Rep*, *43 (26)*, 469-472.

Centers for Disease Control and Prevention, (2008). *Targeting Tobacco Use: The Nation's Leading Cause of Preventable Death*. Atlanta: Centers for Disease Control and Prevention (CDC), National Center for Chronic Disease Prevention and Health Promotion Division of Cancer Prevention and Control.

Chassin, L., Presson, C. C., Sherman, S. J. & Edwards, D. A. (1990). The natural history of cigarette smoking: Predicting young-adult smoking outcomes from adolescent smoking patterns. *Health Psychol, 9 (6)*, 701-716.

Chen, C. Y., Dormitzer, C. M., Bejarano, J. & Anthony, J. C. (2004). Religiosity and the earliest stages of adolescent drug involvement in seven countries of Latin America. *Am J Epidemiol, 159*, 1180–1188.

Chen, C. Y., Dormitzer, C. M., Gutierrez, U., et al. (2004). The adolescent behavioural repertoire as a context for drug exposure: behavioral autarcesis at play. *Addiction, 99*, 897–906.

Cherpitel, C. J., Borges, G. L. & Wilcox, H. C. (2004). Acute Alcohol Use and Suicidal Behavior: A Review of the Literature. *Alcohol Clin Exp Res, 28 (5),* 18S-28S.

Chiles, J. A., Benjamin, G. A. & Cahn T. S. (1990). Who smokes? Why?

Psychiatric aspects of continued cigarette usage among lawyers in Washington State. *Compr Psychiatry, 31*, 176-18.

Cho, H., Hallfors, D. D. & Iritani, B. J., 2007. Early initiation of substance use and subsequent risk factors related to suicide among urban and high school students. *Addict Behav, 32*, 1628–1639.

Choi, W. S., Patten, C. A., Gillin, J. C., 6 et al., (1997). Cigarette smoking predicts development of depressive symptoms among U.S. adolescents. *Ann Behav Med, 19 (1),* 42-50.

Clark, D. B. & Cornelius, J. (2004). Childhood psychopathology and adolescent cigarette smoking: a prospective survival analysis in children at high risk for substance use disorders. *Addict Behav, 29*, 837–841.

Covey, L. S., Glassman, A. H. & Stetner, F. (1997). Major depression following smoking cessation. *Am J Psychiatry, 154 (2)*, 263-5.

Dalack, G. W., Healy, D. J. & Meador-Woodruff, J. H. (1998). Nicotine dependence in schizophrenia: clinical phenomena and laboratory findings. *Am J Psychiat, 155*, 1490-1501.

Davey Smith, G., Phillips, A. N. & Neaton, J. D. (1992). Smoking as 'independent' risk factor for suicide: illustration of an artifact from observational epidemiology? *Lancet, 340*, 709–12.

De Leon, J. & Diaz, F. J. (2005). A meta-analysis of worldwide studies demonstrates an association between schizophrenia and tobacco smoking behaviors. *Schizophr Res, 76 (2-3)*, 135-57.

De Leon, J., Canuso, C., White, A. O., et al. (1995). Schizophrenia and smoking: an epidemiological survey in a state hospital. *Am J Psychiatry, 152*, 453-455.

De Leon, J., Rendon, D. M., Baca-Garcia, E., et al., (2007). Association between smoking and alcohol use in the general population: stable and unstable odds ratios across two years in two different countries. *Alcohol Alcohol, 42 (3),* 252-7.

De Man, A. F. & Leduc, C. P., (1994). Validity and reliability of a self-report suicide ideation scale for use with adolescents. *Soc Behav Pers, 22*, 261–266.

De Man, A. F. & Leduc, C. P. (1995). Suicidal ideation in high school students: depression and other correlates. *J Clinical Psychology, 51*, 173–181.

De Wilde, EJ, Kienhorst, 1CWM, Diekstra, RFW & Wolters, WHG, (1992). The relationship between adolescent suicidal behavior and life events in childhood and adolescence. *Am J Psychiatry, 149*, 45-51.

Degenhardt, L. & Hall, W. (2001). The relationship between tobacco use, substance-use disorders and mental health: results from the National Survey of Mental Health and Well-being. *Nicotine Tob Res, 3 (3)*, 225-34.

'Eramo, D., Prinstein, K. S., Freeman, M. J., et al. (2004). Psychiatric diagnoses and comorbidity in relation to suicidal behavior among psychiatrically hospitalized adolescents. *Child Psychiatry Hum Dev, 35*, 21-35.

Dervic, K., Akkaya-Kalayci, T., Kapusta, N. D., et al. (2007). Suicidal ideation among Viennese high school students. *Wien Klin Wochenschr, 119 (5-6)*, 174-80.

Dervic, K., Csorba, J., Rosza, S., et al., (2005). Attitudes towards suicide and help-seeking in Hungarian adolescents. *J Am Acad Child Adolesc Psychiatry, 44*, 628–629.

Dinn, W. M., Aycicegi, A. & Harris, C. L. (2004). Cigarette smoking in a student sample: neurocognitive and clinical correlates. *Addict Behav, 29*, 107-26.

Doll, R. & Peto, R. (1976). Mortality in relation to smoking: 20 years' observations on male British doctors. *Br Med J, 2*, 1525-1536.

Dong, M., Anda, R. F., Felitti, V. J., et al., (2005). Childhood residential mobility and multiple health risks during adolescence and adulthood: the hidden role of adverse childhood experiences. *Arch Pediatr Adolesc Med, 159 (12)*, 1104-10.

Eaton, D. K., Kann, L., Kinchen, S., et al., (2006). Youth risk behavior surveillance--United States, 2005. *J Sch Health, 76 (7)*, 353-72.

Ellis, T. E. & Trumpower, D. (2008). Health-risk behaviors and suicidal ideation: a preliminary study of cognitive and developmental factors. *Suicide Life Threat Behav, 38 (3),* 251-9.

Eysenck, H. J., Tarrant, M., Woolf, M. & England, L. (1960). Smoking and personality. *Br Med J, 1*, 1456-1460.

Fagerstrom, K. & Hughes, J. R. (2008). Integrating varenicline into the treatment of tobacco dependence. *Neuropsychiatr Dis Treat*, *4*, 1–11

FDA alert 7/2005. Bupropion hydrochloride (marketed as the antidepressant Wellbutrin) Information. *http://www.fda.gov/cder/drug/infopage/bupropion/default.htm*

FDA05/16/2008. Public Health Advisory Important Information on Chantix (varenicline), *http://www.fda.gov/cder/drug/advisory/varenicline.htm*

Fergusson, D. M. & Lynskey, M. T. (1995). Suicide attempts and suicidal ideation in a birth cohort of 16-year-old New Zealanders. *J Am Acad Child Adolesc Psychiatry, 34*, 1308-1317.

Fergusson, D. M., Beautrais, A. L. & Horwood, L. J. (2003). Vulnerability and resiliency to suicidal behaviours in young people. *Psychol Med, 33*, 61–73.

Fergusson, D. M., Goodwin, R. D. & Horwood, L. J. (2003). Major depression and cigarette smoking: results of a 21-year longitudinal study. *Psychol Med, 33*, 1357–1367.

Fergusson, D. M., Horwood, L. J., Ridder, E. M. & Beautrais, A. (2005). Suicidal behaviour in adolescence and subsequent mental health outcomes in young adulthood. *Psychol Med*, *35*, 983–993.

File, S. E., Dinnis, A. K., Heard, J. E. & Irvine, E. E. (2002). Mood differences between male and female light smokers and nonsmokers. *Pharmacol Biochem Behav*, *72*, 681-9.

Fiore, M., Jaen, C., Baker, T., et al. (2008). *Treating Tobacco Use and Dependence: Clinical Practice Guideline*. US Public Health and Human Services, Washington, DC.

Foley, D. L., Goldston, D. B., Costello, E. J. & Angold, A. (2006). Proximal psychiatric risk factors for suicidality in youth. The Great Smoky Mountains Study. *Arch Gen Psychiatry*, *63*, 1017–1024.

Fotti, S. A., Katz., L. Y., Afifi, T. O. & Cox, B. J. (2006). The associations between peer and parental relationships and suicidal behaviours in early adolescents. *Can J Psychiatry*, *51 (11)*, 698–703.

Fowler. J. S., Logan, J., Wang, G. J. & Volkow, N. D. (2003). Monoamine oxidase and cigarette smoking. *Neuro Toxicology*, *24*, 75–82.

Gibbons, R., Hur, K., Bhaumik, D. & Mann, J. (2005). The relationship between antidepressant medication use and rate of suicide. *Arch Gen Psychiatry*, 62, 165–172.

Giovino, G. A., Henningfield, J. E., Tomar, S. L., et al. (1995). Epidemiology of tobacco use and dependence. *Epidemiol Rev, 17 (1)*, 48-65.

Glassman, A. H., (1993). Cigarette smoking: implications for psychiatric illness. *Am J Psychiatry*, *150*, 546-53.

Glassman. A. H., (1988). Heavy smokers, smoking cessation and clonidine. *JAMA*, *259*, 2863-2866.

Glassman, A. H., Helzer. J. E., Covey, L. S., et al., (1990). Smoking, smoking cessation and major depression. *JAMA, 264*, 1549– 1564.

Goff, D. C., Henderson, D. C. & Amico, E. (1992). Cigarette smoking in schizophrenia: relationship to psychopathology and medication side effects. *Am J Psychiatry*, *149*, 1189-94.

Goodman, E. & Capitman, J. (2000). Depressive symptoms and cigarette smoking among teens. *Pediatrics*, *106*, 748-755.

Gorin, S. & Arnold, J. (1998). *Health promotion handbook*. St. Louis: Mosby, Inc.

Gould, M., King, R., Greenwald, S., et al. (1998). Psychopathology associated with suicidal ideation and attempts among children. *J Am Acad Child Adolesc Psychiatry*. 37(9), 915-923.

Gould, M. S., Fisher, P., Parides, M., et al. (1996). Psychosocial risk factors of child and adolescent completed suicide. *Arch Gen Psychiatry 53*, 1155–1162.

Gould, M. S., Greenberg, T., Velting, D. M. & Shaffer, D. (2003). Youth suicide risk and preventive intervention: A review of the past 10 years. *J Am Acad Child Adolesc Psychiatry*, *42*, 386–405.

Gourlay, S. G., Stead, L. F. & Benowitz, N. L., (1999). *Clonidine for smoking cessation*. The Cochrane Library, www.thecochranelibrary.com.

Grant, B. F., Hasin, D. S., Coun, S. P., et al. (2004). Nicotine dependence and psychiatric disorders in the United States: results from the national epidemiologic survey on alcohol and related conditions. *Arch Gen Psychiatry*, *61*, 1107–1115.

Hacker, K. A., Suglia, S. F., Fried, L. E., et al. (2006). Developmental differences in risk factors for suicide attempts between ninth and eleventh graders. *Suicide Life Threat Behav*, *36 (2)*, 154-66.

Hallfors, D. D., Waller, M. W., Ford, C. A., et al. (2004). Adolescent depression and suicide risk: association with sex and drug behavior. *Am J Prev Med*, *27*, 224–231.

Harris, E. C. & Barraclough, B. (1997). Suicide as an outcome for mental disorders. A meta-analysis. *Br J Psychiatry, 170*, 205–228.

Harrison, E. L. Desai, R. A. & McKee, S. A., (2008). Nondaily smoking and alcohol use, hazardous drinking, and alcohol diagnoses amongyoung adults: findings from the NESARC. *Alcohol Clin Exp Res*, *32 (12),* 2081-7.

Heatherton, T. F., Kozlowski, L. T., Frecker, R. C., et al. (1989). Measuring the heaviness of smoking: using self-reported time to the first cigarette of the day and number of cigarettes smoked per day. *Br J Addict*, *84*, 791-800.

Helstrom, A., Bryan, A., Hutchison, K. E., et al. (2004). Tobacco and alcohol use as an explanation for the association between externalizing behavior and illicit drug use among delinquent adolescents. *Prev Sci, 5*, 267–277.

Hemenway, D., Solnick, S. J. & Colditz, G. A. (1993). Smoking and suicide among nurses. *Am J Public Health*, *83 (2)*, 249-51.

Hemmingsson, T. & Kriebel, D. (2003). Smoking at age 18-20 and suicide during 26 years of follow-up-how can the association be explained? *Int J Epidemiol*, *32 (6*), 1000-4.

Henningfield, J. E., Miyasato, K. & Jasinski, D. R. (1985). Abuse liability and pharmacodynamic characteristics of intravenous and inhaled nicotine. *J Pharmacol Exp Ther 234*, 1-12.

Hill, J. P. & Lynch, M. E. (1983). The intensification of gender related role expectations during early adolescence. In J: Brooks-Gunn & A. C. Petersen (Eds.), *Girls at puberty: Biological and psychosocial perspectives* (pp. 201-228). New York: Plenum Press.

Hintikka, J, Pesonen, T, Saarinen, P & et al., (2001). Suicidal ideation in the Finnish general population. A 12-month follow-up study. *Soc Psychiatry Psychiatr Epidemiol, 36*, 590–4.

Hintikka, J., Koivumaa-Honkanen, H., Lehto, S. M., et al. (2009). Are factors associated with suicidal ideation true risk factors? : A 3-year prospective follow-up study in a general population. *Soc Psychiatry Psychiatr Epidemiol, 44 (1)*, 29-33.

Horesh, N., Rolnick T., Iancu, I., et al. (1997). Anger, impulsivity and suicide risk. *Psychother Psychosom, 66 (2)*, 92-96.

Huebner, A. J., Shettler, L., Matheson, J. L., et al. (2005). Factors associated with former smokers among female adolescents in rural Virginia. *Addict Behav, 30*, 167–173.

Hughes, J. R., Hatsukami, D. K., Michell, J. E., & Dahlgren L. A. (1986). Prevalence of smoking among psychiatric outpatients. *Am J Psychiatry, 143*, 993-7.

Hughes, J. R. (2006). Depression during tobacco abstinence. *Nicotine Tobacco Res, 9*, 443–446.

Hughes, J. R. (2007a). The effects of abstinence from tobacco: etiology, determinants, epidemiology, significance. *Nicotine Tobacco Res, 9*, 329–339.

Hughes, J. R., (2007b). The effects of abstinence from tobacco: valid symptoms and time course. *Nicotine Tobacco Res, 9*, 315–327.

Hurford, D. P., Smith, J. V. & Cole A. (2003). The relationship between depression and smoking in adolescents. *Adolescence, 38*, 149-157.

Husain, S. A. (1990). Current perspective on the role of psychological factors in adolescent suicide. *Psychiatr Ann, 32*, 122–7.

Iancu, I., Sapir, A. P. & Shaked, G. (2006). Increased suicidal risk among smoking schizophrenia patients. *Clin Neuropharmacol, 29 (4)*, 230-7.

Istavan, J. & Matarazzo, J. (1984). Tobacco, alcohol and caffeine use: a review of their interrelationships. *Psychol Bull, 16*, 244-273.

Iwasaki, M., Akechi, T., Uchitomi, Y. & Tsugane, S. (2005). Cigarette smoking and completed suicide among middle-aged men: a population-based cohort study in Japan. *Ann Epidemiol, 15 (4)*, 286-92.

Jacobs, M. A., Anderson, L. S., Champagne, E., et al., (1966). Orality, impulsivity, and cigarette smoking in men: further findings in support of a theory. *J Nerv Ment Dis, 143*, 207-19.

John, U., Meyer, C., Rumpf, H. J. Hapke, U. (2003). Probabilities of alcohol high-risk drinking, abuse or dependence estimated on grounds of tobacco smoking and nicotine dependence. *Addiction, 98 (6)*, 805-14.

Johnson, C. C., Myers, L., Webber, L. S. & Boris, N. W. (2004). Profiles of the adolescent smoker: models of tobacco use among 9th grade high school students; Acadiana Coalition of Teens against Tobacco (ACTT). *Prev Med, 39*, 551–558.

Johnston, L. D. (1998). *National survey results on drug use from the monitoring the future study: 1975-1997: Secondary School Students*. Washington, DC: US Government Printing Office.

.Kamali, M., Oquendo, M. A. & Mann, J. J. (2001). Understanding the neurobiology of suicidal behavior. *Depress Anxiety, 14 (3)*, 164-76.

Kandel, D. B., Yamaguchi, K. & Chen, K. (1992). Stages of progression in drug involvement from adolescence to adulthood: Further evidence for the gateway theory. *J Stud Alcohol, 53*, 446–457.

Kann, L., Warren, C. W., Harris, W. A., et al. (1995). Youth risk behavior surveillance–United States, 1993. *J Sch Health, 65 (5)*, 163-170.

Kassel, J. D. (1997). Smoking and attention: a review and reformulation of the stimulus-filter hypothesis. *Clin Psychol Rev, 17 (5)*, 451-78.

Kelly, T. M., Cornelius, J. R. & Clark, D. B. (2003). Psychiatric disorders and attempted suicide among adolescents with substance use disorders. *Drug and Alcohol Dependence, 73*, 87–97.

Kendler, K. S., Neale, M. C., Maclean, C. J., et al., (1993). Smoking and major depression: a causal analysis. *Arch Gen Psychiatry, 50*, 36-43.

Kenny, P. J., File, S. E. & Rattray, M. (2001). Nicotine regulates 5-HT(1A) receptor gene expression in the cerebral cortex and dorsal hippocampus. *Eur J Neurosci, 13 (6)*, 1267-71.

Kessler, R. C., Berglund, P. A., Borges, G., et al. (2007). Smoking and suicidal behaviors in the National Comorbidity Survey: Replication. *J Nerv Ment Dis, 95*, 369–377.

Kessler, R. C., Borges, G., Sampson, N., et al. (2008). The association between smoking and subsequent suicide-related outcomes in the National Comorbidity Survey panel sample. *Mol Psychiatry*.

Khaled, S. M., Bulloch, A., Exner, D. V. & Patten, S. B. (2009). Cigarette smoking, stages of change, and major depression in the Canadian population. *Can J Psychiatry, 54 (3)*, 204-8.

King, C. A., Hill, E. M., Naylor, M., et al. (1993). Alcohol consumption in relation to other predictors of suicidality among adolescent. *J Am Acad Child Adolesc Psychiatry*, *32*(1):82-88.

King, R. A., Schwab-Stone, M., Flisher, A. J., et al. (2001). Psychosocial and risk behavior correlates of youth suicide attempts and suicidal ideation. *J Am Acad Child Adolesc Psychiatry 40*, 837-46.

King, R. A., Schwab-Stone, M., Flisher, A. J., et al. (2002). Psychosocial and risk behavior correlates of youth suicide attempts and suicidal ideation. *J Am Acad Child Adolesc Psychiatry, 40*, 837–46.

Kirmayer, L. J., Brass, G. M. & Tait, C. L. (2000). The mental health of Aboriginal peoples: Transformations of identity and community. *Can J Psychiatry, 45 (7)*, 607–616.

Kotila, L. & Lonnqvist, J. (1988). Adolescent suicide attempts: Sex differences predicting suicide. *Acta Psychiatr Scand, 77*, 264—270.

Lam, T. H., Stewart, S. M., Yip, P. S., et al., (2004). Suicidality and cultural values among Hong Kong adolescents. *Soc Sci Med, 58*, 487-98.

Larsson, B. & Sund, A. M. (2008). Prevalence, course, incidence and 1-year prediction of deliberate self-harm and suicide attempts in early adolescents. *Suicide Life Threat Behav, 38 (2)*, 152–165.

Lasser, K., Boyd, J. W., Woolhandler, S., et al. (2000). Smoking and mental illness: A population-based prevalence study. *JAMA, 284 (20)*, 2606-10.

Laucht, M., Esser, G. & Schmidt., M. (2000a). Longitudinal research on the developmental epidemiology of mental disorders: Aims, concepts, and major results of the Mannheim Study of At Risk Children. *Zeitschrift fur Klinische Psychologie. Forschung und Praxis, 29*, 246–262.

Laucht, M., Esser, G., Baving, L., et al. (2000b). Behavioral sequlae of perinatal insults and early family adversity at 8 years of age. *J Am Acad Child Adolesc Psychiatry, 39*, 1229–1237.

Laucht, M., Schmidt, M. H. & Esser, G. (2002). Motor, cognitive and socio-emotional development of 11-year-olds born with early risks: Late consequences? *Zeitschrift fur Kinder- und Jugendpsychiatrie, 30*, 5–19

Leistikow, B., (2003). Commentary: Questionable premises, overadjustment, and a smoking/suicide association in younger adult men. *Int J Epidemiol, 32(6),* 1005-6.

Leistikow, B. N. & Shipley, M. J. (1999). Might stopping smoking reduce injury death risks? A meta-analysis of randomized, controlled trials. *Prev Med*, 28, 255–259.

Leistikow, B. N., Martin, D. C. & Samuels, S. J., (2000). Injury death excesses in smokers: a 1990–95 United States national cohort study. *Inj Prev, 6,* 277–80.

Lerman, C. & Berrettini, W. (2003). Elucidating the role of genetic factors in smoking behavior and nicotine dependence. *Am J Med Gen B Neuropsychiatr Genet, 118b (1),* 48-54.

Lerman, C., Caporaso, N., Main, D., et al. (1998). Depression and self-medication with nicotine: the modifying influence of the dopamine D4 receptor gene. *Health Psychol, 17(1),* 56-62.

Lewinsohn, P. M., Rohde, P. & Seeley, J. R., (1994). Psychosocial risk factors for future adolescent suicide attempts. *J Consult Clin Psychol, 62 (2),* 297–305.

Lewinsohn, P. M., Rohde, P., Seeley, J. R. & Baldwin, C. L. (2001). Gender differences in suicide attempts from adolescence to young adulthood. *J Am Acad Child Adolesc Psych, 40(4)*, 427–434.

Li, M. D. (2003). The genetics of smoking related behavior: a briefreview. *Am J Med Sci, 326*, 168–173.

Linnoila, V. M. & Virkkunen, M. (1992). Aggression, suicidality, and serotonin. *J Clin Psychiatry, 53*, 46 –51.

Li-Tzy, W. & Anthony, J. (1999). Tobacco smoking and depressed mood in late childhood and early adolescence. *Am J Public Health, 89*, 1837–40.

Lohr, J. & Flynn, K. (1992). Smoking and schizophrenia. *Schizophr Res, 8,* 93-102.

Makikyro, T. H., Hakko, H. H., Timonen M. J., et al. (2004). Smoking and suicidality among adolescent psychiatric patients. *J Adolesc Health, 34,* 250–253.

Malone, K. M., Waternaux, C., Haas, G. L., et al. (2003). Cigarette smoking, suicidal behavior, and serotonin function in major psychiatric disorders.

Am J Psychiatry, 160, 773–779.

Mann, J. (1998). The neurobiology of suicide. *Nature Medicine, 4(1)*, 25–30.

Mann, J. J., Waternaux, C., Haas, G. L., et al. (1999). Toward a clinical model of suicidal behavior in psychiatric patients. *Am J Psychiatry, 156*, 181–9.

Mann, J. J. (2002). A current perspective of suicide and attempted suicide. *Ann Intern Med, 136*, 302–11.

Mann, J. J. (2003). Neurobiology of suicidal behaviour. *Nat Rev Neurosci, 4*, 819–28.

Marcinko, D., Pivac, N., Martinac, M. et al. (2007). Platelet serotonin and serum cholesterol concentrations in suicidal and non-suicidal male patients with a first episode of psychosis. *Psychiatry Res, 150 (1),* 105-8.

Markou, A., Kosten, T. R. & Koob, G. F. (1998). Neurobiological similarities in depression and drug dependence: a self-medication hypothesis. *Neuropsychopharmacology, 18*, 135–174.

Martínez-Ortega, J. M., Jurado, D. & Gurpegui, M. (2008). Nicotine dependence vs. daily smoking as a meaningful variable :implications for clinical and epidemiological psychiatric studies. *Prog Neuropsychopharmacol Biol Psychiatry, 32(8)*, 1972-7.

Marttunen, M. J., Aro, H. M., Henriksson, M. M., et al. (1991). Mental disorders in adolescent suicide. *Arch Gen Psychiatry, 48*, 834–9.

Maser, J. D., Akiskal, H. S., Schettler, P., et al. (2002). Can temperament identify affectively ill patients who engage in lethal or near-lethal suicidal behavior? A 14-year prospective study. *Suicide Life Threat Behav, 32*, 10–32.

McAuliffe, C M., (2002). Suicidal ideation as an articulation of intent: a focus for suicide prevention? *Arch Suicide Res, 6*, 325–338.

McCloud, A., Barnaby, B., Omu, N., et al. (2004). Relationship between alcohol use disorders and suicidality in a psychiatric population. In a patient prevalence study. *Br J Psychiatry, 184*, 439-445.

McEwen, A., Hajek, P., McRobbie, H. & West, R. (2006). *Manual of Smoking Cessation.AGuide for Counsellors and Practitioners.* Blackwell Publishing, Oxford, UK.

McGee, R., Feehan, M., Williams, S., et al. (1990). DSM-III disorders in a large sample of adolescents. *J Am Acad Child Adolesc Psychiatry, 29*, 611–619.

McGee, R., Williams, S. & Nada-Raja, S. (2005). Is cigarette smoking associated with suicidal ideation among young people? *Am J Psychiatry, 162*, 619-20.

McKeown, R. E., Garrison, C. Z., Cuffe, S. P., et al. (1998). Incidence and predictors of suicidal behaviours in a longitudinal sample of adolescents. *J Am Acad Child Adolesc Psychiatry, 37*, 612-9.

McManus, I. C. & Weeks, S. J. (1982). Smoking, personality and reasons for smoking. *Psychol Med, 12*, 349-356.

Menti, E., Lekka, N. P., Assimakopoulos, K., et al., (2007). Smoking, psychosocial factors, psychopathologic behavior, and other related conditions in hospitalized youth suicide attempters. *Compr Psychiatry, 48 (6)*, 522-8.

Meulemans, W., Van den Broeck, J. & Geldhof, K. (1992). Smoking and suicide. *Lancet*, *340*, 1096.

Miller, M., Hemenway, D., Bell, N. S. et al. (2000). Cigarette smoking and suicide: a prospective study of 300 000 male active-duty Army soldiers. *Am J Epidemiol*, *151(11)*, 1060–63.

Miller, M., Hemenway, D. & Rimm, E. (2000). Cigarettes and suicide: a prospective study of 50,000 men. *Am J Public Health*, *90(5)*, 768-73.

Miller, T. R. & Taylor, D. M. (2005). Adolescent suicidality: who will ideate, who will act? *Suicide Life Threat Behav*, *35*, 425–435.

Mino, Y., Shigemi, J., Otsu, T., et al. (2000). Does smoking cessation improve mental health? *Psychiatry Clin Neurosci*, *54(2),* 169–72.

Moriya, F. & Hashimoto, Y. (2005). Do Smokers Who Commit Suicide Have High Blood Levels of Nicotine? *Am J Psychiatry*, *162*, 4.

Moriya, F., Hashimoto, Y. & Furumiya, J. (2007). Nicotine and cotinine levels in body fluids of smokers who committed suicide. *Forensic Sci Int*, *168*, 102–105.

Mück-Seler, D., Jakovljević, M. & Pivac, N. (1996). Platelet 5-HT concentrations and suicidal behaviour in recurrent majordepression. *J Affect Disord*, *39(1),* 73-80.

Murphy, J. M., Horton, N. J., Monson, R. R., et al. (2003). Cigarette smoking in relation to depression: historical trends from the Stirling County Study. *Am J Psychiatry*, *160(9),* 1663-9.

National Center for Health Statistics, (1998). *Health, United States, 1998: Socioeconomic status and health chartbook*. Hyattsville, MD: Public Health Service.

Newcomb, M. D., Huba, G. J. & Bentler, P. M. (1981). A multidimensional assessment of stressful life events among adolescents: Derivation and correlates. *J Health Soc Behav, 22*, 400-415.

Nolen-Hoeksema, S. (1994). An interactive model for the emergence of gender differences in depression in adolescence. *J Res Adolesc*, *4*, 519-534.

Nrugham, L, Larsson, B & Sund, AM, (2008). Predictors of suicidal acts across adolescence: Influences of familial, peer and individual factors. *J Affect Disorder*, 109, 35–45.

Oquendo, M. A., Galfalvy, H., Russo, S. et al. (2004). Prospective study of clinical predictors of suicidal acts after a major depressive episode in patients with major depressive disorder or bipolar disorder. *Am J Psychiatry, 161 (8)*, 1433-41.

Parillo, A. V., Felts, W. M. & Mikow-Porto, V. (1997). Early initiation of sexual intercourse and its co-occurrence with other health risk behaviors in high school students: The 1993 North Carolina youth risk behavior survey. *J Health Educ*, 22(2), 85-93.

Parks, H. S., Schepp, K. G., Jang, E. H. & Koo H. Y. (2006). Predictors of suicidal ideation among high school students by gender in South Korea. *J Sch Health*, *76*, 181-8.

Patten, C. A., Hurt, R. D., Offord, K. P., et al. (2003). Relationship of tobacco use to depressive disorders and suicidality among patients treated for alcohol dependence. *Am J Addict*, *12*, 71–83.

Patton, G., Carlin, J., Coffey, C., et al. (1998). Depression, anxiety, and smoking initiation: a prospective study over 3 years. *Am J Public Health, 88,* 1518–21.

Payci, S. O., Ergin, A., Saatci, E., et al. (2005). Suicidal thought and behaviour in high school students in Adana, Turkey. *Coll Antropol*, *29*, 527– 531.

Pedersen, W. & von Soest, T. (2009). Smoking, nicotine dependence and mental health among young adults: a 13-year population-based longitudinal study. *Addiction*, *104(1),* 129-37.

Piko, B. F. & Fitzpatrick, K. M. (2004). Substance use, religiosity, and other protective factors among Hungarian adolescents. *Addict Behav*, *29*, 1095–1107.

Pivac, N., Jakovljevic, M., Muck-Seler, D. & Brzovic, Z. (1997). Hypothalamic–pituitary– adrenal axis function and platelet serotonin concentrations in depressed patients. *Psychiatry Res*, *73*, 123–32.

Poirier, M. F., Canceil, O, Baylé, F & et al., (2002). Prevalence of smoking in psychiatric patients. *Prog Neuropsychopharmacol Biol Psychiatry*, *26(3),* 529-37.

Rabenstein, R., Caldarone, B. & Bicciotto, M. (2006). The nicotinic antagonist mecamylamine has antidepressant-like effects in wild-type but not _2- or 7-nicotinic acetylcholine receptor subunit knockout mice. *Psychopharmacology*, 189, 395–401.

Reynolds, W., (1999). Assessment of suicidal ideation in inner-city children and young adolescents: Reliability and validity of the suicidal ideation questionnaire-JR. *School Psychology Review*, *28*, 17–30.

Riala, K., Taanila, A., Hakko, H. & Räsänen, P. (2009).Longitudinal smoking habits as risk factors for early-onset and repetitive suicide attempts: the Northern Finland 1966 Birth Cohort study. *Ann Epidemiol, 19(5),* 329-35.

Riala, K., Viilo, K., Hakko, H. & Rasanen, P. (2007). Heavy daily smoking among under 18-year-old psychiatric inpatients is associated with increased risk for suicide attempts. *Eur Psychiatry*, *22*, 219-222.

Ribeiro, E. B., Bettiker, R. L., Bogdanov, M. & Wurtman, R. J. (1993). Effects of systemic nicotine on serotonin release in rat brain. *Brain Res*, *621(2),* 311-8.

Rickelman, B. L. & Houfek, J. F. (1995). Toward an interactional model of suicidal behaviors: Cognitive rigidity, attributional style, stress, hopelessness, and depression. *Arch Psychiatr Nurs*, *9*, 158-168.

Roggenbach, J., Müller-Oerlinghausen, B., Franke, L., et al. (2007). Peripheral serotonergic markers in acutely suicidal patients. 1. Comparison of serotonergic platelet measures between suicidal individuals, nonsuicidal patients with major depression and healthy subjects. *J Neural Transm*, *114(4),* 479-87.

Rohde, P., Seeley, J. S., Rohling, J. & Rohling, M. (2003). The life attitudes schedule-short form: psychometric properties and correlates of adolescent suicide proneness. *Suicide Life Threat Behav*, *(3)*, 249-260.

Rossow, I, Grohølt, B. & Wichstrøm, L. (2005). Intoxicants and suicidal behaviour among adolescents: changes in levels and associations from 1992 to 2002. *Addiction*, *100(1)*, 79–88.

Royal College of Physicians, (1977). *Smoking or Health*. London, UK: Pitman Medical.

Rutter, M. (2000). Psychosocial influences: Critiques, findings, and research needs. *Dev Psychopathol*, *12*, 375–405.

Salin-Pascual, R. J., Rosas, M., Jimenez-Genchi, A., et al. (1996). Antidepressant effect of transdermal nicotine patches in non-smoking patients with major depression. *J Clin Psychiatry*, *57*, 387–389.

Schneider, B., Wetterling, T., Georgi, K., et al. (2009). Smoking differently modifies suicide risk of affective disorders, substance use disorders, and social factors. *J Affect Disord*, *112 (1-3),* 165-73.

Schuman, H. & Johnson, M. P. (1976). Attitudes and behaviour. *Ann Rev Sociol*, *2*, 161–207.

Shaffer, D., Gould, M., Fisher, P., et al. (1996). Psychiatric diagnosis in child and adolescent suicide. *Arch Gen Psychiatry*, *53*, 339– 344.

Sher, L. (2006a). Alcohol consumption and suicide. *QJM*, *99(1),* 57-61.

Sher, L, (2006b). Alcohol and suicide: neurobiological and clinical aspects. *ScientificWorldJournal*, *6,*700-6.

Shneidman, E. S. (1985). Definition of suicide. New York: Wiley

Silagy, C., Lancaster, T., Stead, L., et al. (2004). *Nicotine replacement therapy for smoking cessation*. The Cochrane Library, *www.thecochranelibrary.com*.

Smith, G. D., Phillips, A. N. & Neaton, J. D. (1992). Smoking as "independent" risk factor for suicide: illustration of an artifact from observational epidemiology? *Lancet*, *340(8821),* 709-12.

Smith, G. M. (1969). Relations between personality and smoking behavior in preadult subjects. *J Consult Clin Psychol*, *33*, 710-715.

Smith, S. & Fiore, M. (1999). The epidemiology of tobacco use, dependence, and cessation in the United States. *Primary Care Clinics in Office Practice*, *26 (3)*, 100-123.

Smith, R C., Singh, A., Infante, M., et al. (2002). Effects of cigarette smoking and nicotine nasal spray on psychiatric symptoms and cognition in schizophrenia. *Neuropsychopharmacology*, *27 (3),* 479–497.

Spijkerman, R., van den Eijnden, R. J., Vitale, S. & Engels, R. C. (2004). Explaining adolescents' smoking and drinking behavior: the concept of smoker and drinker prototypes in relation to variables of the theory of planned behavior. *Addict Behav*, *29*, 1615–1622.

Stålenheim, E. G. (2001). Relationships between attempted suicide, temperamental vulnerability, and violent criminality in a Swedish forensic psychiatric population. *Eur Psychiatry*, *16(7),* 386-94.

Stanley, B., Gameroff, M. J., Michalsen, V., et al. (2001). Are suicide attempters who self-mutilate a unique population? *Am J Psychiatry 158*, 427–32.

Statham, D. J., Heath, A. C., Madden, P. A., et al. (1998). Suicidal behaviour: an epidemiological and genetic study. *Psychol Med*, *28*, 839–855.

Sullivan, P. F., Neale, M. C. & Kendler, K. S. (2000). Genetic epidemiology of major derpression: review and meta-analysis. *Am J Psychiatry*, *157,*1552–1562.

Takakura, M., Ueji, M. & Sakihara, S. (2001). Covariation of cigarette smoking and other health-risk behaviours among Japanese high school students: a preliminary study. *J Epidemiol*, *11*, 224–228.

Tanskanen, A., Tuomiletho, J., Viinamaki, H. et al. (2000). Smoking and the risk of suicide. *Acta Psychiatr Scand*, 101, 243–45.

Tanskanen, A., Viinamaki, H., Hintikka, J., et al. (1998). Smoking and suicidality among psychiatric patients. *Am J Psychiatry*, *155 (1)*, 129-130.

Taylor, J. E., Conard, M. W., Koetting, O., Byrne, K., et al. (2004). Saturation of tobacco smoking models and risk of alcohol and tobacco use among adolescents. *J Adolesc Health,* 35, 190–196.

Tercyak, K. P. & Audrain-McGovern, J. (2003). Personality differences associated with smoking experimentation among adolescents with and without comorbid symptoms of ADHD. *Subst Use Misuse*, *38*, 1953-70.

Terracciano, A. & Costa, Jr P. T. (2004). Smoking and the five-factor model of personality. *Addiction*, *99*, 472-81.

Tomori, M., Zalar, B., Kores Plesnicar, B., et al. (2001). Smoking in relation to psychosocial risk factors in adolescents. *Eur Child Adolesc Psychiatry*, *10*, 143–150.

Toros, F., Bilgin, N. G., Sasmaz, T. et al. (2004). Suicide attempts and risk factors among children and adolescents. *Yonsei Med J*, *45*, 367–374.

Trauth, J. A., Seidler, F. J., Ali, S. F., et al. (2001). Adolescent nicotine exposure produces immediate and long-term changes in CNS noradrenergic and dopaminergic function. *Brain Res*, *892*, 269–80.

Tsoh, J. Y., Humfleet, G. L., Munoz, R. F., et al. (2000). Development of major depression after treatment for smoking cessation. *Am J Psychiatry*, 157, 368–374.

Undheim, A. M. & Sund, A. M. (2005). School factors and the emergence of depressive symptoms among young Norwegian adolescents. *Eur Child Adolesc Psychiatry, 14*, 446– 453.

Upadhyaya, H. P., Deas, D., Brady, K. T. & Kruesi, M. (2002). Cigarette smoking and psychiatric comorbidity in children and adolescents. *J Am Acad Child Adolesc Psychiatry, 41*, 1294–1305.

US Department of Health and Human Services, (1990a). Psychological and behavioral consequences and correlates of smoking cessation. In: *Health Benefits of Smoking Cessation: A Report of the US Surgeon General. Office on Smoking & Health* (pp. 517–578.), Rockville, MD: US Department of Health and Human Services.

US Department of Health and Human Services, (1990b). *The Health Benefits of Smoking Cessation. A Report of the US Surgeon General. Office on Smoking & Health*. Rockville, MD: US Department of Health and Human Services.

Verkes, R. J,, Van der Mast, R. C., Kerkhof, A. J., et al. (1998). Platelet serotonin, monoamine oxidase activity, and [3H]paroxetine binding related to impulsive suicide attempts and borderline personality disorder. *Biol Psychiatry, 43(10)*, 740-6.

Vinod, K. Y. & Hungund, B. L. (2006). Role of the endocannabinoid system in depression and suicide. *Trends Pharmacol Sci*, 27, 539–545.

Wadsby, M., Sydsjo, G. & Svedin, C. G. (1998). Evaluation of a short term intervention program for psychosocial-risk mothers and their infants. *Nord J Psychiatry, 52*, 501–511.

Wadsby, M. Sydsjo, G. & Svedin, C. G. (2001). Evaluation of an intervention programme to support mothers and babies at psychosocial risk: assessment of mother/child interaction and mother's perception of benefit. *Health Soc Care Community, 9*, 125–133.

Wadsby, M., Svedin, C. G. & Sydsjö, G. (2007). Children of mothers at psychosocial risk growing up: a follow up at the age of 16. *J Adolesc, 30 (1)*, 147-64.

Weiser, M., Reichenberg, A., Grotto, I., et al. (2004). Higher rates of cigarette smoking in male adolescents before the onset of schizophrenia: a historical-prospective cohort study. *Am J Psychiatry*, 161, 1219–1223.

Weiss, J. W., Mouttapa, M., Chou, Z. C., et al. (2005). Hostility, depressive symptom, and smoking in early adolescence. *J Adolesc, 28*, 49-62.

West, R. & Shiffman, S. (2001). Effect of oral nicotine dosing forms on cigarette withdrawal symptoms and craving: a systematic review. *Psychopharmacology*, 155, 115–122.

Whitfield, J. B., Pang, D., Bucholz, K. K., et al. (2000). Monoamine oxidase: associations with alcohol dependence, smoking and other measures of psychopathology. *Psychol Med, 30(2),* 443-54.

WHO, (2008). Statement World Suicide Prevention Day 10 September.

Wichstrøm, L. & Rossow, I. (2002). Explaining the gender difference in self-reported suicide attempts: A nationally representative study of Norwegian adolescents. *Suicide Life Threat Behav*, *32(2)*, 101–116.

Wichstrøm, L., (2000). Predictors of adolescent suicide attempts: a nationally representative longitudinal study of Norwegian adolescents. *J Am Acad Child Adolesc Psychiatry, 39 (5)*, 603–610.

Wilson, K. G., Stelzer, J., Bergman, JN & et al., (1995). Problem solving, stress, and coping in adolescent suicide attempts. *Suicide Life Threat Behav*, *25*, 241-252.

Windle, M., (1992). A longitudinal study of stress buffering for adolescent problem behaviors. *Dev Psychology, 28*, 522-530.

Windle, RC & Windle, M, (1997). An investigation of adolescents' substance use behaviors, depressed affect, and suicidal behaviors. *J Child Psychol Psychiatry*, *38*, 921-9.

Woods, E. R., Lin, Y., Middleman, A., et al. (1997). The associations of suicide attempts in adolescents. *Pediatrics*, *99*, 791–796.

Wu, P., Hoven, C. W., Liu, X., et al. (2004). Substance use, suicidal ideation and attempts in children and adolescents. *Suicide Life Threat Behav*, *34*, 408–420.

Xu, J., Mendrek, A., Cohen, M. S., et al. (2007). Effect of cigarette smoking on prefrontal cortical function in nondeprived smokers performing the Stroop Task. *Neuropsychopharmacology*, *32(6),* 1421-8.

Xu, Z., Seidler, F., Cousins, M., et al. (2002). Adolescent nicotine administration alters serotonin receptors and cell signaling mediated through adenyl cyclase. *Brain Res*, *951*, 280 –292.

Yang, Y. K., Nelson, L., Kamaraju, L., et al. (2002). Nicotine decreases bradykinesia-rigidity in haloperidol-treated patients with schizophrenia. *Neuropsychopharmacology*, *27(4),* 684–686.

In: Smoking Relapse: Causes, Prevention ... ISBN: 978-1-60876-580-5
Editors: J. Egger and M. Kalb

Chapter 2

Cultural Barriers to Treating Tobacco Dependence: An Evidence-Based Review with Clinical and Health Policy Recommendations

Megan J. Engelen[1] and John E. Snyder[2*]
[1]New Hanover Regional Medical Center. Wilmington, NC.
[2] University of North Carolina School of Medicine,
SEAHEC Department of Internal Medicine.

Abstract

Although entirely preventable, smoking is one of the most common causes of morbidity and mortality in the United States. As a result it creates a significant financial burden on the health care system. This creates an obligation and urgency on the part of health care providers, public health officials, and government leaders to address the causes of smoking and identify the populations most susceptible, common barriers to quitting smoking, and strategies for improving success rates of cessation. Tobacco policy must address all of these concerns. To most effectively accomplish these tasks we must better understand influences that encourage smoking and barriers to successful cessation in at-risk

---

* Corresponding author: University of North Carolina School of Medicine at Chapel Hill. South East Area Health Education Center (SEAHEC).

patient populations. This requires a multifaceted, individualized, and culturally-sensitive approach.

Patients in certain at-risk cultural groups are uniquely vulnerable to tobacco dependence for many reasons. Factors such as directed and aggressive tobacco industry marketing techniques, barriers to accessing health care providers who provide treatment for tobacco dependence, inequitable access to pharmacological treatment options, and a limited availability of culture-specific support resources play significant roles. In this chapter, we identify six distinctive patient subpopulations, each with unique cultural characteristics to consider during the effective treatment of tobacco dependence. These include patient groups based on a patient's gender, age, race and ethnicity, native language, and sexual orientation. We first present an evidence-based approach for providers that helps identify the most at-risk patients. We then offer specific clinical strategies for approaching tobacco cessation which are proven to be the most effective in overcoming the existing cultural barriers. Lastly, we propose a number of health policy recommendations which can assist with breaking down barriers to care for each cultural group and result in more effective cessation programs on the population level.

Background - Tobacco Dependence and Culture

In 2006 the Centers for Disease Control estimated that about 21% of the United States population currently smoked tobacco [1]. The health impacts of tobacco dependence are vast and create a burden on society in caring for the people who develop chronic and life-threatening diseases as a consequence of smoking. Although overall 70% of smokers express a desire to quit, only about 2.5 million out of the 30 million total smokers who each year attempt to quit are successful [2]. Since the success rate of quitting smoking is so low, and the morbidity and mortality associated with tobacco dependence is so high, it has become a national health priority to address the barriers that prevent people from quitting smoking. The health benefits that can be achieved from tobacco cessation are very cost-effective. Studies suggest that the estimated cost-per-life-year saved ranges from $2,300-4,200 [3]. In comparison, screening and treatment for hypertension costs $14,000-30,000 per quality-adjusted life year.

Treatment of tobacco dependence in clinical practice is best served by using the "five A's." They are: *Ask* about smoking, *Advise* smokers to quit, *Assess* readiness to quit, *Assist* patients to quit, and *Arrange* follow up [4]. The provider interventions that tend to lead to increased success rates include when the physician or other health care provider always asks about the patient's desire to quit smoking *and* advises them to quit, when the provider refers the patient to tobacco cessation resources such as a telephone quit line or behavioral counseling, and when the provider offers the patient nicotine replacement or other pharmacotherapy [4]. Studies suggest that 28% of patients will quit when they have access to both professional counseling and pharmaceutical aides [5] – over three times the current national quit rate [2]. As smoking cessation often involves repeated quit attempts interjected with periods of relapse, it is important to note that continued intensive support programs, with the assistance of pharmacotherapeutic agents, may lead to greater periods of abstinence [5]. Generally, with the right support, most smokers are willing to continue trying to quit smoking with this high-intensity level of disease management.

However, not all patients will respond similarly to different tobacco cessation strategies. Therein lies the challenge for providers, as assisting individuals with tobacco dependence requires a customized approach to prevention, education, and assistance with cessation. Patient cultural factors additionally seem to play an important role in successful tobacco cessation. Culture is a broad term, defined as "*the sum of attitudes, customs, and beliefs that distinguishes one group of people from another [sic] transmitted through language, material objects, ritual, institutions, and art, from one generation to the next*" [6]. Cultural groups include those united by similarities such as those of gender, age, race, ethnicity, sexual orientation, religion, geography, native language, and socioeconomic status – among others, such as shared life experiences. Cultural factors play an important and increasingly recognized role in an individual's belief system, and understanding a patient's cultural background may help aide in individualizing their medical needs and optimizing their care.

The effect of patient cultural background appears to be particularly important when it comes to the treatment of tobacco dependence. Both differences in the prevalence of tobacco use and in the success rates of different cessation techniques seem to exist among different culturally-based subpopulations of patients. In addition, there is a discrepancy seen in the frequency of tobacco cessation counseling done by physicians to patients in different sociocultural subpopulations. For example, women, ethnic minorities, persons with Medicaid, and patients who are uninsured are all less likely to receive appropriate tobacco counseling and cessation services by physicians [7]. Due to the health consequences of smoking, those in the medical profession and in the public health field need to work harder to augment the numbers of people who try and successfully quit smoking. But in order to accomplish this task, we must better understand the factors associated with smoking in specific target patient populations as well as the barriers of these patients to successfully quit smoking.

Tobacco Dependence Treatment and Female Gender

Tobacco Use Patterns and Public Health Impact for the Female Gender

Males have always been more prevalent smokers than females. In the most recent survey by the CDC, the smoking rate for men is 22.3% and for women is 17.4% [8]. The highest prevalence of female smokers is amongst American Indian or Alaska Native women (34.5%), then white women (23.5%), then black women (21.9%). The lowest prevalence is among Hispanic (13.8%) and Asian women (11.2%) [9]. Additionally, women who have achieved a lower education level (9-11 years of school) have a prevalence rate of 30.9%, and those with 16 or more years of school have a 10.6% prevalence rate of smoking [9].

An important reason to advocate for cessation in both men and women is that heart disease is the primary cause of death in the United States and smoking contributes to the morbidity and mortality of heart disease. There are also specific health consequences of smoking that tend to disproportionately affect women. Young female smokers tend to have more significant early deleterious changes in their lung function, noted during pulmonary function testing, than their male counterparts [10]. In women who are actively smoking, the annual risk of death is double that of their non-smoking peers, and they have an average of a 14 year shorter lifespan [9]. Lung cancer rates have increased 600% in women over the last 50 years, surpassing breast cancer as the most common cause of cancer death in women [9]. The lung cancer rate in black females is 42.6 cases per 100,000 population and in white females is 45 cases per 100,000 population [9]. Women who smoke are also at higher risk for cervical and vulvar cancer, stroke, heart disease, peripheral vascular disease, colon cancer, pancreatic cancer, dysmenorrhea, menstrual irregularities, infertility, ectopic pregnancy, decreased bone mineral density, and increased risk of hip fracture [11]. Tobacco dependence treatment is critical in women not only for the overall adverse health effects for themselves, but also for the consequences in pregnancy and to the unborn child. There have been countless studies on the negative effects of smoking on the fetus, including low birth weight, premature rupture of membranes, preterm delivery, abruptio placentae, and placenta previa [12].

Population-Specific Barriers to Treatment of Tobacco Dependence

Women tend to be influenced by factors that limit smoking avoidance, diminish successful cessation, and that are unique from men. Studies suggest that women are often influenced by the advertising media's depiction of desirable, attractive, and independent women in cigarette ads that portray themes of social desirability and independence, even though the consequences of smoking are much the opposite [9]. Tobacco advertising also targets women by sponsorship of women's fashion, artistic, athletic, and political events [9]. Data also suggest that women are more likely to continue smoking due to the desire to be thin and the thought that quitting smoking will cause them to gain weight [13], [14]. Women also generally have a tendency to need more social support in quitting tobacco [11]. Patient gender can often additionally play a role in access to general medical care. Numerous studies show that a woman’s health and nutrition are often devalued and that female patients do not always receive the same medical treatments as male counterparts [see, for example, 12].

Clinical Solutions

Clinical recommendations for treating women smokers include involving them in counseling and support groups, referring them for cognitive behavioral therapy, offering them pharmacological interventions such as bupropion and varenicline, and encouraging them to partake in adjunctive exercise programs. Significant gender-based differences in long-term cessation rates when using the nicotine patch have been seen. In one clinical study, women had worse outcomes than men when treated with the nicotine patch, whether or not formal counseling was also provided [15]. Multiple other clinical trials have compared the efficacy of nicotine replacement therapy in the quit rates of women versus men. Some of these studies have found that these treatments are less successful in maintaining long-term abstinence in women compared with men [16]. Gender-based differences seen in the efficacy of nicotine replacement treatment can be partly explained by the fact that women may tend to experience more severe nicotine withdrawal symptoms and also greater adverse effects of nicotine replacement therapy than men [16]. Women have a tendency to have lower compliance rates with this treatment, as well as a higher attachment to the behaviors associated with smoking beyond simply the addiction to nicotine [16].

Bupropion has been studied in women and most placebo-controlled trials show no gender differences in the treatment of tobacco cessation with this medication. A prospective trial showed that, in pregnancy, giving bupropion was associated with a 45% quit rate as compared with a 14% quit rate in controls [17]. Gender differences in varenicline therapy have been evaluated in at least one clinical trial, which showed that abstinence rates for men and women at 9-12 weeks were equivocal [18].

In women, there is a high association of weight gain with smoking cessation. This precludes many women from quitting, and may also decrease the long term compliance if there is subsequent weight gain [19]. Studies have found that not only is there a higher tobacco cessation rate but also that actual weight loss is associated with multifaceted smoking cessation programs that include a combination of exercise, counseling, and nicotine replacement therapy [19].

When choosing pharmacotherapeutic agents for female smokers of child-bearing age, it is important to consider the drugs' safety profiles during pregnancy and breast-feeding. In general, women who are pregnant or breast-feeding should attempt smoking cessation without the use of medications. Bupropion [20] and varenicline [21] have not been adequately studied in pregnant or lactating women. They are both currently classified in pregnancy class 'C' and should be used during pregnancy only if the potential benefit justifies the potential risk to the fetus. Bupropion is secreted in human milk, and it is not known if the same occurs for varenicline; generally neither should be taken while breast feeding. Nicotine replacement aides are believed to be safer than smoking in pregnancy, however the risks of using such products during pregnancy or breast-feeding are not completely understood [22]. The use of any pharmacotherapeutic agent for tobacco cessation during pregnancy or lactation should be done with extreme caution and only with the explicit direction of a patient's trained health care provider.

Health Policy Recommendations

There are many opportunities to affect health policy for tobacco dependence in women. Programs to counteract female-targeted advertising, and particularly geared toward young women, may aid in greater smoking prevention. Initiatives such as the youth-oriented 'TheTruth.com' campaign tend to focus on racial diversity, but could be easily adapted to be more gender-based. Educating primary care providers to remember to counsel women on smoking cessation and on what techniques are most effective for women is essential.

Policy also should be targeted at tobacco cessation during pregnancy and on maintaining that cessation thereafter. Currently one-third of women who quit tobacco during pregnancy go back to using tobacco after they have delivered [12]. Hospitalization for labor and delivery is an important opportunity to impact the smoking rates of women, because they are unlikely to be able to smoke while in the hospital, and they can be encouraged to maintain tobacco cessation for the health and wellbeing of their newborn child. Implementing a solid post-partum support plan for new mothers who quit smoking, including close primary care follow-up, would likely be the key to the success of such an initiative. This is particularly true given the stress, exhaustion, "maternity blues," and even post-partum depression that can follow childbirth. Additionally, increasing the number of and access to prenatal and postnatal support groups could improve adherence to cessation. Studies suggest that women may be more influenced by emotional ties than men, and hence may need stronger social support systems during smoking cessation [18].

Key Points

- The prevalence of smoking among women is not seeing the corresponding decreases seen in men. This is especially true among American Indian/Alaskan Natives, blacks, and white women.
- Women tend to be specifically targeted by tobacco advertising, have lesser access to health care overall than their male counterparts, and may be driven to continue smoking out of fear that cessation may result in weight gain.
- Involving women in counseling/support groups, cognitive behavioral therapy, and using medical interventions such as bupropion and

varenicline seem to be the most effective tools for tobacco cessation. Caution must be used with pharmacological agents during pregnancy and lactation. Adjunctive exercise programs may result in weight loss rather than gain. For various reasons, nicotine replacement therapy is not necessarily as effective for women as it is for men.

- Counteracting gender-based tobacco advertising, increasing primary care-based interventions, and assisting female smokers in the peri-partum period are key to successful health policy initiatives for women.

Tobacco Dependence Treatment in Adolescents and Young Adults

Tobacco Use Patterns and Public Health Impact in Adolescents and Young Adults

Adolescent and young adult smoking is quite prevalent, estimated at a rate of about 21.9% in 2003, and most smokers start using tobacco before they are 18 years old [23], [24]. Fortunately, these rates represent an overall decline from the 36.4% prevalence rate seen in 1997 [24]. Tobacco use rates are highest among white youths (30.9%) when compared to African American (12.6%) and Hispanic youth (25.3%). The Surgeon General's Report on youth and smoking from 1994 revealed that an increased risk of smoking in adolescents and young adults was associated with family structure. Youth who lived alone were the most likely to smoke, followed by those who lived in a single parent home in which the mother was absent, and then by youth who were home alone while their parents worked [23]. The report also noted an inverse relationship between smoking and population density, with the highest smoking rates seen in rural areas [23]. The lowest smoking rates were seen in youth with plans for attending college after high school graduation and in those with strong religious beliefs [23]. Smoking initiation also seems to be associated with inadequate parental monitoring, homes in which the parents are smoking, and having peers and friends who smoke [10]. Most of the factors that tend to contribute to youth smoking are universal throughout different socioeconomic levels and demographic groups. The key underlying theme is that youth who have role models that smoke (such as parents and peer influences) may find it harder to understand the reasons to never start smoking, or to appreciate the long-term health consequences of smoking.

The immediate health impacts of youth tobacco use are increased rates of chronic cough, acute bronchitis, and chest illness [10]. Young smokers, and in particular young females, can often already demonstrate detrimental changes in lung function as seen by pulmonary function testing [10]. In addition to causing a shortened life expectancy, many of the specific negative health effects from smoking have a dose-response relationship. Cancer of the nasopharynx, larynx, lung, esophagus, stomach, pancreas, bladder, and cervix all tend to have such an association, and are related to long-term tobacco use [10]. Hence, youth and adolescents have the most to lose with the initiation of smoking.

Population-Specific Barriers to Treatment of Tobacco Dependence

Although a visit to the pediatrician's office provides an occasion to counsel on smoking prevention and cessation, many pediatricians do not routinely address tobacco use with their patients [25]. If they do, they are more likely to counsel their patients on prevention rather than discuss cessation. Many adolescents may not be honest with their pediatricians about their use of tobacco, and an opportunity for tobacco dependence treatment is lost.

Despite this, studies have found that 75% of high school students who smoke have tried to quit smoking, and that most students are interested in cessation [26]. However, certain unique barriers to successful cessation exist in the adolescent and young adult population. For one, youth may be less likely to identify themselves as a "smoker" because they may only smoke when they are with friends or if they feel the need to fit in with a crowd [27]. When polled, most adolescents who currently smoke do not believe they will continue to do so long-term [25]. However, even "social" tobacco use may lead to more regular smoking and eventual addiction. Between 33 and 50% of adolescents who experiment with tobacco become regular smokers [23]. Studies suggest that 75% of current youth smokers are still smoking when re-polled five years later [25]. Despite an intention to not smoke long-term, or even a belief that "social" smoking is not a habit, many youth still seem to become dependent on tobacco in this way.

Youth and young adults seem to be one of the most vulnerable populations to the influences of peer pressure, directed advertising, and the presence of tobacco in entertainment and other media [27], [28], [29]. Studies have demonstrated that cartoon characters used in tobacco advertising, such as "Joe Camel," are not only easily recognizable by minors but also are strongly associated with the initiation of tobacco use [29], [30]. In movies, for another example, the smoking message is more hidden and therefore doesn't get the same criticism as direct advertising to youth from tobacco companies [31]. A study of the top-grossing twenty-five films in the U.S., in each year over a ten year period from 1988 to 1997, found tobacco use in 85% of the films and the presence of brand name products in 28% [32]. Brand products were present even in 20% of the films that were specifically rated for children. Despite 1998 settlement agreements prohibiting tobacco manufacturers from paid advertising of brand tobacco products in movies, television, video games, or similar media [33], these products still find their way into such media outlets. In the top five grossing U.S. films of 2000, there were an average of 10.9 instances of smoking per hour, compared to 7.3 instances in the top films of 1960 [34], [35]. In one study, a dose-response relationship was measured between exposure to movie smoking and initiation of smoking in youth [31]. Households with children tend to watch an average of three movies per week [31]. Movie stars may be inspirational role models for children and adolescents, and stars that smoke on-screen may be sending the message to youth that smoking is socially desirable. Tobacco companies have also targeted general-audience public entertainment venues such as sporting events, spending $30.6 million on these events in 2005 [36]. Star athletes likely have similar social influences on youth as movie actors.

Evidence is mounting that directed tobacco industry marketing also strengthens cigarette addiction in young adults, in a time period where experimentation may occur and lead to more regular usage [37]. A Cochrane Systematic Review examining nine longitudinal studies and including over 12,000 youth concluded that nonsmoking adolescents with greater exposure to and receptiveness toward this sort of marketing are more likely to eventually become smokers [38]. Promotions often target youth and young adults via the military, colleges, the workplace, and bars [37]. Cigarette brands that are more popular in young smokers are more heavily advertised in magazines with high readership in this age group [39]. College students are a particularly frequent target of tobacco industry promotions. In one study of 119 colleges and universities [40], 99.2% of students reported the presence of tobacco-sponsored social events at bars, nightclubs, or on campus where free cigarettes were distributed. Attendance rates at these events were approximately 8.5%, and attendance was associated with higher prevalence rates of smoking.

Clinical Solutions

In pediatrics and adolescent medicine, there is a great opportunity to intervene in smoking prevention and cessation. One reason is that, in most states, children under 18 are covered by state health insurance plans and hence have access to affordable medical care even if they are in a low socioeconomic class. Also, between 63-85% of adolescents are seen for preventive care each year [25]. Since access to affordable care is a lesser problem in this patient population, there is a greater opportunity to screen for tobacco use and to intervene early on smoking cessation. Pediatricians usually have a long-term relationship with their patients and may have a greater influence on certain risk behaviors than even the patient's parents do.

Evidence suggests that the best clinical solutions for tobacco cessation in adolescents and young adults include the use of nicotine replacement therapy (such as the nicotine patch), counseling, and cognitive-behavioral therapy. The rates of tobacco cessation by adolescents with the patch are similar to that of the adult population [27]. However, it is important to note that the sale of nicotine and nicotine-containing products such as gum is prohibited in persons under 18 years of age in the United States [22]. In addition to nicotine replacement therapy, there are other strategies to tobacco cessation in adolescents. Counseling from health care providers and peers can improve quit rates [25]. It has also been shown that cognitive behavioral therapy can improve cessation in adolescents and young adults [41]. Evidence also overall supports the clinical benefit of computer- and internet-based smoking cessation programs [42], which may appeal to youth who have grown up with these technologies and tend to be more savvy with them.

A randomized controlled trial looked at practice-based smoking prevention and cessation techniques for adolescents using the "5A approach" and included referring patients to peer counselors in order to develop a personalized approach for cessation or sustained abstinence [25]. Counseling was first done in-person, and then with follow-up phone conversations four times over the next 5 months. For the non-smokers in the trial, 95.5% in the usual care group continued to be abstinent at 12 months, compared with 96.8% in the intervention group. Quit rates for smokers were 24.6% at six months' time in the usual care cohort, and 36.4% in the intervention group. However, at 12 months the sustained quit rates were 27.7% and 25.3%, respectively. One might infer from this study that provider-initiated cessation, supplemented with counseling, can improve young adults' cessation rates, but only in the first few months after intervention. There needs to be continued and frequent re-evaluation and abstinence counseling to improve the long term cessation rates in this population.

Pharmacological treatment of tobacco dependence in persons less than 18 years of age, and particularly with bupropion [21] and varenicline [20], is currently limited since the safety and efficacy of these agents have not been well-studied in younger patients. These agents are not currently approved by the FDA for tobacco dependence treatment in this population. Although bupropion has been studied in adolescents, and its side effect profile was felt to be tolerable, it has not been consistently demonstrated to increase smoking cessation in this population [43], [44]. Anti-depressants, such as bupropion, also carry a "black box" warning that they may increase suicidal thoughts and actions in about 1 out of 50 people who are 18 years old or younger [21].

Health Policy Recommendations

The health impact of tobacco addiction at an early age is a significant public health crisis. It is critically important to understand what influences young people to start smoking so that we can both prevent smoking and also create policy directed towards cessation. It is estimated that teenagers smoke 1.1 billion packs of cigarettes annually and the eventual health costs from this, added to the subsequent loss of productivity, will amount to over $200 billion per year [10]. Although laws prevent the sales of tobacco products to persons under 18, stronger enforcement of these regulations is necessary to keep cigarettes out of the hands of minors.

A meta-analysis of smoking cessation in teens suggested that, across 48 studies, the probability of successful cessation was improved by 46% when interventions were school- or clinic-based, when there were at least five sessions, and when they used motivation-enhancement, cognitive-behavioral techniques, or social influence approaches [27], [41]. Hence, promoting policy directed at school-based avoidance and cessation programs might be the best strategy. In contrast, a systematic review of randomized controlled trials of smoking prevention interventions at primary care clinics and dentist offices for pediatric patients showed very limited evidence for efficacy of smoking prevention, low efficacy of smoking cessation interventions, and no evidence of long-term effectiveness of either intervention [45]. The controversy in the medical literature about the effectiveness of various tobacco cessation programs in youth suggests that there needs to be more research and larger studies on the methods and results of different tobacco cessation models.

In addition to primary care clinics offering cessation and abstinence counseling, there are other provider sites, including dental offices and emergency departments, which can play a role in influencing the smoking prevalence in this population. Young adults tend to be very aware of their own general and dental appearance, and seem to feel significant appearance-related concerns [46], [47]. Therefore, they may to respond to health campaigns using imagery that depicts stained fingers, wrinkled skin, and the changes of gum disease and stained teeth resulting from continued tobacco use. In emergency departments, there is an additional opportunity to make a difference – for example, when youth are presenting with symptoms of diseases such as asthma that may be exacerbated by tobacco abuse. A contact person such as a case manager or social worker in an emergency department could direct such patients into peer counseling programs and make weekly phone calls to see how they were doing with quitting.

Health care policy initiatives must also be directed at other significant influences on tobacco abuse in younger populations, such as the entertainment media and movie industry. Changing behaviors and influences in the movie industry could prove to be very difficult due to the constitutional rights of free speech. The counterargument to that would be that there has been a precedent set with the restriction of tobacco advertising on radio and television advertisements and that this is an extension of that restriction. To restrict tobacco smoking in movies that are geared toward children and teens would decrease the "normalization" of tobacco use and thus may decrease the receptiveness of adolescents and young adults to cigarettes. Limiting tobacco advertising in a way to completely exclude cartoon characters additionally seems essential.

Key Points

- The prevalence of smoking among adolescents and young adults is high, especially among white youth. Despite laws preventing the sale of tobacco to minors, children are indirectly targeted by tobacco advertising through the entertainment industry and the use of cartoon characters in advertisements.
- Most adult smokers begin their habit before they are 18 years old. There are a number of significant health impacts of tobacco use on youth.

- Evidence suggests that the best clinical solutions for tobacco cessation in adolescents and young adults include the use of counseling, cognitive-behavioral therapy, and nicotine replacement therapy. However, nicotine products and pharmacological agents are not approved for use in persons under 18 years of age.
- Counteracting tobacco advertising that affect youth and increasing interventions at the level of primary care, dental offices, and emergency departments may be successful health policy initiatives for this patient population.

Tobacco Dependence Treatment in Older Adults

Tobacco Use Patterns and Public Health Impact in Older Adults

Older smokers are at greater risks from smoking for many reasons. For one, they have generally smoked for much longer periods of time, with an average tobacco use history of 40 years [48]. The current generation of older adults in the U.S. had smoking rates among the highest of any U.S. generation – in the 1960's, 54 percent of adult males in this generation were active smokers and 21 percent were former smokers [49]. This generation also tends to be heavier smokers and its members are more likely to already suffer from a smoking-related illness [48]. Currently, twenty-two percent of adults age 45-65 smoke, but that number decreases drastically to only 9.1% of adults over the age of 65 [50]. One of the reasons for this sharp decline is that mortality is increased in smokers, and users of cigarettes die an average of 13-14 years earlier than nonsmokers [50], [51]. A substantial number of adults in the 45 to 65 year old age range have already started suffering the long-term health consequences of smoking. For those over 65, the health consequences are even greater and persons are dying sooner. Tobacco-related diseases, including heart disease, cancer, and stroke, are the leading cause of disease, disability, and death in the United States [52]. Annually, an estimated 443,000 persons die prematurely in the U.S. from smoking or exposure to secondhand smoke [54]. Another 8.6 million persons have a serious illness caused by smoking [52]. The diseases caused by smoking are numerous and are extensively reviewed elsewhere (see, for example, [48] and [52]).

Population-Specific Barriers to Treatment of Tobacco Dependence

Adults that have been smoking all of their lives are a challenging subset of the population to assist in terms of tobacco cessation. With an average tobacco use history of 40 years and a much longer history of addiction, tobacco dependence may be a harder habit and routine for older adults to break [48], [52]. Older smokers continue to smoke for various reasons, including "habit," for "relaxation," and for "pleasure" [53]. Additionally, older smokers are significantly less likely than younger smokers to believe that smoking harms their health [53], [54]. They also may fear imagined potential health risks from smoking cessation aides, such as nicotine replacement therapy [55], although such worries are often based on inaccurate information. They may also believe that quitting smoking offers no benefit at an advanced age, or that the damage from smoking "has already been done," even though there is robust evidence to suggest that smoking cessation at any age will both prolong life and improve overall quality of life [55]. After one year has passed from quitting tobacco, the added risk of heart disease from smoking is cut almost by 50%, and the risk of stroke, lung disease, and cancer decreases as well [56]. In fact, research suggests that most of the reasons that older adults cite for not wanting to quit tobacco are based on erroneous beliefs [55]. Other barriers to treatment of tobacco addiction in the older age group may overlap with barriers from other population subsets, such as those based on gender or race. In addition, the cost of health care may play a role. For older adults who do have health care insurance such as Medicare, tobacco cessation-related expenses may not always be covered by their plan. If they are living off of a fixed and limited budget from retirement savings or Social Security payments, and particularly if their medication costs are already high, they may not be willing to take on the additional medical- and drug-related costs associated with tobacco cessation.

Clinical Solutions

Motivation to quit seems to be a major factor in assisting older adults with tobacco cessation, and studies suggest that persons with higher levels of medical problems and psychological stress seem to have the greatest desire to quit smoking [59]. Hence, motivational methods may be necessary for those who do not report the same levels of illness and stress. Another important factor in smoking cessation is ensuring that clinicians counsel older patients about quitting. In a study of older adults admitted with acute myocardial infarction, only 40% of these patients had gotten smoking cessation counseling upon discharge from the hospital [51].

Overall, the clinical recommendations for helping older adults quit smoking include the use of counseling and social support, supplemented with nicotine replacement aides and pharmacotherapy. In a recent study of smoking cessation in older adults, nicotine replacement improved cessation rates by four-fold when combined with counseling and ongoing telephone support [58]. Behavior therapy on its own doubles success rates for cessation [59]. Most of the research that focuses on older adults and smoking cessation has been done with nicotine replacement therapy, and there is a relative paucity of research on older adults and newer pharmacologic therapies such as varenicline. Although data are limited, there seems to be no need for dose-adjustment of varenicline in older patients based on age alone, and that the drug may be overall well-tolerated in these patients [60]. Bupropion has been shown to double quit rates and has a low drop-out rate from adverse events [59]. Since various methods are considered to be both efficacious and safe, treatment regimens can be individually tailored to the needs of each patient. However, drug therapies must be used with caution in the older population due to the high incidence of polypharmacy and the potential for adverse inter-drug reactions.

Health Policy Recommendations

The public health effect of smoking on older adults is staggering. To combat this, ensuring that providers counsel older patients on tobacco cessation is essential. Additionally, for older adults who do have health insurance, mandating that insurers cover pharmacologic agents and services such as behavioral therapy may improve the access of patients to these proven interventions for tobacco cessation. At this time, less than half of insured persons have coverage for counseling services related to tobacco cessation [61].

A strategy to assist older adults who are still in the workforce could be to promote workplace incentives for quitting smoking. A randomized, controlled study in the *New England Journal of Medicine* suggested that this method can be highly successful [62]. In this study, enrollees were provided cessation education and then were randomized to one of two treatment arms. One arm offered a financial incentive of $250 for cessation of smoking within 6 months, and $400 for sustained abstinence for another 6 months. The other treatment arm offered no financial incentive. The group receiving the financial incentive had a statistically-significant, 2- to 3-time higher rate of success than the other group, both in the short term and after 15-18 months of follow-up. The cost of these incentives seems to be reasonably small in comparison to the costs associated with tobacco-related illness, such as lost productivity and increased numbers of sick days. However, incentive programs may have additional expenses, such as random blood testing, which are done to ensure that people who are surreptitiously still smoking do not get the incentives. Further analysis of the savings benefits from an expanded, incentive-based model could be investigated in the future.

Key Points

- Older persons often continue smoking, and cite reasons for not wanting to quit, based on erroneous beliefs that treatment is harmful and that quitting offers them little benefit. Missed opportunities by clinicians to counsel older patients on smoking cessation compound the problem. Financial considerations may also play a role.
- Motivation to quit seems to be a major factor in assisting older adults with tobacco cessation, and many tools are available to help these patients quit once they have committed to the idea. Behavioral therapy seems to be beneficial, and pharmacologic agents appear to be safe and well-tolerated. Caution must be used to avoid polypharmacy and drug-drug interactions.

Tobacco Dependence Treatment and Patient Race and Ethnicity

Tobacco Use Patterns and Public Health Impact by Patient Race and Ethnicity

The United States is composed of a racially- and ethnically-diverse population. An individual's *race* is an arbitrary and self-designated classification often based on phenotypic characteristics related to a common heredity or descent; *ethnicity* is an arbitrary and self-designated classification often based on common cultural, religious, or linguistic traditions [63]. A person's *culture* may often embody belief systems, attitudes, or behaviors shared by members of groups united by race, ethnicity, or other factors [6], [63]. Cultural factors such as race and ethnicity appear to be important when considering the scope of tobacco abuse and its treatment. Different cultural, racial, and ethnic groups often have a higher prevalence of tobacco dependence than the general population, and share unique influences on tobacco-related behavior or even distinctive responses to different tobacco cessation techniques.

For one example, African American smoking rates in 1995 were 31.4% for males and 22.7% for females [64], whereas 21% of the overall United States population smokes tobacco [1]. Data suggest that African Americans may be less dependent on nicotine because they smoke fewer cigarettes per day, but they are also less likely to successfully quit smoking, perhaps due in part to decreased access to preventative health services [64]. Despite these statistics, the prevalence of smoking among African American youth (16.7%) is less than that for white youth (45.4%). African American youth appear to be less likely than whites to believe that cigarettes control their weight, and African American parents seem more likely than their white counterparts to maintain a clear anti-tobacco message for their children [64].

Race may also play a role in the susceptibility to different to diseases caused by tobacco abuse. Even with a lower pack-year history of smoking, African American smokers tend to have a higher incidence of lung cancer than white smokers [65]. Native Hawaiian smokers have a higher rate of lung cancer than whites, Japanese Americans, and Latinos [65]. What predisposes certain racial groups to higher incidences of lung cancer with the same past amount of tobacco exposure is not clear. Environmental factors such as exposure to other lung carcinogens may play a role, and it is possible that there may be an inherent biological difference between races in the ability to metabolize some of the carcinogens and other materials found in cigarettes. It has been shown that even after the same number of cigarettes smoked, African Americans have a higher serum level of cotinine than white or Hispanic smokers [66].

American Indians and Alaska Natives have the highest smoking prevalence rates among all of the racial and ethnic populations in the United States. In American Indian and Alaskan natives, 45.4% of men and 34.2% of females smoke tobacco [64]. Cessation rates are significantly lower in both American Indians and Alaskan natives than in the general population [64].

These communities have had a long history of traditions, passed down through generations, which can include gathering around ceremonial pipes – as there is a belief that smoking rituals connect individuals to their spirituality. Smoking has been used in medicinal and healing rituals, in ceremonial and religious practices, as a symbol of peace, and is considered a gift of the earth [67]. Some American Indians may believe that they must continue to smoke, at least traditionally, because it helps them maintain their spirituality and their identity as an Indian [68]. However, there is a great difference between ceremonial smoking and habitual tobacco dependence involving commercial tobacco products. Health care providers must understand this difference well in order to be able to influence Native American patients to quit smoking but at the same time to not criticize or interfere with Indian cultural beliefs and traditions. Of note, ceremonial smoking typically does not involve inhaling the smoke [67].

Asian and Pacific Islanders have an overall lower rate of smoking than the rest of the population, but there is a disparity in the percentage of men versus women smoking. In this group 25.1% of men and only 5.8% of women smoke tobacco [64]. In the Hispanic population, 22.9% of men and 15.1% of Hispanic women smoke tobacco [64]. After adjusting for education level, Hispanics have been found to be more likely than whites to be able to quit smoking [64]. When education is not adjusted for, the overall quit rates are higher for whites than they are for African American and Hispanic populations [64].

Population-Specific Barriers to Treatment of Tobacco Dependence

The 1998 Surgeon General's report on tobacco use in racial and ethnic minority groups shed a great deal of light on how the tobacco industry has in many ways targeted minority groups with directed marketing campaigns and by other methods of influence [64]. For example, one highlighted study found that three major African-American magazines (*Ebony*, *Jet*, and *Essence)* were paid disproportionately higher amounts than other publications for cigarette advertisements [64]. The tobacco industry has supported African-American cultural events, community organizations, elected political figures, and has made donations to predominantly African-American institutions of higher education and scholarship programs. In regard to the Latino community, the tobacco industry has contributed financial support to primary and secondary schools, colleges, and universities, as well as funded scholarship programs targeting Latinos [64]. Tobacco products have been disproportionately promoted to the Latino community through advertising in community publications and by sponsorship of cultural events. Cigarette brands with names like "*Dorado*" and "*Rio*" have been specifically marketed to the Latino community [64]. The tobacco industry has also focused efforts toward American Indians and Alaskan natives by funding cultural and sporting events, and by developing the "*American Spirit*" brand [64], whose package features both an Indian in a headdress smoking a pipe and other culturally-inspired symbols. In one San Diego study [64], it was found that more tobacco advertising billboards were placed in neighborhoods with higher populations of racial and ethnic minorities, with the highest proportion placed in Asian-American neighborhoods. More tobacco advertising displays were also placed in stores catering to primarily Asian-American clientele.

Access to tobacco products may be greater in areas with higher percentages of minority patients as well. Several studies out of the University of Iowa suggest that this is true [69]. Researchers found that there was a higher density of tobacco outlet stores in counties with a greater percentage of African American residents, and that these counties also had greater prevalence rates of smoking. Areas with the lowest average household incomes and areas with the highest proportions of African American and Latino residents had more than twice as many tobacco outlets along major roadways when compared to wealthier, less diverse areas. The researchers in these studies proposed that tobacco companies may be seeking financial gains by purposefully increasing their presence in financially-disadvantaged areas and in more racially-diverse communities.

Beyond directed marketing, many other barriers clearly exist for racial and ethnic minorities to access health care in general, beyond even that for treatment of tobacco dependence. Although the medical system as a whole may have egalitarian goals, numerous studies have shown that racial minorities are treated differently than their white counterparts for the same medical problems. This issue is beyond that of access to physicians, as even at single institutions, article after article has demonstrated a lack of access to surgeries and procedures, immunizations and other preventive services, radiological studies, and even pain medication by non-white patients [70]. Patients that do not speak or have literacy in English, and especially if they also do not speak Spanish, may also find it difficult to get medical assistance or have interpreter services available to them if they do. Issues can also include fear of coercive treatment [71] and mistrust of the health care system [72].

Clinical Solutions

The use of various techniques for treatment of tobacco dependence in certain racial and ethnic groups has been studied, although not extensively or in large-scale clinical trials. The use of sustained-release bupropion has been specifically examined in African-American patients, with a 21% quit rate observed at 26 weeks. Participants also reported a reduction of depressive symptoms and no associated weight gain [73]. Even though these results are lower than the 30.3% quit rate seen in studies of bupropion in white patients, it still appears to be an important treatment modality for this patient group [74]. Combination treatment with bupropion, nicotine patch, and behavioral counseling shows disproportionately lower success rates among racial and ethnic minorities when compared to white patients [75], but are still overall recommended in nonwhite patients [76] due to a lack of proven alternatives.

In addition to counseling and pharmacological aides, cessation strategies should be catered to individuals and should keep cultural factors in mind. For example, clinical solutions specific to American Indians might include group and individual counseling along with support from the family and community at large [68]. It is also important not to discourage ceremonial use of tobacco because of its significance in the culture of the American Indian. In this population there may also be financial barriers related to the cost and accessibility of nicotine replacement therapy and other pharmacotherapeutic agents [68].

There are a few studies that can help guide specific clinical recommendations in the Latino population, but no large-scale trials that are definitive in nature. A ten-week randomized, double-blind, placebo-controlled trial compared the use of the nicotine patch and counseling with placebo and counseling in Latino patients. It was found that the nicotine patch with counseling improved the abstinence rate, and that the highest abstinence rates were in those Latinos with greater integration into American culture [76], [77]. One of the barriers to addressing tobacco use in the Latino population is that Latinos may perceive smoking as a weakness and not a medical condition that needs to be treated [78]. Studies have suggested that the Latino population has an overall distrust for medical treatments and has a specific aversion to bupropion because of its association with the treatment of mental illness [78].

The efficacy of varenicline for smoking cessation in minority groups has not been well studied, although in a largely white population it seems to be effective and achieved abstinence rates of around 23% at 52 weeks, compared with bupropion (14.6% abstinence), and placebo (10.3% abstinence) [74].

Although no specific data exists to support or oppose varenicline use in Asian Americans, the drug has been shown to be efficacious and well-tolerated in Asian persons hailing from Taiwan and Japan [79], [80].

Health Policy Recommendations

Race and ethnicity play an important role in how individuals respond to assistance and clinical advice related to smoking cessation. Policy makers must take into account differences in race and ethnicity when determining solutions for this problem, and not offer blanket recommendations they believe will work for everyone. Numerous studies have demonstrated that demographic subgroups of the general population (based on race, culture, gender, age, and sexual orientation) do not always receive the same diagnostic studies, treatment options, or even preventive care. As tobacco dependence clearly has different characteristics and treatment intricacies among different racial and ethnic groups, it is vital that clinical studies are more inclusive of minorities in the future. Since the health consequences of smoking vary among racial and ethnic groups, this should be highlighted in educational material. There needs to be culturally-sensitive educational materials on quitting smoking that appeal to common beliefs and that doesn't attack or offend a group's identity or spirituality. Language barriers need to be considered for non-English speaking patients, who may benefit from linguistically-appropriate educational materials. Educational programs, pamphlets and other materials written in Spanish or geared toward minority groups can be disseminated through churches or community centers catering to non-white and non-English speaking persons.

Race and ethnicity play an important role in how we must approach challenges in treating tobacco dependence due to cultural barriers. Initiatives such as the youth-oriented 'TheTruth.com' campaign tend to focus their efforts on racial diversity and inclusiveness. A study in the journal *Ethnicity and Health* assessed the impact of the national 'TheTruth.com' antismoking campaign on beliefs, attitudes, and intent to smoke within different racial and ethnic groups [81]. This study suggested that the campaign inspired anti-tobacco beliefs in youth across different races and ethnicities. The campaign tended to have similar impact on both African American and white youth in transmitting a message that cigarette companies lie about the fact that cigarettes are addictive and cause cancer [81]. The impact was slightly less significant in Hispanic and Asian youth. Similar campaigns geared toward adults and parents may have a broad appeal across racial and ethnic groups, and may help influence individuals who do not normally feel that public health outreach is geared toward their needs.

Key Points

- Different cultural, racial, and ethnic groups have varied prevalence rates of smoking, share unique influences on tobacco-related behavior, are affected by tobacco-related diseases differently, and may even have distinctive responses to different tobacco cessation techniques.
- The use of various techniques for treatment of tobacco dependence in certain racial and ethnic groups has been studied, although not extensively or in large-scale clinical trials. Combination treatment with bupropion, nicotine patch, and behavioral counseling shows disproportionately low success rates among racial and ethnic minorities when compared to white patients, but is still supported due to a lack of proven alternatives. Varenicline may be useful in minority patients, but data specific to these patients is lacking. Culture and language should be considered when tailoring a smoking cessation plan to an individual patient.
- Significant public health policy is needed to address barriers to care for minority groups in general, including but certainly not limited to the treatment of tobacco dependence.

Tobacco Dependence and Patient Sexual Orientation

Tobacco Use Patterns and Public Health Impact and Patient Sexual Orientation

Persons who self-identify as lesbian, gay, bisexual, or transgendered (LGBT) compose a large and diverse cultural group [82]. LGBT persons cannot be uniformly characterized, as much as members of any cultural group can be, and factors such as racial and ethnic associations may contribute to an individual's cultural identity. Nonetheless, LGBT persons may share certain cultural bonds and belief systems due to similar sociocultural experiences. LGBT persons are also generally united in the idea that their gender identity and sexual orientation are innate and cannot be changed.

LGBT persons, as a cultural group, may have unique risks for certain disease conditions that are different than those of the general population (see, for example, [83] through [91]), and these risks may be based on both heritable and cultural factors. Physicians must remain attentive to and screen for disease processes that are highly prevalent amongst individuals of cultural groups within their patient population. One example is the disproportionately increased rate of smoking observed in the gay, lesbian, and bisexual communities. The prevalence rate of tobacco use among LGBT persons has been quoted as high as 50% in some studies, as compared with 21% of the general population [1]. The public health impact of this high rate of smoking is not yet known, as this has not been a widely published area of research [82], [92], [93]. However, it is likely that there are several resulting and serious health consequences from this degree of tobacco exposure.

Population-Specific Barriers to Treatment of Tobacco Dependence

It has been proposed that several barriers to accessing health care in general exist for LGBT patients, and that these negatively affect both acute medical care and preventive services [94]. A major identified barrier has been that of bias on the part of health care providers, and the resulting fear of discriminatory treatment on the part of patients. Improving access of LGBT patients to high quality health care will require active education of providers to assist in overcoming such biases. Providing a safe and accepting health care environment will allow for more opportunities to address health issues, such as tobacco cessation, with LGBT patients.

One of the identifiable barriers to the treatment of tobacco dependence in LGBT persons is that the tobacco industry specifically targets this population in advertising [51]. There is a significant amount of both commercial and noncommercial imagery and text relating to tobacco and smoking in gay, lesbian, and bisexual magazines and newspapers, which tend to shed a positive light on smoking or associate tobacco use with celebrities [52]. Some media marketing is targeted toward LGBT youth smokers [93]. The effect of this is a relative normalization of tobacco use in this population. Tobacco companies have also sponsored LGBT events [95], offered disproportionately high amounts of free product samples to LGBT persons [96], and in 1990, Philip Morris gained LGBT support by pledging to donate large sums of money in the fight against HIV/AIDS [92]. The end result is that tobacco companies have been to some degree welcomed by the LGBT population, being touted for having a strong commitment to diversity and overall support for the LBGT community.

Clinical Solutions

Clinical recommendations for patients in the lesbian, gay, bisexual, transgender population are similar as to those in the general population, and include the use of nicotine replacement therapy, counseling, and pharmacotherapeutic agents such as bupropion and varenicline. However, in research involving bupropion and varenicline, there have not been specific studies looking at this target subpopulation. In general, there needs to be more research directed at tobacco cessation in this high-risk group.

One of the important factors to emphasize in the LGBT population is the importance of peer support. A pilot study investigating smoking cessation in gay men found that, with ongoing peer support and nicotine replacement therapy, there was a 76% rate of abstinence after 7 weeks [97]. This success rate is far higher than the overall national data for this combined approach, which has up to a 53% success rate. Although studies in the LGBT population are still limited by number and scope, the available information to date suggests that this population can be quite successful in tobacco cessation with peer support and nicotine replacement therapy.

Health Policy Recommendations

Most importantly, improving overall access to medical care to LGBT persons needs to be a public health priority. This requires providing a safe and accepting environment for LGBT patients so that access to care and preventive services, including tobacco cessation, will increase. Educational material on providing welcoming care for the LGBT patient is available from many sources, including the website for the Gay and Lesbian Medical Association (glma.org).

Focusing on the differences in exposure to tobacco products and marketing in the LGBT population can give direction of creating policy and strategies for tobacco cessation. Policy must be directed at both limiting the tobacco industry's targeting of this cultural group and also by counter-advertising in directed media, publications, and events. In addition focus should be on educating the influential leaders in the gay, lesbian, and bisexual community to actively oppose use of tobacco advertising in print media that is directed towards that population. Historically, LGBT persons have been successfully able to organize around a cause when they feel that they have been exploited [90]. Hence, a successful approach may be to improve information flow to LGBT persons on how the tobacco companies are exploiting them by directly marketing a product to them which is known to cause one in five deaths in this country each year [11]. This may help decrease the normalization of tobacco use that is seen with overwhelming incidence in directed media. The 'Truth.com'campaign attempted to transmit the message, particularly to youth from diverse racial and ethnic backgrounds, that tobacco companies lie about the fact that cigarettes are addictive and cause cancer [81]. Given the particularly high prevalence rate of smoking in LGBT persons, and the significant media targeting to young and adult LGBT persons, a similar campaign could be geared toward this patient subpopulation. Public health efforts directed toward the LGBT community may strengthen goodwill within this population of people who do not normally feel that their needs are adequately respected and addressed by society and government.

Key Points

- The prevalence rate of tobacco use among LGBT persons has been quoted as high as 50% in some studies; hence it is likely that this population is at high risk for the serious health consequences of tobacco exposure. The true impact is not known as public health studies for this patient population are lacking.
- Providing a safe and accepting health care environment will allow for more opportunities to address health issues, such as tobacco cessation, with LGBT patients.
- Clinical recommendations for LGBT patients include the use of nicotine replacement therapy, counseling, and pharmacotherapeutic agents such as bupropion and varenicline. Preliminary data suggests that peer support, combined with nicotine replacement therapy, appears to have a very high rate of success.

TOBACCO DEPENDENCE TREATMENT AND PATIENT NATIVE LANGUAGE

Tobacco Use Patterns and Public Health Impact by Patient Native Language

Although all non-English speakers do not share a unified cultural bond, their native language creates a similar demographic and systematic barrier for them, and one that places them at a disadvantage for maneuvering the increasingly complex U.S. health care system. Patients that do not speak or have literacy in English, and especially if they also do not speak Spanish, may find it difficult to obtain medical assistance or have interpreter services available to them if they do. According to data from the U.S. Census Bureau, in the year 2000, 47 million U.S. residents – nearly one in five persons – speak a language other than English at home [98]. This was a 46% increase from 1990 data, and the number of Spanish speakers within that group rose by 62% to a total of 28.1 million persons. Of the Hispanic population in the United States, 41% speak only Spanish or have limited proficiency in English [99]. There are additionally many persons in the U.S. who don't speak English or Spanish. Two million persons identified by the Census Bureau in 2000 spoke Chinese, the third most common language from the survey data [98].

Data on the public health impact of smoking in non-English speakers have not been previously well-characterized. The largest group of non-English speakers has Spanish as their native language, and greater data is available on persons of Hispanic ethnicity. Limited data analyzed from the 2001 The California Health Interview Survey (CHIS) suggests that smoking prevalence rates among Californian Asian Americans differs on the basis of ethnic origin, gender, and level of English proficiency [100]. In that study, Asian men who had high English proficiency were less likely to be smokers than those with lower English proficiency, but the opposite effect was seen among Asian women. Clearly, much more needs to be understood on the public health impact that native language has on health and health care disparities, including that of tobacco dependence.

Population-Specific Barriers to Treatment of Tobacco Dependence

With English as the official language in the United States, most health care information is primarily available in that language. Although a great deal of services may be available to patients in English and Spanish, access to these services is not universal, and there are a large number of persons in the U.S. who speak neither English nor Spanish. Some of the barriers to receiving health care services in patients with non-English native languages are the same barriers that are seen in other cultural groups, such as those united by race or gender. Low socioeconomic status can also play a significant role. In major U.S. cities such as New York and Los Angeles, the most powerful predictor of poverty and hardship, including low income, lacking health insurance, and food insecurity, is having limited English skills [101]. In one study of race, ethnicity, and native language and their effects on health care access for insured patients [102], data suggested that disparities in care for Hispanic patients were largely explained by differences in English proficiency. Spanish-speakers in that study were significantly less likely to have had a physician visit, mental health visit, or influenza vaccination than non-Hispanic white patients. Other studies, however, have conflicting results to this. One such study suggested that although the majority of U.S. Hispanics speak English at home or comfortably in society, they were at increased risk for not receiving recommended health care services whether they were comfortable in speaking English or not [102]. Thus, the issue remains complex and unclear. It seems than other cultural characteristics of non-English speaking persons, in addition to native tongue, may play a significant role in access to health care.

Clinical Solutions

The obvious major barrier to treatment of patients with a native language other than English is communication difficulty. To treat tobacco use effectively, there must be good communication between the provider and patient, both in terms of counseling and in instructions for using nicotine replacement therapy or medications such as varenicline and bupropion. Data on the efficacy of pharmacotherapeutic agents in non-English speakers is not available. Therefore, clinical solutions would be the same for non-English speakers as it would be in the general population. These would include treating patients with counseling, nicotine replacement therapy, and pharmacotherapeutic agents. The caveat is that there must be culturally-sensitive education for patients in their native language, and that takes other aspects of culture (such as race and gender) into consideration. It would also be ideal to have community support groups with the same native language to help with peer counseling for smoking cessation. A trial through the National Cancer Institute's Cancer Information Service has also shown that one way to work around the language barrier in Spanish-speaking smokers is to provide counseling services over the phone in Spanish [99]. As evidence also supports the clinical benefit of computer- and internet-based smoking cessation programs [42], this modality could be easily adapted to languages other than English.

Health Policy Recommendations

Increasing access to interpreter services at health care centers would be an important start in providing improved outreach to non-English-speaking patients. Data suggest that this intervention alone can significantly decrease disparities for non-English-speaking patients in clinical service use, screening tests, and preventive services such as immunization [103]. Training initiatives for bilingual social workers and other persons capable of smoking cessation counseling would also be beneficial. Educational programs using pamphlets and books written in Spanish and other languages can be not only made available at physician's offices and health care clinics, but can also be disseminated through churches and community centers catering to non-English speaking communities. Informing health care providers about counseling services available in other languages, such as telephone quit lines, may also increase their utilization.

Key Points

- Nearly one in five persons speaks a language other than English at home. Other cultural characteristics of non-English speaking persons, in addition to native tongue, may both play a significant role in access to health care and smoking cessation services.

- Clinical solutions for treatment of tobacco dependence are the same for non-English speakers as in the general population, and include counseling, nicotine replacement therapy, and use of pharmacotherapeutic agents. Patient education must be culturally-sensitive and offered, if possible, in a patient's native language. Other aspects of culture (such as race and gender) should be taken into consideration.

CONCLUSION

Culture plays an important role in the management of tobacco dependence. Different cultural groups are individually targeted by tobacco industry marketing. Addiction to nicotine and response to pharmacotherapeutic agents may be different based on a person's cultural background, although research in these areas has been limited. Due to various barriers, different cultural groups have unequal access to treatment, medications, support, and other health care resources. As a result, the prevalence of smoking and tobacco-related diseases, as well as the overall burden of these diseases, is higher within these patient populations.

The solutions for these problems lie in the hands of three different parties. The health care provider must be willing and able to offer culturally-competent care and treatment recommendations to assist individual patients with tobacco cessation. The policy-maker must assist in breaking down barriers to fair and equitable access within the health care system. And researchers need to consider the unique qualities and needs of various cultural groups when conducting studies on tobacco dependence, and further assess the efficacy of various interventions within these groups.

Hundreds of thousands of persons die annually in the U.S. alone from tobacco-related diseases, resulting in billions of dollars spent in yearly health care costs. Tobacco is a leading cause of death and disability, and yet tobacco dependence is a completely preventable and treatable disease. The cost-per-life-year saved for treatment is negligible compared to that of other common diseases. In order to ensure that the health care provider, the policy maker, and the researcher all coordinate their efforts to make the greatest impact on this crisis, public health leaders must take charge and champion this cause. Through tobacco taxation, and directed efforts with the collected capital, a true difference can be made. Education can help prevent smoking initiation in youth and to motivate all smokers to quit. Learning opportunities will also strengthen providers' efforts and abilities to assist their patients in cessation. Medications and support resources can be made available at low- to no-cost for those who need them. And public smoking bans can be imposed across the nation. Through such efforts, significant strides can be made to help persons from all cultural backgrounds achieve better opportunities for improved health and well-being.

REFERENCES

[1] U. S. Centers for Disease Control and Prevention (CDC), "Cigarette Smoking in Adults – -- United States 2006." *Morbidity and Mortality Weekly Report (MMWR).* 56(44), 1157-1161, November 9, 2007. Acquired on June 4, 2009 at: *http://www.cdc.gov/mmwr/preview/* mmwrhtml/mm5644a2.htm.

[2] Gollust, S; Schroeder, S; Warner, K. Helping Smokers Quit: Understanding the Barriers to Utilization of Smoking Cessation Services. *The Milbank Quarterly.* 86(4): 60-627, 2008.

[3] Warner, KE; Mendez, D; Smith, DG. The Financial Implications of Coverage of Smoking Cessation Treatment by Managed Care Organizations. 2004. Inquiry 41 (1): 57-69.

[4] Fiore, MC; Bailey, WC; Cohen, SF. Treating Tobacco Use and Dependence: A Clinical Practice Guideline. Rockville, MD. U.S. Department of Health and Human Services. 2000.

[5] Ellerbeck, EF; Mahnken, JD; Cupertino, P; Sanderson, Cox, L; Greiner, KA; Mussulman, LM; Nazir, N; Shireman, TI; Resnicow, K; Ahluwalia, JS. Effect of Varying Levels of Disease Management on Smoking Cessation: A Randomized Trial. *Annals of Internal Medicine.* 150(7): 437-446, 2009.

[6] culture. (n.d.). The American Heritage® New Dictionary of Cultural Literacy, Third Edition. Retrieved May 17, 2009, from Dictionary.com website: http://dictionary1.classic.reference.com/browse/culture.

[7] Report of the Surgeon General on Tobacco Use Among US Racial/Ethnic Minority Groups. Washington DC : US Department of Health and Human Services 1998.

[8] U.S. Centers for Disease Control and Prevention (CDC), "Cigarette Smoking Among Adults- United States 2007." *Morbidity and Mortality Weekly Report (MMWR).* Nov 14, 2008. 57(45): 1221-1226. Acquired on June 4, 2009 at *http://www.cdc.gov/mmwr/preview/mmwrhtml/*

mm5745a2.htm.

[9] Office of the Surgeon General. Women and smoking: A Report of the Surgeon General. Retrieved June 4, 2009 from: http://www.surgeongeneral.gov/library/womenandtobacco/.

[10] Woolf, A. Smoking and Nicotine Addiction: A Pediatric Epidemic with Sequelae in Adulthood. *Current Opinion in Pediatrics*. 9:470-477, 1997.

[11] U.S. Centers for Disease Control and Prevention (CDC), "Women and smoking: A Report of the Surgeon General. Chapter 5: Efforts to reduce tobacco use among women." *Morbidity and Mortality Weekly Report (MMWR)*. 51(RR12):1-30, August 30, 2002. Acquired on June 4, 2009 at: http://www.cdc.gov/mmwr/preview/mmwrhtml/rr5112a4.htm.

[12] World Health Organization. Gender or women's health: why should WHO work on this? WHO role as an advocate for gender equality and women's health. Retrieved June 4, 2009 from: *http://www.who.int/gender/* about/gender_or_womens_health/en/index.html.

[13] Levine, MD; Perkins, KA; Marcus, MD. The Characteristics of Women Smokers Concerned about Postcessation Weight Gain. *Addicitive Behaviors*. 26(5): 749-756, 2001.

[14] Clark, MM; Hurt, RD; Croghan, IT; Patten, CA; Novotny, P; Sloan, JA; Dakhil, SR. et al. The Prevalence of Weight Concerns in a Smoking Abstinence Clinical Trial. *Addictive Behaviors*. 31(7): 1144-1152, 2006.

[15] Perkins, KA; Scott, J. Sex differences in long-term smoking cessation rates due to nicotine patch. *Nicotine & Tobacco Research*. 10(7): 1245-50, 2008 Jul.

[16] Schnoll, RA; Patterson, F; & Lerman, C. Treating Tobacco Dependence in Women. *Journal of Women's Health*. 16(8): 1211-1217, 2007 Nov 8.

[17] Chan, B; Einarson, A; Koren, G. Effectiveness of bupropion for smoking cessation during pregnancy. *Journal of Addicitive Diseases*. 20:19, 2005.

[18] Gonzales, D; Rennard, SI; Nides, M; Oncken, C; Azoulay, S; Billing CB; Watsky, EJ; Gong, J; Williams, KE; Reeves, KR. Varenicline an $\alpha 4\beta 2$ Nicotinic Acetylcholine Receptor Partial Agonist, vs Sustained-Release Bupropion and Placebo for Smoking Cessation: A Randomized Controlled Trial. 2006. *JAMA*. 296:47-55.

[19] Chaney, SE; Sheriff, S. Weight Gain Among Women During Smoking Cessation: Testing the Effects of a Multifaceted Program. *AAOHN Journal*. 56(3), March 2008.

[20] Prescribing Information: CHANTIX® (varenicline) Tablets. Dosage and Administration. Retrieved May 17, 2009 from *https://www.pfizerpro.*

com/sites/pfp/pages/product_info/Chantix_pi_dosage_and_adminiadmin ist.aspx and http://www.pfizer.com/files/products/uspi_chantix.pdf.

[21] Bupropion hydrochloride drug information. Retrieved May 17, 2009 from http://www.fda.gov/cder/drug/infopage/bupropion/default.htm.

[22] Nicorette Stop Smoking Gum. Frequently asked questions. Retrieved May 24, 2009 from http://www.nicorette.com/Faqs.aspx#21 and http://www.nicorette.com/Nicorette_Know.aspx.

[23] Elders, MJ; Perry, CL; Eriksen, MP; Giovino, GA. The report of the Surgeon General: Preventing tobacco use among young people. *American Journal of Public Health. 84*(4): 543-547, 1994.

[24] Centers for Disease Control and Prevention. Cigarette Use Among High School Students- United States, 1991-2007. *Morbidity and Mortality Weekly Reports (MMWR)*. 57(25), June 27, 2008.

[25] Pbert, L; Flint, A; Fletcher, K; Young, M; Drunker, S. Effect of a Pediatric Practice Based Smoking Prevention and Cessation Intervention for Adolescents: A Randomized, Controlled Trial. *Pediatrics*. 121; e738-e747, 2008.

[26] Centers for Disease control and Prevention. Selected cigarette smoking initiation and quitting behaviors among high school students – United States 1997. *Morbidity and Mortality Weekly Reports (MMWR)*. Vol 47, 1998.

[27] McVea, K. Evidence for Clinical Smoking Cessation for Adolescents. *Health Psychology*. 25(5): 558-562, 2006.

[28] Hutcheson, T; Greiner, KA; Ellerbeck, E. Understanding smoking cessation in rural communities. Spring 2008 National Rural Health Association.

[29] Pierce, JP; Choi, WS; Gilpin, EA; Farkas, AJ; Berry CC. Tobacco Industry Promotion of Cigarettes and Adolescent Smoking. *JAMA*. 279: 511-515, 1998.

[30] Waxman, H. Tobacco marketing. Profiteering from children [comment]. *JAMA*. 266(22): 3185-6, 1991 Dec 11.

[31] Sargent, J; Gibson, J; Heatherton, TF. Comparing the effects of entertainment media and tobacco marketing on youth smoking. *Tobacco Control*. 18: 47-53, 2009.

[32] Dalton, MA; Tickle, JJ; Sargent, JD; Beach, ML; Ahrens B; Heatherton TF. The Incidence and Context of Tobacco Use in Popular Movies from 1988 to 1997. *Preventive Medicine*. 34(5): 516-23, May 2002.

[33] III.(e) Prohibition on Payments Related to Tobacco Products and Media. *Master Settlement Agreement*, November 23, 1998. Retrieved May 17,

2009 from http://www.naag.org/upload/1032468605_cigmsa.pdf.
[34] National Center for Tobacco-Free Kids. Campaign for Tobacco-Free Kids. Factsheets. Acquired on April 7, 2009 at: http://www.tobaccofreekids.org/research/factsheets/.
[35] Kacirk, K; Glantz, S. Smoking in Movies in 2000 Exceeded Rates in the 1960s. Letter. *Tobacco Control.* 10: 397-98, 2001.
[36] Federal Trade Commission Cigarette Report for 2004-2005. Acquired on May 30, 2009 at: http://www.ftc.gov/reports/tobacco/2007cigarette2004-2005.pdf.
[37] Ling, PM; Glantz, SA. Why and How the Tobacco Industry Sells Cigarettes to Young Adults: Evidence from Industry Documents. *American Journal of Public Health*. 92(6): 908-916, June 2002.
[38] Lovato, C; Linn, G; Stead, LF; Best A. Impact of tobacco advertising and promotion on increasing adolescent smoking behaviors (Review). *Cochrane Database of Systematic Reviews*. 2003, Issue 3. Art. No. CD003439. The Cochrane Collaboration.
[39] King, C; Siegel, M; Celebucki, C; Connolly, G. Adolescent Exposure to Cigarette Advertising in Relation to Youth Readership. *JAMA*. 279(7): 516-520, 18 February 1998.
[40] Rigotti, NA; Moran, SE; Wechsler, H. US College Students' Exposure to Tobacco Promotions: Prevalence and Association With Tobacco Use. *American Journal of Public Health*. 95(1): 138-144, January 2005.
[41] Sussman, S; Sun, P; Dent, CW. A Meta-Analysis of Teen Smoking Cessation. *Health Psychology*. 25(5): 549-557, 2006.
[42] Myung, SK; McDonell, DD; Kazinets, G; Seo, HG; Moskowitz JM. Effects of Web- and Computer-Based Smoking Cessation Programs. Meta-analysis of Randomized Controlled Trials. *Archives of Internal Medicine*. 169(10): 929-937, May 25 2009.
[43] Killen, JD; Robinson, TN; Ammerman, S; Hayward, C; Rogers J; Stone C; Samuels, D; Levin, SK; Green, S; Schatzbert, AF. Randomized Clinical Trial of the Efficacy of Bupropion Combined with Nicotine Patch in the Treatment of Adolescent Smokers. *Journal of Consulting and Clinical Psychology*. 72(4): 729-735, 2004.
[44] Colby, SM; Gwaltney, CJ. Pharmacotherapy for Adolescent Smoking Cessation. *JAMA*. 298: 2182-2184, 2007.
[45] Christakis, D; Garrison, M; Ebel, B; Wiehe, S; Rivara, F. Pediatric Smoking Prevention Interventions Delivered by Care Providers: A Systematic Review. *American Journal of Preventative Medicine*. 25(4): 358-362, 2003.

[46] Simis, KJ; Koot, JM; Verhulst, FC; Hovius, SER; and The Adolescence Plastic Surgical Research Group. Assessing adolescents and young adults for plastic surgical intervention: pre-surgical appearance ratings and appearance-related burdens as reported by adolescents and young adults, parents and surgeons. *British Journal of Plastic Surgery*. 53(7): 593-600, October 2000.
[47] Espeland, LV, Stenvik, A; Medi, L. Concern for dental appearance among young adults in a region with non-specialist orthodontic treatment. *The European Journal of Orthodontics*. 15(1): 17-25, 1993.
[48] Smoking Among Older Adults Fact Sheet. American Lung Association. Retrieved May 24, 2009 from: *http://www.lungusa.org/site/* c.dvLUK9O0E/b.39862.
[49] Centers for Disease Control and Prevention. National Center for Health Statistics. National Health Interview Survey, 1965-2006. Calculations for 1997-2006 were performed by the American Lung Association Research and Program Services Division using SPSS and SUDAAN software. Retrieved May 24, 2009 from: *http://www.lungusa.org/* site/c.dvLUK9O0E/b.39862.
[50] U.S. Centers for Disease Control and Prevention (CDC). "Cigarette Smoking Among Adults - United States, 2003." *Morbidity and Mortality Weekly Report (MMWR)*. 54(20); 509-513. Retrieved May 24, 2009 from: http://www.cdc.gov/mmwr/preview/mmwrhtml/mm5420a3.htm.
[51] Doolan, D; Froelicher, E. Effficacy of Smoking Cessation Intervention Among Special Populations. *Nursing Research*. July/August 2006. 55(4S): pS29-S37.
[52] United States Center for Disease Control and Prevention. 2009. State Specific Prevalence and Trends in Adult Cigarette Smoking - United States - 1998-2007. *Morbidity and Mortality Weekly Report (MMWR)*. 58(09): 221-226, March 13 2009.
[53] Donze, J; Ruffieux, C; Cornuz, J. Determinants of smoking and cessation in older women. *Age Ageing*. 36: 53-57, 2007.
[54] Rimer, BK; Orleans, CT; Keintz, MK; Cristinzio, S; Fleisher, L. The older smoker: status, challenges and opportunities for intervention. *Chest*. 97: 547-53, 1990.
[55] Kerr, S; Watson, H; Tolson, D; Lough, M; Brown, M. Developing Evidence-Based Smoking Cessation Training/Education Initiatives in Partnership with Older People and Health Professionals. Caledonian Nursing & Midwifery Research Centre: Glasgow 2004. Retrieved May 24, 2009 from http://www.lungusa.org/site/c.dvLUK9O0E/b.39862.

[56] Taylor, DH; Hasselblad, V; Henley, J; Thun, MD; Sloan, FA. Benefits of Smoking Cessation for Longevity. *American Journal of Public Health*. 92: 990-6, 2002.
[57] Sachs-Ericsson, N; Schmidt, NB; Zvolensky, MJ; Mitchell, M, Collins, N, Blazer, DG. Smoking cessation behavior in older adults by race and gender: The role of health problems and psychological distress. *Nicotine Tob Res.* 11: 433-443, 2009.
[58] Tait, RJ, Hulse, GK; Waterreus, A; Flicker, L; Lautenschlager, NT; Jamrozik, K; Almeida, OP. Effectiveness of a Smoking Cessation Intervention in Older Adults. *Addiction*. 102: 148-155, 2006.
[59] Hughes, JR. New treatments for smoking cessation. *CA Cancer J Clin.*, 50: 143, 2000.
[60] Burstein, AH; Fullerton, T; Clark, DJ; Faessel, HM. Pharmacokinetics, Safety, and Tolerability After Single and Multiple Oral Doses of Varenicline in Elderly Smokers. *J Clin Pharmacol.* 46: 1234-1240, 2006.
[61] McPhilips-Tangum, C; Rehm, B; Carreon, C; Erceg, CM; Bocchino, C. Addressing Tobacco in Managed Care: Results of the 2003 Survey. *Preventing Chronic Disease*. 3(3), July 2006.
[62] Volpp, K; Troxel, A; Pauly, M. A. Randomized, Controlled trial of Financial Incentives for Smoking Cessation. *NEJM*. 360(7): 699-709, Feb 12, 2009.
[63] *Evidence-Based Medical Ethics: Cases for Practice-Based Learning.* Snyder JE and Gauthier CC. Humana Press, 2008. Page 136.
[64] U.S. Department of Health and Human Services. Tobacco Use Among U.S. Racial/Ethnic Minority Groups—African Americans, American Indians and Alaska Natives, Asian Americans and Pacific Islanders, and Hispanics: A Report of the Surgeon General. Atlanta: U.S. Department of Health and Human Services, Centers for Disease Control and Prevention, 1998 [cited 2007 May 10]. Retrieved May 24, 2009 from: http://www.cdc.gov/tobacco/data_statistics/sgr/sgr_1998/index.htm.
[65] Haiman, C; Daniel, S; Wilkens, L. Ethnic and Racial Differences in the Smoking-Related Risk of Lung Cancer. *NEJM*. 354(4): 333-342, Jan 26, 2006.
[66] Caraballo, RS; Giovino, GA; Pechacek, TF; Mowery, PD; Richter, PA; Strauss, WJ; Sharp, DJ; Eriksen, MP; Pirkle JL; Maurer, KR. Racial and Ethnic Differences in Serum Cotinine Levels of Cigarette Smokers: Third National Health and Nutrition Examination Survey, 1988-1991. *JAMA*. 280: 135-139, 1998.

[67] Struthers, R; Hodge, F. Sacred, Tobacco Use in Ojibwe Communities. *Journal of Holistic Nursing*. 22: 209-225, 2004.

[68] Choi, WS; Daley, CM; James, A; Thomas, J; Schupbach, R; Segraves M; Barnoskie, R; Ahluwalia, JS. Beliefs and Attitudes Regarding Smoking Cessation Among American Indians: A Pilot Study. *Ethnicity and Disease*. 16: 35-40, Winter 2006.

[69] UI Health Care News: Week of December 5, 2005. UI Researchers Examine Effect of Race on Smoking, Tobacco Outlet Density. Retrieved May 24, 2009 from *http://www.uihealthcare.com/news/* news/2005/12/05tobacco.html

[70] Friedman, E. Money isn't everything. Nonfinancial barriers to access. *JAMA*. 271(19): 1535-8, 1994 May 18.

[71] Hahm, HC; Segal, SP. Failure to seek health care among the mentally ill. *American Journal of Orthopsychiatry*. 75(1): 54-62, 2005 Jan.

[72] Chadda, RK; Agarwal, V; Singh, MC; Raheja, D. Help seeking behaviour of psychiatric patients before seeking care at a mental hospital. *International Journal of Social Psychiatry*., 47(4): 71-8, 2001.

[73] Ahluwalia, JS; McNagny, SE; Clark WS. Smoking Cessation among Inner-City African Americans Using the Nicotine Transdermal Patch. *JGIM*. 13(1): 1-8, 1998.

[74] Jorenby, DE; Hays, JT; Rigotti, NA; Azoulay, S; Watsky, EJ; Williams KE; Billing CB; Gong J; Reeves KR. Efficacy of Varenicline, an $\alpha 4\beta 2$ Nicotinic Acetylcholine Receptor Partial Agonist; vs Placebo or Sustained-Release Bupropion for Smoking Cessation. *JAMA*. 296(1): 56-63, 2006.

[75] Covey, LS; Botello-Harbaum, M; Glassman, AH; Masmela, J; LoDuca, C; Salzman, V; Fried, J. Smoker's response to combination bupropion, nicotine patch, and counseling treatment by race/ethnicity. *Ethnicity and Disease*. 18(1): 59-64, 2008 Winter.

[76] Robles, GI; Singh-Franco, D; Ghin, HL. A review of efficacy of smoking-cessation pharmacotherapies in nonwhite populations. *Clin. Ther.* 30(5): 800-812, 2008 May.

[77] Leischow, SJ; Hill, A; Cook, G. The Effects of Transdermal Nicotine for the Treatment of Hispanic Smokers. *American Journal of Health Behavior*. 20(5): 304-311, 1996.

[78] Levinson, AH; Borrayo, EA; Espinoza, P; Flores, ET; Perez-Stable, EJ. An Exploration of Latino Smokers and the Use of Pharmaceutical Aids. *American Journal of Preventive Medicine*. 31(2): 167-171, 2006.

[79] Nakamura, M; Oshima, A; Fujimoto, Y; Maruyama, N; Ishibashi, T;

Reeves, KR. Efficacy and tolerability of varenicline, an alpha4beta2 nicotinic acetylcholine receptor partial agonist, in a 12-week, randomized, placebo-controlled, dose-response study with 40-week follow-up for smoking cessation in Japanese smokers. *Clinical Therapeutics*. 29(6): 1040-56, 2007 Jun.

[80] Tsai, ST; Cho, HJ; Cheng, HS; Kim, CH; Hsueh, KC; Billing, CB; Williams, KE. A randomized, placebo-controlled trial of varenicline, a selective alpha4beta2 nicotinic acetylcholine receptor partial agonist, as a new therapy for smoking cessation in Asian smokers. *Clinical Therapeutics*. 29(6): 1027-39, 2007 Jun.

[81] Cowell, A; Farrelly, MC; Chou, R; Vallone, DM. Assessing the impact of the national 'truth' antismoking campaign on beliefs, attitudes, and intent to smoke by race/ethnicity. *Ethnicity and Health*. 14(1), 75-91, 2009 Feb.

[82] Snyder, JE. A Review and Analysis of Medical Publications about LGBT Patients. Unpublished data. Submitted to the *Journal of Homosexuality*, under review, 2009.

[83] Brandenburg, DL; Matthews, AK; Johnson, TP; Hughes, TL. Breast cancer risk and screening: a comparison of lesbian and heterosexual women. *Women Health*. 45(4): 109-30, 2007.

[84] Case, P; Austin, SB; Hunter, DJ. et al. Sexual orientation, health risk factors, and physical functioning in the Nurses' Health Study II. *J Womens Health (Larchmt)*. 13(9): 1033-47, 2004 Nov.

[85] Chin-Hong, PV; Vittinghoff, E; Cranston, RD; et al. Age-related prevalence of anal cancer precursors in homosexual men: the EXPLORE study. *J Natl Cancer Inst*. 97(12): 896-905, 2005 Jun 15.

[86] Daling, JR; Weiss, NS; Hislop, G; Maden, C; Coates, RJ; Sherman, KJ; Ashley, RL; Beagrie, M; Ryan, JA; Corey, L. Sexual practices, sexually transmited diseases, and the incidence of anal cancer. *NEJM*. 317: 973–7, 1987.

[87] Denenberg, R. Report on lesbian health. *Womens Health Issues*. 5(2): 181–91, 1995.

[88] Dibble, SL; Roberts, SA; Robertson, PA; Paul, SM. Risk factors for ovarian cancer: lesbian and heterosexual women. *Oncol Nurs Forum*. 29(1): E1-7, 2002 Jan-Feb.

[89] Goldstone, SE; Hundert, JS; Huyett, JW. Infrared coagulator ablation of high-grade anal squamous intraepithelial lesions in HIV-negative males who have sex with males. *Dis Colon Rectum*. 50(5): 565-75, 2007 May.

[90] Lesbian Health Fact Sheet. Office on Women's Health, U.S. Department

of Health and Human Services. Retrieved May 22, 2008 from http://www.glma.org/_data/n_0001/resources/live/lesbian1.pdf.

[91] Robertson, P; Schacter, J. Failure to identify venereal disease in a lesbian population. *Sex Transm Dis*. 8(2): 75–6, 1981.

[92] Stevens, P; Carlson, L; Hinman, J. An Analysis of Tobacco Industry Marketing to Lesbian, Gay, Bisexual, and Transgender Populations: Strategies for Mainstream Tobacco Control and Prevention. *Health Promotion Practice*. 5(3) (Supplement): S129-S134, July 2004.

[93] Washington, HA. Burning Love: Big Tobacco Takes Aim at LGBT Youth. *American Journal of Public Health*. 92(7):1086-1095, July 2002.

[94] Dean, L; Meyer, IH; Robinson, K; Sell, RL; Sember, R; Silenzio,VMB, Bowen, DJ; Bradford, J; Rothblum, E; White, J; Dunn, P; Lawrence, A; Wolfe, D; Xavier, J. Lesbian, Gay, Bisexual, and Transgender Health: Findings and Concerns. *J Gay Lesbian Med Assoc*. 4(3): 101-151, 2000.

[95] Smith, EA; Malone, RE. The Outing of Philip Morris: Advertising Tobacco to Gay Men. *American Journal of Public Health*. 93(6), 988-993, June 2003.

[96] Dilley, JA; Spigner, C; Boysun, MJ; Dent, CW; Pizacani, BA. Does tobacco industry marketing excessively impact lesbian, gay and bisexual communities? *Tobacco Control*. 17: 385-390, 2008.

[97] Harding, R; Bensley, J; Corrigan, N. Targeting Smoking Cessation to High Prevalence Communities: Outcomes from a Pilot Intervention for Gay Men. *BMC Public Health*. 4: 43, 2004.

[98] Bergman, M. Nearly 1-in-5 Speak a Foreign Language at Home; Most Also Speak English 'Very Well,' Census Bureau Reports. Public Information Office, U.S. Census Bureau, U.S. Department of Commerce. Retrieved May 25, 2009 from http://www.census.gov/Press-Release/www/releases/archives/census_2000/001406.html.

[99] Wetter, D; Mazas, C; Daza, P; Nguyen, L; Fouladi, R; Li, Y; Cofta-Woerpel, L. Reaching and Treating Spanish-Speaking Smokers Through the National Cancer Center Institute's Cancer Information Service: A Randomized Controlled Trial. *Cancer*. 109(2 Suppl): 406-413, 2007 Jan 15.

[100] Cheng, EM; Chen, A; Cunningham, W. Primary Language and Receipt of Recommended Health Care Among Hispanics in the United States. *JGIM*. 22(Suppl 2): 283–288, 2007 November.

[101] Fix, M; Capps, R. "Immigrant Well-Being in New York and Los Angeles;" Policy Brief No. 1 in series "Immigrant Families and Workers: Facts and Perspectives," Aug. 7, 2003, Retrieved May 25,

2009 from http://www.urban.org/url.cfm?ID=310566.

[102] Fiscella, K; Franks, P; Doescher, MP; Saver, BG. Disparities in Health Care by Race, Ethnicity, and Language Among the Insured: Findings From a National Sample. *Medical Care*. 40(1): 52-59. January 2002.

[103] Jacobs, EA; Lauderdale, DS; Meltzer, D; Shorey, JM; Levinson, W; Thisted, RA. Impact of interpreter services on delivery of health care to limited-English-proficient patients. *JGIM.* 16: 468-74, 2001.

Disclaimer: It is important to note that information contained in this document is not intended to replace professional medical advice. Any questions regarding a medical diagnosis or treatment should be directed to a medical practitioner.

In: Smoking Relapse: Causes, Prevention ... ISBN: 978-1-60876-580-5
Editors: J. Egger and M. Kalb

Chapter 3

Systematic Barriers to Treating Tobacco Dependence: An Evidence-Based Review with Clinical and Health Policy Recommendations

Megan J. Engelen[1] and John E. Snyder[2*]
[1]New Hanover Regional Medical Center. Wilmington, NC.
[2] University of North Carolina School of Medicine,
SEAHEC Department of Internal Medicine.

Abstract

Tobacco dependence is a chronic illness with severe, adverse implications on the smoker's health and well-being. Additionally, the public health impact of tobacco-related illness is staggering. The highly preventable nature of this disease spectrum makes smoking cessation a major public health priority. Health care providers must address smoking on the level of the individual patient, while policy makers and government leaders need to address the issue on the population level. To make the biggest impact on tobacco-related disease, we must better understand the influences that encourage smoking and the barriers to successful cessation in the most at-risk patient populations.

---

* Corresponding author: University of North Carolina School of Medicine at Chapel Hill. South East Area Health Education Center (SEAHEC)

Patients in certain socioeconomic and demographic groups are uniquely vulnerable to tobacco dependence for many reasons. Barriers within the health care system at-large play a significant role, as do geographic and economic factors, insurance status, ability to read, and the presence of underlying mental illness. Other factors include directed and aggressive tobacco industry marketing techniques, barriers to accessing health care providers who provide treatment for tobacco dependence, inequitable access to pharmacological treatment options, and a limited availability of or access to support resources. In this chapter, we first present an evidence-based approach for providers that helps identify the most at-risk patients. We then offer specific clinical strategies for approaching tobacco cessation which are proven to be the most effective in overcoming these systematic barriers. Lastly, we propose a number of health policy recommendations which can assist with breaking down barriers to care for each patient group and result in more effective cessation programs on the population level.

Background - Tobacco Dependence and Systematic Barriers

Each year, 8 million Americans suffer from tobacco-related diseases and 400,000 Americans die as a result – more than from any other cause [1], [2]. There are $96.7 billion in annual health care costs associated with tobacco use, $38 billion of which are funded by U.S. taxpayer dollars [3]. A disproportionate burden of these illnesses is carried by low-income and uninsured persons, who have decreased access to health care services. The estimated cost-per-life-year saved from tobacco cessation ranges from $2,300-4,200 [4]. However, although the majority of all smokers express a desire to quit (around 70%), only about 8% of all smokers who attempt to quit each year are successful [5].

The health care provider's office provides the perfect opportunity for the initiation of discussions with an individual about quitting smoking. However, clinicians must do a better job in identifying which patients are smokers, offering assistance and tools for tobacco cessation, and following through with counseling at subsequent appointments. Clinical experience has revealed that most patients will not initiate a discussion about their tobacco use or smoking habits unless their provider prompts them. Therefore there are many guidelines, including from the Agency for Health Care Policy and Research, which suggest that clinicians should identify a patient's smoking status and counsel them on smoking cessation at each visit [6]. In a national survey of physicians, 62% of specialists determined smoking status during clinical visits, compared to 67% of primary care physicians [6]. Even though most physicians do ask their patients if they are smoking, studies also suggest that less than 40% of physicians actually provide them with assistance in quitting [7]. The percent of clinical visits that included time spent on smoking counseling was only 15% among specialists and 33% among primary care providers [6].

The disconnect between asking a patient about smoking and actually providing them with counseling and assistance with smoking cessation has been studied, and there are many barriers that affect this trend. In one study, clinicians agreed that barriers included having an inadequate amount of time, patients being unready to quit, inadequate patient resources for both the underserved and insured, inadequate provider resources (educational materials and staff), and inadequate clinical skills to deal with tobacco cessation [8]. One study on tobacco cessation counseling showed that providers are more likely to address smoking cessation in patients with diseases and diagnoses related to smoking such as COPD, alcohol and drug abuse, peptic ulcer disease, respiratory infections, asthma, and heart disease [6]. They are also more likely to discuss cessation with patients that are sicker, rather than healthy patients [9]. Even though it is important to address smoking cessation in patients with specific tobacco-related diseases, care needs to be taken that smoking cessation be addressed in all patient encounters. Smoking cessation is becoming an increasingly emphasized part of medical training curricula and should be equally emphasized in continuing medical education on this subject.

Other factors play a role as well. Persons with comorbid psychiatric illnesses are more likely to be smokers and statistically tend to have less success in quitting. Tobacco dependence rates are also higher within specific low-income groups, such as the rural and urban poor. There is also often decreased access to preventative health care in these areas, as well as a greater peer influence component that affects an individual's smoking habits. Higher rates of tobacco dependence within patient subpopulations put patients in those groups at higher risk for the health consequences associated with smoking.

In addition to varied smoking prevalence rates, there is also a discrepancy seen in the frequency of tobacco cessation counseling done by physicians to patients in different sociocultural subpopulations. For example, women, ethnic minorities, persons with Medicaid, and patients who are uninsured are all less likely to receive appropriate tobacco counseling and cessation services by physicians [10]. Due to the health consequences of smoking, those in the medical profession and in the public health field need to work harder to augment the number of people who try and successfully quit smoking. But in order to accomplish this task, we must better understand the factors associated with smoking in specific target patient populations, as well as the barriers of these patients to successfully quit smoking.

Tobacco Dependence Treatment in the Urban Poor

Tobacco Use Patterns and Public Health Impact in the Urban Poor

Urban poverty has been argued to be tantamount to a situation of exclusion from the basic rights of citizenship – including exclusion from having a political voice, quality housing and education, safety, transportation, goods and services, legal protection, and opportunities for income and self-betterment [11], [12]. The health care impact of living in low-income urban settings is apparent in many disease processes, such as the higher rates observed for cardiovascular heart disease (CHD) [13]. Smoking among the urban poor is of particular concern because smokers have a higher rate of CHD and hypertension, hence socioeconomic status may put individuals in this population at particularly high risk for the adverse effects of smoking [13]. There are higher overall rates of high cholesterol, hypertension, physical inactivity, and poor diet in these communities [14]. Overall, the urban poor tend also to have a disproportionably high rate of tobacco abuse [15]. In one study of the urban poor in Houston, the nation's 4th largest city, smoking prevalence rates were measured to be 53% among white residents, 42% among black residents, and 24% in the Hispanic population [13]. Residents of public housing also have higher reported rates of tobacco abuse [15].

Population-Specific Barriers to Treatment of Tobacco Dependence

Access to health care in the urban poor is a critical public health issue, with large systematic barriers at play. In urban populations where the average household income is below $15,000, the rate of uninsured can be as high as 75% [16]. Nearly half of persons in these conditions, even if they have access to public health clinics, may avoid health services completely due to financial concerns [16]. Even among the urban poor and near-poor who are privately insured, the cost of co-pays and deductibles limits their usage of health care services [17].

The difference in smoking prevalence rates in low socioeconomic urban areas appears to be due to a greater smoking initiation rate and a lower quit rate [13]. This may be due to the increased targeting of tobacco company advertising in these areas, the social structure that supports an environment of smoking, and the increased stress rates of living in these environments. The poor in general are targeted by the tobacco companies by some of their biggest promotional offers, including by offering cheaper cigarettes, multi-pack discounts, and coupons to make cigarettes more affordable [18]. Tobacco companies spent $13.11 billion (U.S.) in 2005 on advertising and promotion, with the largest amount of those expenditures being discounts to retailers to decrease the price of tobacco [19]. It has been observed that stores actively participating in tobacco company incentive programs often have lower prices for cigarettes and are more likely to feature cigarettes and advertising materials in a prominent manner [20]. Discounts target the low socioeconomic class as this population is likely to be highly sensitive to price increases and taxing on cigarettes.

The main barriers to tobacco cessation in underserved communities appear to be lack of time to undertake the cessation process, patients not feeling ready to quit smoking, inadequate access to patient resources, inadequate provider resources that are available, and inadequate clinical skills of providers that offer cessation [8]. Additionally, patients without insurance are more likely to be unable to afford the pharmacological options for helping with smoking cessation, such as nicotine replacement therapy, bupropion, and varenicline. Patients with low income may have a lesser willingness to sacrifice the money that they would be paying for cigarettes for medications to help them quit. Surveyed providers for this population feel that there are not enough community resources that they can refer their patients to for help, and that there is inadequate time to do all of the necessary tobacco cessation counseling required in a 15 minute office visit [8]. There may also be frustration among providers serving patient populations with low quit rates, with the feeling that their efforts in trying to get patients to quit smoking are not often enough successful. Yet persistence, including continued discussion about tobacco cessation at every single office visit, may eventually lead to more successful quit rates for patients.

Clinical Solutions

Clinical solutions for the treatment of tobacco dependence are the same for the urban poor as in the general population, and include counseling and peer support, nicotine replacement therapy, and the use of pharmacotherapeutic agents such as bupropion and varenicline. However, barriers to care for the urban poor must be considered when initiating a tobacco cessation plan. Patients may not have time outside of work to participate in individual or group quit programs. Patients also may be unable to afford prescribed medications or nicotine replacement therapy.

In research involving varenicline and bupropion, there have not been specific studies looking at this target subpopulation. In general, there needs to be more research directed at tobacco cessation in this high-risk group that carries such a high burden of disease related to tobacco use. One study in urban, low-income, African American patients examined the use of nicotine replacement therapy (via the patch) in combination with counseling versus placebo and counseling, and found that the short-term quit rates are significantly improved from the use of nicotine replacement (21.5% versus 13.7% respectively) [21]. In another study of low-income, African American, inner-city smokers, there was an increased quit rate associated with culturally-sensitive self-help tobacco cessation literature combined with a single phone contact [22]. Computer- and internet-based smoking cessation programs may be of benefit as well [23].

Health Policy Recommendations

The poor are targeted by tobacco company promotions and discounts, which make cigarettes more affordable for this population [18]. One of the ways to counteract such incentives and decrease tobacco dependence is to create policy to increase tobacco taxation. This approach may be of particular benefit to lower socioeconomic groups. One New Zealand study calculated that a tax increase of 16% decreased the national rate of tobacco consumption over the following year by 10% [24]. Another study out of the United Kingdom found that as the price of cigarettes rose 342% over a 15 year period, from $3.39 to $11.60, the prevalence of smoking decreased more dramatically in poorer populations (36.5% to 28.4%) when compared to higher income groups (21.5% to 16.6%) [25]. Since increases in tobacco taxation are directly related to decreases in tobacco consumption, this appears to be the most effective strategy for global tobacco cessation.

Even though with taxation there is still disparity seen in the prevalence of smoking between different socioeconomic classes, taxation tends to narrow this gap. Increases in tobacco taxation may have a greater deleterious financial impact on the poor than on wealthier persons since they spend a higher percentage of their total income on cigarettes. However, the poor also carry a higher burden of disease that is a direct effect of tobacco use. The goal of cigarette taxation is to discourage all purchasers of tobacco products from continued use. Additionally, tax monies raised can be aimed at media and other campaigns that promote tobacco cessation, and these efforts can be particularly directed toward poorer populations. Policy makers have a duty to protect this particularly vulnerable population.

Key Points

- Smoking among the urban poor is of particular concern because low socioeconomic status puts individuals in this population at very high risk for the adverse effects of smoking.
- Access to health care in the urban poor is a critical public health issue, with large systematic barriers at play. The poor in general are additionally targeted by the tobacco companies by some of their biggest promotional offers.
- Clinical solutions for treatment of tobacco dependence are the same for the urban poor as in the general population, and include counseling and peer support, nicotine replacement therapy, and the use of pharmacotherapeutic agents such as bupropion and varenicline. However, patients also may be unable to afford prescribed medications or nicotine replacement therapy.
- Barriers to care for the urban poor must be considered when initiating a tobacco cessation plan. Culturally-sensitive self-help tobacco cessation literature and phone support may be effective strategies.

Tobacco Dependence and the Rural Poor

Tobacco Use Patterns Public Health Impact in the Rural Poor

Cigarette smoking is more prevalent among both adults and adolescents in rural regions than it is in suburban or urban communities. In rural areas, there is a 25% smoking prevalence rate, compared with 22% in urban communities and 21% in the general United States population [26]. Additionally, the overall decreased prevalence of smoking in the U.S. during the last 40 years has not seen as sharp of a decline in rural communities [28]. In some rural areas, the prevalence has actually seen increases by as much as two percentage points [27]. On average, the rural smoker also tends to consume more cigarettes per day [28].

The most rural counties in the American south have the highest regional rates of heart disease-related deaths for men and the second highest rates for women [29], [30]. Additionally, the smallest mortality declines for premature coronary heart disease among both white and African American persons are in these areas [30], [31]. Lung cancer rates are also higher among both white and African American males in certain rural areas in the South, such as in Georgia, when compared to urban areas [32]. Poor survival from lung cancer in rural areas seems to be associated with low socioeconomic class and inadequate supply of health care providers [33].

Population-Specific Barriers to Treatment of Tobacco Dependence

Rural regions of the country face unique barriers to health care access related to geographic isolation. Patients (or families of patients) that are unable to take time off from work, that are housebound, that lack transportation access, who live in remote rural areas or regions with weather and terrain barriers, or who have no nearby providers may not be able to access the health care they need [34]. In other words, even if health care could be provided at low or no cost, that does not mean that a patient will be able to receive it. Rural communities are affected by greater distances from health care facilities, lower rates of health insurance coverage, inadequate access to specialty and mental health care, and limited options for smoking cessation programs and interventions [28].

A study involving rural communities in Kansas identified several individual barriers to smoking cessation, such as the belief that the damage from smoking was already done, that smoking is enjoyable and it helps with boredom and loneliness, and that tools that help with tobacco cessation may be of uncertain benefit [28]. Additional systematic barriers that were identified included inadequate finances to visit a physician, a paucity of local cessation programs, and poor knowledge about available products and services for quitting [28]. Other community-related and social factors also played a role. These included a lack of alternative activities to smoking, the absence of public smoking restrictions, and having friends and family who smoke [28]. In addition, patients from rural areas were less likely than those from urban settings to report that they received consistent advice and assistance on smoking cessation from their physicians [28].

Clinical Solutions

For low-income rural populations, telephone-based tobacco quit lines can be of significant benefit because these work around the need for traveling to physician visits and can be offered as a free service. The hours for quit lines can also be flexible so that participants can use the program despite work and childcare obligations. Telephone quit lines provide individualized assistance to patients and have been shown improve cessation rates [5].

Other clinical solutions for treating tobacco cessation in the rural poor include internet- and email-based counseling programs and telemedicine. These are all cost-effective solutions for bringing tobacco education and cessation counseling to geographical areas that have poor access to health care [28]. Nicotine replacement therapy is important for cessation in rural populations as it can be purchased over the counter and may be readily accessible. However the utility of this recommendation may be limited by its associated expense. Cost also limits the access of pharmacological interventions such as bupropion and varenicline, although these medications may be very helpful for patients in rural areas.

Health Policy Recommendations

The greatest barriers to assisting the rural poor with tobacco cessation appear to be related to decreased access to adequate care and a limited education about tobacco cessation programs and resources. Currently several programs exist to improve primary medical care to rural areas in the United States, such as the National Health Service Corps and the Indian Health Service. Providers are often incentivized to join these programs by being given significant reductions in their student loan debt. The Health Resources and Services Administration (HRSA) branch of the U.S. Department of Health and Human Services also provides a number of grants and training opportunities for rural health care, particularly through the Office of Rural Health Policy (ORHP). Improved access to motivated, well-trained providers will help to promote tobacco cessation programs and other critical health care initiatives in rural regions. Educational programs, offered to youth at early ages in the public school system, can also be used to help educate them about avoiding the initiation of smoking altogether. Drug programs that offer discounted or free medications would also be helpful in this population.

Key Points

- Cigarette smoking is more prevalent in rural regions than in suburban or urban communities. The overall decreased prevalence of smoking in the U.S. over the last 40 years has not seen as sharp of a decline in rural communities, and some rural areas are actually seeing increased prevalence of tobacco use.
- The greatest barriers to assisting the rural poor with tobacco cessation appear to be related to decreased access to adequate care and a limited education about tobacco cessation programs/resources and their effectiveness.
- Patients in rural areas may be unable to access or afford prescribed medications or nicotine replacement therapy. Telephone counseling, internet and email based programs, and telemedicine are practical solutions to assist patients with tobacco cessation.

Tobacco Dependence Treatment in the Illiterate

Tobacco Use Patterns and Public Health Impact in the Illiterate

There are an estimated 42 million U.S. adults who cannot read and an additional 50 million who are considered to be functionally illiterate, having a reading level below the 5th grade reading level [35]. As one in four teenagers drop out of high school annually, and one in four of those who remain in school only reach the equivalent of an 8th grade education, it is estimated that the number of functionally illiterate Americans is growing by 2.25 million persons per year [35]. Literacy level has a significant effect on health care. In a study of patients at two public hospitals, a large number were deemed to have functional health illiteracy as they were unable to read and comprehend basic medical instructions – totalling 35% of all English-speaking and 61% of all Spanish-speaking patients [36]. In the patient groups examined, 41% of individuals were unable to understand directions for taking a prescription on an empty stomach, 26% could not understand when their next appointment was scheduled, 59% could not understand a standard informed consent document, 23% could not understand how to take a prescription four times per day, and 81% could not understand the rights and responsibilities of a Medicaid application. Data from this and other studies [37] suggest that the elderly are the highest at-risk group with regard to literacy status – up to 80% of both English- and Spanish-speaking patients are considered to read at a low literacy level.

Findings such as these suggest that literacy plays a major role in public health. The illiterate and non-English speaking subjects should generally not be excluded from research studies based on the fundamental principles of the Belmont Report. However, research inclusive of the illiterate may be limited by an inability to provide true informed consent, or in the fact that participants may avoid participation in survey-based research out of fear or embarrassment. There has not been much research specifically into the tobacco use patterns in the illiterate population, hence the public health impact of smoking in this population is not truly known. Even in the most recent data from the Centers for Disease Control [26], the prevalence rates of tobacco use were classified in many ways, but the closest category to illiteracy was education level. In that data, smoking prevalence was found to be highest among adults who had earned a General Educational Development (GED) diploma (46.0%) or who had only 9 to 11 years of formal education (35.4%), and prevalence of tobacco use decreased as individuals' education levels increased. Since, as mentioned previously, up to one in four teenagers who remain in high school only reach the equivalent of an 8th grade education [35], and 18% of people with low literacy hold a high school diploma [37], education level and degree literacy do not perfectly correlate. In one study at a public hospital clinic, the reading levels of smokers and the readability of smoking cessation materials was examined [38]. In this study group, the participants' number of years completed in school was not a reliable predictor of their reading ability.

Population-Specific Barriers to Treatment of Tobacco Dependence

A significant amount of patient educational resources and media-based tobacco cessation campaigns are provided via printed educational materials. This approach will have limited effect on the illiterate and functionally illiterate. Health care literature is generally written at the 10th grade level or above [39]. It has been found that up to 30-50% of the target audience for these materials is unable to read at this level, and therefore is unable to understand the message [39]. Additionally, misconceptions on the part of health care providers may play a role, including those that illiterate persons are likely to be poor, intellectually-impaired, immigrants, minorities, or that they will forthcoming about their inability to read [37]. In terms of absolute numbers, low literacy levels are actually more common in white, native-born Americans [37]. Health care providers must recognize the problems associated with care for persons with low literacy, and take pro-active steps to address tobacco cessation specifically in this population.

Clinical Solutions

Clinical solutions for treating tobacco cessation in the low literacy and illiterate patient population include the use of group support, cognitive behavioral therapy, nicotine replacement therapy, and pharmacologic treatment such as bupropion and varenicline. These recommendations are based on those for the general population as there have been no studies on tobacco cessation that specifically target low-literacy persons. It is important for the physician to assess their patient's literacy status and tailor their recommendations for these patients to a lower reading level. This may include having educational handouts that are largely pictorial. Group and individual sessions for cognitive behavioral therapy could be successful in this population as they are discussion-based. Patients with low levels of literacy may also need individual demonstration of the proper use of nicotine replacement therapy agents and other medications, and not be left to rely on written instructional materials.

Health Policy Recommendations

There are a number of national campaigns to address literacy in general. It appears that initiatives to inform health care providers on how to identify and address the needs of persons with low literacy levels will be key to improved patient counseling and education, medication adherence/compliance and error reduction, means of obtaining informed consent, and perhaps even improved access to and utilization of payer sources such as Medicaid. Revision of forms and printed materials, including those present in medication packaging, must be done to consider the needs of low literacy persons. Experts in literacy, and specifically health care literacy, can be utilized to break down systematic barriers to care for this vulnerable patient population. All of these policy movements for health care in general can also be applied specifically to tobacco cessation campaigns.

Key Points

- Over 90 million Americans are considered illiterate or functionally illiterate. Literacy level has a significant effect on health care. Up to 30-50% of the target audience for tobacco cessation materials is unable to adequately read them or understand their message. Additionally, misconceptions on the part of health care providers about low literacy persons may play a role.
- Group support and cognitive behavioral therapy, nicotine replacement therapy, and pharmacologic treatment with bupropion and varenicline are all recommended for persons with low literacy levels.
- Educational handouts for this patient population should be largely pictorial. Group and individual sessions for cognitive behavioral therapy could be helpful in this population as they are discussion-based. Individual demonstration of the proper use of nicotine replacement therapy agents and other medications may be necessary.

Tobacco Dependence Treatment in those with Comorbid Mental Illness

Tobacco Use Patterns and Public Health Impact in those with Comorbid Mental Illness

Persons carrying a psychiatric diagnosis have a very high prevalence of concurrent tobacco abuse, with reported smoking rates in this population ranging from 52%-90% [40]. Treatment for mental health disorders in the previous year is associated with an Adjusted Odds Ratio for daily smoking of 1.16, for alcohol abuse or dependence of 1.86, and for illicit drug abuse or dependence of 2.80 [41]. The tobacco, alcohol, and illicit drug use in this population places this group at tremendous risk for the adverse health effects of these substances. However, there have not been significant research data reported that specifically examined the public health impact of smoking in this population.

Population-Specific Barriers to Treatment of Tobacco Dependence

Systematic barriers often prevent persons with mental illness from accessing the health care they need in general. Since its creation in 1965, the Medicaid program has significantly expanded access to mental health care for low-income patients, and mental health care represents a significant chunk of the Medicaid budget [42]. Medicaid assists patients with the cost of both acute and chronic care as well as prescription drugs. Despite the successes of the Medicaid program, patients with mental disorders make up a disproportionate part of the uninsured population [42]. Those who are uninsured are more likely to have not received outpatient mental health care prior to a first hospitalization for psychotic illness [43], suggesting a missed opportunity for care. A critical point to be made is that insurance coverage of patients with mental illness does not ensure that they will have access to care [34] as many other issues are also at play. The chronically mentally ill and the confused may find it difficult to navigate an increasingly complex health care and insurance system [34]. The social stigma of mental illness and issues including fear of coercive treatment [44], mistrust of the health care system, and even a belief in supernatural causation of their mental illness [45] have been shown to drive patients away from obtaining psychiatric care.

The highest rates of persons seeking mental health treatment in the U.S. are seen among adults aged 26 to 49, in women more than in men, in American Indians/Alaska Natives or persons reporting more than one race, in divorced/separated persons, in persons with at least some college education, in the unemployed, in habitants of small metropolitan areas, in those with less than $20,000 family income, and in members of families who receive government assistance [41]. Hence, patients with tobacco dependence and underlying mental illness may face additional cultural and systematic barriers to successful smoking cessation.

Another hindrance to smoking cessation in persons with psychiatric illness is their understanding of the harms of tobacco use. In one study of inpatients at a psychiatric facility, 68% of the patients interviewed believed that smoking was harmful to their health and quitting would be beneficial to their health [40]. This is in contrast to national data that show 93.4% of the smoking population believes that smoking is harmful to their health [46], [47]. One of the first steps to tobacco cessation is contemplation of quitting, and often the main reason for this is health concerns. If persons with mental illness do not fully understand the short- and long-term health effects of smoking, they may be less inclined to enter the contemplation phase of cessation. Mental illness is associated with fewer quit attempts and a lower cessation success rate than in the general population [48]. Additional factors include the perceptions of providers and mental health institutions that this population is unmotivated to quit smoking, lacks the cognitive function and necessary insight to quit smoking, and that tobacco cessation would take away one of the patient's only "pleasures" [40].

Persons with depression have a high prevalence of smoking and a low likelihood of quitting successfully [49]. And conversely, major depression is present in 6.6% of smokers and 2.9% of nonsmokers. Smokers carrying a diagnosis of depression only have a 14% success rate in smoking cessation attempts [49]. Nicotine may play a role in these findings as it may have the benefit of reducing negative affect [40] and increasing the release of dopamine in the brain [50]. Smoking may also complicate the treatment of depression, as it has been shown to decrease the blood levels of some antidepressants [40]. In addition, hepatic microsomal enzymes are activated by nicotine and tar, increasing the metabolism of neuroleptic medications and hence blunting the effect of these medications [50]. Therefore these medications need to be titrated to effect more closely in smokers. As tobacco actually improves some of the symptoms experienced by persons with psychiatric disorders, nicotine withdrawal can lead to exacerbation of some psychiatric disorders [48]. Smokers also have two to three times' higher risk of tardive dyskinesia with dopamine-blocking neuroleptic drugs, perhaps due to the higher doses that are required by smokers or to the increased dopaminergic activity induced by nicotine [51]. All of these factors need to be taken into account by health care providers that treat smokers with a psychiatric diagnosis.

Clinical Solutions

In patients with psychiatric illness, clinical recommendations for treating tobacco dependence include the use of cognitive behavioral therapy, nicotine replacement therapy, and bupropion. Nortriptyline has also been studied in patients with psychiatric illness who smoke – a small trial in 2004 showed that adding nortriptyline to nicotine replacement therapy and counseling resulted in a 50% reduction in smoking at one year [52]. In patients with major depression, integration of cognitive behavioral therapy with standard smoking cessation treatment has the greatest success [53]. Bupropion has also been studied in patients with depression and has been shown to improve smoking cessation rates [52]. In patients with schizophrenia, atypical antipsychotics in combination with nicotine replacement therapy or bupropion may be efficacious [53].

It is important to note that the use of any pharmacotherapeutic agent for tobacco cessation must be done with caution and vigilance in patients with underlying psychiatric illness. All patients on varenicline, including those with underlying mental illness, must be monitored for side effects such as agitation, depressed mood, atypical changes in behavior, or suicidal thoughts/behavior [54]. Patients with depression or other mental illnesses may have suicidal thoughts, and must be watched very closely for clinical worsening when taking antidepressant medications, including bupropion [55] and nortriptyline [56], especially early in their treatment or when their dose is adjusted. Additional caution must be used to avoid potential drug-drug interactions between different psychiatric medications.

Health Policy Recommendations

It used to be the case that patients in inpatient psychiatric facilities were allowed to smoke, and smoking breaks were actually used as a reward for good behavior [40]. Over the past several years there has been more research into smoking and mental illness. Studies have shown that bans on smoking for patients going through substance abuse and alcohol treatment programs actually increase the interest and success in quitting substance abuse and alcohol abuse [57], [58]. Over the past few years, as more hospitals have banned smoking for inpatients, so have mental health facilities. This is an important step to decreasing the acceptability of smoking by health care professionals. Smoking cessation in the inpatient setting can be beneficial because of the existing network of support (such as counseling), the availability of nicotine replacement and other medications, and the provision of a social environment that does not pressure an individual to restart smoking.

Tobacco dependence treatment is especially challenging in persons with mental illness. Even though the majority of persons with mental illness realize that smoking is detrimental to their health, there is generally less insight into this than in the general population. Additionally, mental illness is associated with fewer quit attempts and a lower cessation success rate than in the general population. Better access to mental health care and psychiatric medications is essential to mental health policy in general. Greater incorporation of tobacco cessation into mental health visits, inpatient psychiatric treatment plans, and substance abuse programs will likely have a significant impact on smoking prevalence rates.

Key Points

- Persons carrying a psychiatric diagnosis have a high prevalence of concurrent tobacco abuse, with reported smoking rates in this population ranging from 52%-90%.
- Systematic barriers often prevent persons with mental illness from accessing the health care they need in general. Additional cultural barriers may play a role, and persons with psychiatric illness may have less insight into the harms of tobacco use.
- The chemicals in cigarettes affect brain neurochemistry and the metabolism of psychiatric drugs in a way that makes management of

both the underlying mental illness and tobacco dependence more challenging.

- Clinical recommendations for treating tobacco dependence include cognitive behavioral therapy and nicotine replacement therapy. Nortriptyline may be another viable option. However, caution must be used with bupropion, varenicline, and nortriptyline in this population as worsening of psychiatric symptoms may occur. Drug interactions may additionally limit treatment choices.

TOBACCO DEPENDENCE TREATMENT IN THE UNDER AND UNINSURED

Tobacco Use Patterns and Public Health Impact in the Under- and Uninsured

Currently, there is an estimated 15.3% rate of uninsured persons in the U.S. – totaling 45.7 million people without insurance – and this number is growing [59]. Approximately two-thirds of the uninsured are low-income individuals and families [60]. Uninsured status is highest in African Americans, Hispanics, persons aged 18 to 29, those with incomes of less than $25000 annually, the self-employed, and the unemployed [61]. The prevalence of tobacco abuse is higher amongst the under- and uninsured (estimated at 39%) than in the general population (estimated at 21-23%) [62], [63].

Given the wide range of serious adverse health effects from smoking, and the limited access to health care amongst the under- and uninsured, the public health impact of tobacco use in this population is significant. Although there are no perfect estimates of the true financial impact of all tobacco-related health problems, almost half of all such costs are thought to be covered by federal programs (such as Medicare and Medicaid), and approximately $38 billion in federal tax dollars are spent annually on this alone – the equivalent of $320 in federal taxes per household [3]. This does not take into consideration the cost of health care for persons without a payer source at all. Beyond cost, low-income smokers suffer more health complications from tobacco because of greater tobacco use. Additionally, persons working in "blue collar" jobs are also more likely to be exposed to second-hand smoke [3]. Limited access to health care due to under- and uninsured status also means that persons in this group are more likely to be diagnosed at advanced stages of tobacco-related illness and will therefore ultimately need greater amounts of health care services [64]. Reports also suggest that this population tends overall to receive poor quality health services, and that many ultimately go without treatment at all [65].

Population Specific Barriers to Treatment

Barriers to treatment of tobacco abuse are similar to those of the rural and urban poor, which have been previously reviewed. Overall, there is decreased access to health care services as a result of an inability to pay for those services, and an inability to afford the recommended treatments to assist with cessation. In addition, although the under- and uninsured and population has a higher prevalence of tobacco use, some studies suggest that these patients, even when able to access outpatient health care, tend to receive less counseling on tobacco cessation [62]. It is felt that this inequity is due in part to decreased access to cessation interventions, and also due to the lesser quality of care that underserved patients often receive.

Clinical Solutions

Clinical solutions to improving the cessation rate of the under and uninsured who smoke include increasing the access to tobacco cessation counseling on telephone quit lines and community outreach and support. There also needs to be increased access to primary care and drug assistance programs so that these persons can receive tobacco cessation counseling, nicotine replacement, and opportunities to benefit from pharmacotherapeutics such as bupropion and varenicline. There have been no specific studies targeting tobacco cessation treatment in people who are under- and uninsured, but more research needs to be done to improve the care provided to this population.

Policy Recommendations

A study by the Kaiser Commission found that close to 25% of the approximately 46.1 million (non-elderly) uninsured Americans, or around 11.5 million persons in total, actually qualified for government funded health insurance but were simply not enrolled [66]. Barriers to enrolling these persons in health care programs must be identified and broken down – and this should be a major public health priority. Costs put forward to increase enrollment in health insurance programs would likely result in significant cost savings in return, particularly by improving access to primary care and preventive services. Policy changes are key to improving the access to care for the under- and uninsured patients.

As discussed in previous sections, increased tobacco taxation may in the long-term be of particular benefit to persons in lower socioeconomic groups, as taxation tends to result in decreased tobacco consumption [23]. In January of 2008, the state of Indiana raised the tax on cigarettes and used that money to fund preventative services such as tobacco cessation programs, incentives for small business to offer health insurance to employees, and a plan to allow employers and employees to purchase health insurance on a pre-tax basis [67]. This is a good example of how an increase of tax on cigarettes can both discourage tobacco use and direct money to programs that increase access to health coverage and hence tobacco cessation programs.

Key Points

- There are around 45.7 million people in the U.S. without insurance and this number is growing. The prevalence of tobacco abuse is higher amongst the under- and uninsured (estimated at 39%) than in the general population (estimated at 23%).
- This group has decreased access to health care services and an inability to afford recommended treatments. Also, some data suggests that underserved patients often receive lower quality health services.
- Clinical recommendations for treating tobacco dependence are similar to those for the general population and include cognitive behavioral therapy, nicotine replacement therapy, bupropion, and varenicline. Tobacco cessation counseling on telephone quit lines and community outreach and support are options for those with particularly limited resources.
- Assisting those who qualify for government-funded health insurance will improve access to primary care, preventive services, and tobacco cessation interventions.

CONCLUSION

The burden of tobacco-related diseases is inequitably divided, with a disproportionate share falling upon those with inadequate resources and poor access to quality health care. Limitations to health care access occur for various reasons – comorbid illness, financial hardship, insurance status, geographic barriers, resource availability, sociocultural factors, and decreased ability to navigate through an increasingly complex health care system. And for unclear reasons, the degree of tobacco counseling and cessation assistance offered to patients of limited means tends to be less than that for other patients. While access to affordable tobacco products exists, fair access to the treatment of tobacco dependence does not.

To successfully make an impact on the public health burden of tobacco in underserved patient populations, far greater outreach must be done. Tobacco taxation is a proven method to decrease smoking prevalence rates. Increasing the availability of medications and other cessation services to those of limited means or access can be done with the collected tax revenues. Banning smoking, certainly in hospitals but additionally in the workplace, schools, and other public areas, will likely also have a significant impact. Expanding free services which have been shown to be effective, such as telephone- and internet-based counseling, can be done for those with cost, geographic, language, literacy, or time barriers. And incentivizing health care providers to train and work in programs, such as the National Health Service Corps, will improve the quality of health care for people living in isolated regions. Through concerted efforts, large strides can be made in combating this preventable disease that results in substantial mortality, disability, and spent resources.

REFERENCES

[1] U.S. Centers for Disease Control and Prevention (CDC), "Annual Smoking-Attributable Mortality, Years of Potential Life Lost, and Economic Costs—United States 1997-2001." *Morbidity and Mortality Weekly Report (MMWR).* 54(25), 625-628, July 1, 2005, Acquired on May 30, 2009 at: http://www.cdc.gov/mmwr/preview/mmwrhtml/mm5425a1.htm.

[2] U.S. Centers for Disease Control and Prevention (CDC), "Cigarette smoking Attributable Morbidity – United States, 2000," *Morbidity and Mortality Weekly Report (MMWR).* 52(35): 842-844, September 5, 2003. Acquired on May 30, 2009 at: http://www.cdc.gov/mmwr/PDF/wk/mm5235.pdf.

[3] National Center for Tobacco-Free Kids. Campaign for Tobacco-Free Kids. Factsheets. Acquired on April 7, 2009 at: http://www.tobaccofreekids.org/research/factsheets/.

[4] Warner, KE; Mendez, D; Smith, DG. The Financial Implications of Coverage of Smoking Cessation Treatment by Managed Care Organizations. *Inquiry.* 41(1): 57-69, 2004.

[5] Gollust, S; Schroeder, S; Warner, K. Helping Smokers Quit: Understanding the Barriers to Utilization of Smoking Cessation Services. *The Milbank Quarterly.* 86(4): 601-627, 2008.

[6] Thorndike, A, Rigotti, N, Stafford, R, Singer, D. National Patterns in the Treatment of Smokers by Physicians. *JAMA*. 279(8): 604-608, 1998.

[7] Association of American Medical Colleges (AAMC). Physician Behavior and Practice Patterns Related to Smoking Cessation. A Report Prepared for the American Legacy Foundation by the Association of Medical Colleges. May 17, 2007. Acquired on June 2, 2009 at: http://www.americanlegacy.org/261.aspx.

[8] Blumenthal DS. Barriers to the Provision of Smoking Cessation Services Reported by Clinicians in Underserved Communities. *Journal of the American Board of Family Medicine.* 20: 272-279, 2007.

[9] Houston, TK; Scarinci, IC; Person, SD; Greene, PG; Patient Smoking Cessation Advice by Health Care Providers: The Role of Ethnicity, Socioeconomic Status, and Health. *American Journal of Public Health.* 95(6): 1056-61, 2005.

[10] Report of the Surgeon General on Tobacco Use Among US Racial/Ethnic Minority Groups. Washington DC: US Department of Health and Human Services 1998.

[11] Mercado, S; Havernann, K; Sami, M; Ueda, H; Urban Poverty: An Urgent Public Health Issue. *Journal of Urban Health*. 84(1): 7-15, May 2007.

[12] Garau, P; Sclar, ED. Interim Report of the Millennium Development Goal Task Force 8 on Improving the Lives of Slum Dwellers. New York: United Nations; 2004.

[13] Hyman, DJ; Simons-Morton, DG; Dunn, JK; Ho, K; Smoking, Smoking Cessation, and Understanding of the Role of Multiple Cardiac Risk

Factors Among the Urban Poor. *Preventive Medicine*. 25: 653-659, 1996.

[14] Diez-Roux, AV; Nieto, FJ; Muntaner, C; Tyroler, HA; Comstock, GW; Shahar, E; Cooper, LS; Watson, RL; Szklo, M. Neighborhood Environments and Coronary Heart Disease: A Multilevel Analysis. *American Journal of Epidemiology*. 146(1): 48-63, 1997.

[15] Lee, D. The Urban Poor's Economic Profile of Tobacco Use. *The American Journal of Drug and Alcohol Abuse*. 34: 626-633, 2008.

[16] Kiefe, CT; Hyman, DJ. Do public clinic systems provide health care access for the urban poor? A cross-sectional survey. *J. Community Health*. 21(1): 61-70, 1996 Feb.

[17] Freeman, HE; Corey, CR. Insurance status and access to health services among poor persons. *Health Serv Res*. 28(5): 531-41, 1993 Dec.

[18] Hyland, A; Bauer, JE; Li Q; Abrams, SM; Higbee, C; Peppone, L; Cummings, KM. Higher cigarette prices influence cigarette purchase patterns. *Tobacco Control*. 14: 86-92, 2005.

[19] Federal Trade Commission Cigarette Report for 2004-2005. Acquired on May 30, 2009 at: http://www.ftc.gov/reports/tobacco/2007cigarette2004-2005.pdf.

[20] Feighery, EC; Ribisl, KM; Schleicher, NC; Clark, PI. Retailer participation in cigarette company incentive programs is related to increased levels of cigarette advertising and cheaper cigarette prices in stores. *Preventive Medicine*. 38(6): 876-884, June 2004.

[21] Ahluwalia, JS; McNagny, SE; Clark, WS. Smoking Cessation Among Inner-City African Americans Using the Nicotine Transdermal Patch. *Journal of General Internal Medicine*. 13(1): 1-8, 1998.

[22] Resnicow, K, Vaughan, R; Futterman, R; Weston, RE; Royce, J; Parms C; Hearn MD; Smith M; Freeman HP; Orlandi MA. A Self-Help Smoking Cessation Program for Inner-City African Americans: Results from the Harlem Health Connection Project. *Health Education & Behavior*. 24(2): 201-17, 1997.

[23] Myung, SK; McDonell, DD; Kazinets, G; Seo, HG; Moskowitz, JM. Effects of Web- and Computer-Based Smoking Cessation Programs. Meta-analysis of Randomized Controlled Trials. *Arch Int Med*. 169(10): 929-937, May 25, 2009.

[24] Wilson, N; Thomson, G. Tobacco, tax as a health protecting policy: a brief review of the New Zealand evidence. *The New Zealand Medical Journal*. 118: 1213, April 2005.

[25] Siahpush, MS; Wakefield, MA; Spittal, MJ; Durkin SJ; Scollo MM.

Taxation Reduces Social Disparities in Adult Smoking Prevalence. *American Journal of Preventive Medicine*. 36(4), 285-291, 2009.

[26] U.S. Centers for Disease Control and Prevention (CDC), "Cigarette Smoking in Adults – -- United States 2006." *Morbidity and Mortality Weekly Report (MMWR)*. 56(44): 1157-1161, November 9, 2007. Acquired on June 4, 2009 at: http://www.cdc.gov/mmwr/preview/mmwrhtml/mm5644a2.htm.

[27] Doescher, MP; Jackson, JE; Jerant, A; Hart, L. Prevalence and Trends in Smoking: A National Rural Study. *The Journal of Rural Health*. 22(2): 112-118, 2006.

[28] Hutcheson, T; Greiner, KA; Ellerbeck, E. Understanding smoking cessation in rural communities. *The Journal of Rural Health*. 24(2): 116-124, 2008.

[29] Eberhardt, M; Ingram, D; Makuc, D; Pamuk, ER; Freid, VM; Harper, SB; Schoenborn, CA; Xia H. Urban and Rural Health Chartbook. *Health United States, 2001*. Hyattsville, MD: National Center for Health Statistics, 2001.

[30] Zuniga, M; Anderson, D; Alexander, K. (2003). Heart Disease and Stroke in Rural America. Rural Healthy People 2010: A companion document to Healthy People 2010. Volume 1. College Station, TX: The Texas A&M University System Health Science Center, School of Rural Public Health, Southwest Rural Health Research Center. Retrieved May 25, 2009 from http://www.srph.tamhsc.edu/centers/rhp2010/06Volume1heart.htm

[31] Barnett, E; Halverson, J. Disparities in premature coronary heart disease mortality by region and urbanicity among black and white adults ages 35-64, 1985-1995. *Public Health Reports*. 115(1): 52-64, 2000.

[32] Singh, S; Bayakly, AR; McNamara, C; Redding, K. Lung Cancer in Georgia, 1999-2002. Georgia Department of Human Resources, Division of Public Health, Chronic Disease, Injury, and Environmental Epidemiology Section, February, 2005. Publication number DPH06/006W. Retrieved May 25, 2009 from http://health.state.ga.us/pdfs/chronic/cancer/lungCancer99_02.pdf.

[33] Shugarman, LR; Sorbero, MES; Tian, H; Jain, AK; Ashwood, JS. An Exploration of Urban and Rural Differences in Lung Cancer Survival Among Medicare Beneficiaries. *American Journal of Public Health*. 98(7): 1280-1287, July 2008.

[34] Friedman, E. Money isn't everything. Nonfinancial barriers to access. *JAMA*. 271(19): 1535-8, 1994 May 18.

[35] Sweet, RW. Illiteracy: An Incurable Disease or Education Malpractice? 1996. The National Right to Read Foundation. Retrieved May 27, 2009

from http://www.nrrf.org/essay_Illiteracy.html.

[36] Williams, MV; Parker, RM; Baker, DW; Parikh, NS; Pitkin, K; Coates, WC; Nurss, JR. Inadequate Functional Health Literacy Among Patients at Two Public Hospitals. *JAMA*. 274(21): 1677-1682.

[37] Roter, D, Rude, R; Comings, J. Patient Literacy: A Barrier to Quality of Care. *Journal of General Internal Medicine*. 13(12): 850-851, 1998 December.

[38] Meade, C; Byrd, J. Patient Literacy and the Readability of Smoking Education Literature. *American Journal of Public Health*. 79(2), Feb 1989.

[39] Plimpton, S; Root, J. Materials and Strategies That Work in Low Literacy Health Communication. *Public Health Reports*., 109(1): 86-92, Jan-Feb 1994.

[40] Carosella, A; Ossip-Klein, D, Owens, C. Smoking Attitudes, Beliefs, and Readiness to change among Acute and Long Term Care inpatients with psychiatric diagnoses. *Addictive Behaviors*. 24(3): 331-344, 1999.

[41] Prevalence of Mental Health Treatment among Demographic and Socioeconomic Subgroups. Demographic and Socioeconomic Characteristics of Adults Receiving Mental Health Treatment. SAMHSA, Office of Applied Studies, National Household Survey on Drug Abuse, 2000 and 2001. U.S. Department of Health and Social Services, Office of Applied Studies website. Acquired on February 15, 2009 at: http://www.oas.samhsa.gov/mhtx/ch2.htm#2.3.1

[42] Frank, RG; Goldman, HH; Hogan, M. Medicaid and mental health: be careful what you ask for. *Health Affairs*. 22(1): 101-13, 2003 Jan-Feb.

[43] Rabinowitz, J; Bromet, EJ; Lavelle, J; Severance, KJ; Zariello, SL; Rosen, B. Relationship between type of insurance and care during the early course of psychosis. *American Journal of Psychiatry*. 155(10): 1392-7, 1998 Oct.

[44] Hahm, HC; Segal, SP. Failure to seek health care among the mentally ill. *American Journal of Orthopsychiatry*. 75(1): 54-62, 2005 Jan.

[45] Chadda, RK; Agarwal, V; Singh, MC; Raheja, D. Help seeking behaviour of psychiatric patients before seeking care at a mental hospital. *International Journal of Social Psychiatry*. 47(4): 71-8, 2001.

[46] Fiore, MC; Bailey, WC; Cohen, SF. 2000. Treating Tobacco Use and Dependence: A Clinical Practice Guideline. Rockville, MD. U.S. Department of Health and Human Services.

[47] US Department of Health and Human Services. The health consequences of smoking: nicotine addiction. A report of the Surgeon General. Atlanta

(GA): US Department of Health and Human Services. Public Health Service, Centers for Disease Control, Center for Chronic Disease Prevention and Health Promotion, Office of Smoking and Health. DHHS Publication No. (PHS) (CDC) 88-8406. 1988.

[48] Fagerstrom, K; Aubin, HJ. Management of smoking cessation in patients with psychiatric disorders. *Current Medical Research Opinion.* 25 (2): 511-8, 2009 Feb.

[49] Glassman, AH; Cigarette Smoking: Implications for Psychiatric Illness. *American Journal of Psychiatry.* 150(4): 546-553, April 1993.

[50] Salokangas, RK; Saarijarvi, S; Taimien, T; Lehto, H; Niemi, H; Alola, V; Syvalahti, E. Effect of Smoking on Neuroleptics in Schizophrenia. *Schizophrenia Research.* 23: 55-60, 1997.

[51] Binder, RL; Kazamatsuri, H; Nishimura, T; McNiel, D. Smoking and Tardive Dyskinesia. *Biological Psychiatry.* 22(10): 1280-1282, 1987.

[52] Hall, SM; Tsoh, JY; Prochaska, JJ; Eisendrath, S; Rossi, JS. Redding CA; Rosen, AB; Meisner, M; Humgleet, GL; Gorecki, JA. Treatment for Cigarette Smoking Among Depressed Mental Health Outpatients: A Randomized Clinical Trial. *American Journal of Public Health.* 96(10): 1808-14, 2006.

[53] Kisely, S; Campbell, LA; Use of Smoking Cessation Therapies in Individuals with Psychiatric Illness : An Update for Prescribers. *CNS Drugs.* 22(4): 263-73, 2008.

[54] Prescribing Information: CHANTIX® (varenicline) Tablets. Dosage and Administration. Retrieved May 17, 2009 from https://www.pfizerpro.com/sites/pfp/pages/product_info/Chantix_pi_dosage_and_adminiadminist.aspx.

[55] Bupropion hydrochloride drug information. Retrieved May 17, 2009 from http://www.fda.gov/cder/drug/infopage/bupropion/default.htm.

[56] Nortriptyline. Drugs.com Drug Information Online. Acquired June 2, 2009 at: http://www.drugs.com/pro/nortriptyline.html.

[57] Joseph, AM; Nichol, KL; Willenbring, ML; Korn, JE; Beneficial effects of treatment of nicotine dependence during an inpatient substance abuse treatment program. *JAMA*. 263: 3043-3046, 1990.

[58] Miller, WR; Hedrick, KE; Taylor, CA; Addictive Behaviors and Life Problems Before and After Behavioral Treatment of Problem Drinkers. *Addictive Behaviors.* 8: 403-412, 1983.

[59] U.S. Census Bureau. Income, Poverty, and Health Insurance Coverage in the United States: 2007. Issued August 2008. Retrieved April 7, 2009 from: http://www.census.gov/prod/2008pubs/p60-235.pdf.

[60] Urban Institute and Kaiser Commission on Medicaid and the Uninsured, analysis of March 2002 Current Population Survey, 2002. Retrieved May 17, 2009 from http://www.kff.org/uninsured/loader.cfm?url=/commonspot/security/getfile.cfm&PageID=14185.

[61] Nelson, DE; Bolen, J; Wells, HE; Smith, SM; Bland, S. State Trends in Uninsurance Among Individuals Aged 18-64 Years: United States, 1992-2001. *American Journal of Public Health*. 94(11): 1992-97, 2004.

[62] Parnes, B; Main, D; Holcomb, S; Pace, W. Tobacco Cessation Counseling Among Underserved Patients: A Report from CaReNet. *The Journal of Family Practice*. 51(1): 65-69, 2002.

[63] U.S. Centers for Disease Control and Prevention (CDC). "Self-assessed Health Status and Selected Behavioral Risk Factors Among Persons With and Without Health-care Coverage- United States, 1994-1995. *Morbidity and Mortality Weekly Report.* 47(9): 176-180, 1998. Retrieved June 2, 2009 from http://www.cdc.gov/mmwr/preview/mmwrhtml/00051507.htm.

[64] Adler, NE; Boyce, WT; Chesney, MA; Folkman, S; Syme, SL. Socioeconomic inequalities in health: No easy solution. *JAMA*. 269: 3140-5, 1993.

[65] Fiscella, K; Franks, P; Gold, MR; Clancy, CM. Inequality in quality: Addressing socio-economic, racial, and ethnic disparities in health care. *JAMA*. 283(19): 2579-2584, May 17, 2000.

[66] Dubay, L; Holahan, J; Cook, A. The Uninsured And The Affordability Of Health Insurance Coverage. *Health Affairs*. 26: w22-w30, 2007.

[67] "Healthy Indiana Plan" to Go Live in January. No author listed. *Healthcare Financial Management*. 61(10): 13-14, 2007.

Disclaimer: It is important to note that information contained in this document is not intended to replace professional medical advice. Any questions regarding a medical diagnosis or treatment should be directed to a medical practitioner.

In: Smoking Relapse: Causes, Prevention ... ISBN: 978-1-60876-580-5
Editors: J. Egger and M. Kalb

Chapter 4

Factors Associated with Trying to Quit or Cut Down on Smoking in a Community-Based Sample of Adult Persistent Smokers

[1]Hugh Klein*, [2]Claire E. Sterk and [2]Kirk W. Elifson

[1]Rollins School of Public Health, Emory University, Atlanta, GA, USA and Kensington Research Institute, Silver Spring, MD, USA

[2]Rollins School of Public Health, Emory University, Atlanta, GA, USA

Abstract

Despite 50+ years of public health campaigns to reduce the rates of smoking in the United States, approximately one-quarter of the adults living in this country continue to use tobacco. Most of these persons have tried to quit smoking, typically more than once in their lives. The present paper examines the factors associated with trying to quit or cut down on tobacco use in a community-based sample of 485 adult persistent smokers recruited from the Atlanta, Georgia metropolitan area between 2004 and 2007. Both active and passive recruiting approaches were used, along with a targeted sampling strategy.

The data revealed that 90.9% of the smokers interviewed said that they had tried at least once before to quit or cut down on their smoking,

---

* Corresponding author: 401 Schuyler Road, Silver Spring, MD 20910, Phone: 301-588-8875, Email: hughk@aol.com

with the "average" person having attempted to do this seven previous times. Multivariate analysis of the factors associated with the number of times that people reported having tried to quit or cut down on their tobacco use yielded three similar but not identical models. All three models contained two items in common, age (older age = more cessation/reduction attempts) and the number of reasons for wanting to quit/cut down on smoking (more reasons = more cessation/reduction attempts). Model 1 contained one additional item pertaining to viewing oneself negatively as a result of one's smoking and/or viewing one's tobacco use behaviors negatively (greater negative perception = more cessation/reduction attempts). Model 2 contained a different third measure, pertaining to the number of tobacco dependency symptoms that had been experienced (more symptoms = more cessation/reduction attempts). Model 3 contained both of these additional measures.

Keywords: Smokers; smoking; tobacco use; smoking cessation; reduction in use.

Factors Associated with Trying to Quit or Cut Down on Smoking in a Community-Based Sample of Adult Persistent Smokers

Despite approximately 45 years of small but fairly steady declines, more than 1 in 4 American adults (28.6%) still currently uses tobacco, with most of these persons (84.6% of them, or 24.2% of the total) being cigarette smokers (Substance Use and Mental Health Services Administration [SAMHSA], 2008). Evidence shows that most of these persons either say that they want to quit using tobacco and/or that they recently have tried to do so (Centers for Disease Control and Prevention [CDC], 2002a). More than half of all current smokers report wanting to quit smoking or cut down on their tobacco use, but being unable to do so (Hebert, 2004; SAMHSA, 1998).

Given this high percentage, it is somewhat surprising that, compared to other topics reported on in the smoking literature, relatively little has been written about the factors that are associated with wanting to quit or cut down on tobacco use. This is particularly true with regard to adult (versus adolescent) smokers. Evidence from the studies that ***have*** been published suggests that concerns about the effects of second-hand smoke increases some smokers' likelihood of wanting to quit or cut down on their tobacco use (Hyland, Rezaishiraz, Bauer, Giovino, & Cummings, 2005; Milberger, Davis,

& Holm, 2009). Receiving information about the dangers associated with smoking has also been linked with an increased desire to quit or cut down on smoking (Tingen, Waller, Smith, Baker, Reyes, & Treiber, 2006; Willemsen, 2005), as has experiencing adverse health effects as a result of one's smoking (Clark, Hogan, Kviz, & Prohaska, 1999; Hebert, 2008). Some studies have identified various demographic and personal characteristics that are associated with a greater desire to quit smoking, too, including being: female (Harris, Schwartz, & Thompson, 2008), older (Harris, Schwartz, & Thompson, 2008; Yong, Borland, & Siahpush, 2005), pregnant (Haviland, Thornton, Carothers, Hund, Allen, Kastens, Wojciak, Hamasaka, & Healton, 2004), and a nondaily smoker (Tong, Ong, Vittinghoff, & Perez-Stable, 2006).

In the present study, we examine the factors that are associated with wanting to quit or cut down on one's tobacco use, relying upon a community-recruited sample of adult persistent smokers. Three types or categories of factors are considered: demographic traits, measures of psychological and psychosocial functioning, and various tobacco use-related items. As discussed later in this paper, these potential influences were chosen for examination, in part, because of previous research that has linked these types of influences to actual smoking behaviors. These potential influences were also chosen for examination, in part, because of their relevance to the Health Belief Model, which is the principal theoretical paradigm guiding the present research.

This theoretical paradigm posits that people's behaviors can be understood, at least in part, based on their behavioral intentions–that is, the specific things that people plan to do regarding engaging/not engaging in a specific behavior ***or*** regarding modifying their practice of a particular behavior (see, for example, Banyard, 2002). The Health Belief Model postulates that intentions precede behaviors, and that the former strongly predicts the latter. Applied to tobacco use and smoking cessation, the Health Belief Model predicts that there will be a link between behavioral intentions (measured by constructs such as wanting to quit or cut down on one's tobacco use, actively devising a strategy to quit smoking) and smoking related behaviors (such as amount of tobacco use, bonafide attempts to quit/reduce smoking, etc.). Additionally, the Health Belief Model also includes a component tenet predicting a relationship between perceptions about engaging in a particular behavior and actual involvement in that behavior (Banyard, 2002). Here, the model hypothesizes that negative perceptions will be associated with a diminished likelihood of engaging in a particular behavior, whilst positive perceptions will increase the likelihood of engaging in a behavior. Applied to tobacco use and smoking cessation, this part of the Health Belief Model would posit that smokers who perceive their smoking negatively (perhaps because of experiencing health-related problems rom tobacco use, or because of receiving negative feedback from friends and family members as a result of their smoking) are more likely to take action to stop smoking than those who do not perceive their tobacco use in a negative manner. Likewise, smokers who perceive themselves likely to derive benefits from quitting or cutting down on their tobacco use (e.g., improved health, support from friends, diminished hassling from nonsmoking strangers with whom they have contact) will be the individuals who are most likely to try to quit/reduce their cigarette usage. Also worth noting is the fact that the Health Belief Model operates on the assumption that people's behavioral intentions and their perceptions of the benefits/risks of engaging/not engaging in a particular behavior will differ based on their personal experiences and on their demographic characteristics (Banyard, 2002).

METHODS

Subjects and Design

The data presented in this study were collected in Atlanta, Georgia between September 2004 and July 2007 as part of the *Persistent Smokers Project (PSP)*. This was a community-based sample, and was not derived from clinical or other institutional settings. To be eligible, the participants had to be aged 18 years or older and reside in the Atlanta metropolitan area. As a study of persistent smokers, study participants had to have smoked at least 100 cigarettes during their lifetime [which is consistent with the National Health Interview Survey (NHIS) classification (CDC, 2002b) as "ever smoked"] and have smoked in the last week [which is consistent with the NHIS classification (CDC, 2002b) as "current smoker"].

Participant recruitment involved purposive sampling, including a combination of active and passive recruitment techniques. Using a short screening form, potential study participants were screened in the setting where they were recruited, such as near office buildings or other work locations, at restaurants, in social entertainment settings, in parks, and in other public settings. Passive recruitment involved posting flyers in local venues such as stores, restaurants, and community centers. Interested individuals, who called the project phone line listed on the flyers, initially were screened over the phone using the same short form used in the active recruitment. Two-thirds of the respondents were brought into the study via active recruitment, with the remaining one-third being identified through passive recruitment. We did not identify any significant difference in the sample characteristics or in the outcome variables based on the recruitment strategy.

Once a person was identified as eligible, the staff member described the study and time required to participate. The most common reason for ineligibility was having smoked an insufficient number of cigarettes to qualify, either during the person's lifetime or during the preceding week. The interviews took place at a mutually-convenient location, such as one of the project offices, the respondent's home, a local restaurant or coffee shop, or at community centers. Additional information was provided on the nature of the study, the time required, and the informed consent and other confidentiality procedures. The questionnaire contained items covering the respondent's social background characteristics, smoking behaviors, attitudes, and opinions, as well as items about alcohol and other drugs, a health inventory, and self and identity items.

The targeted sampling design and data collection procedures (Watters & Biernacki, 1989) yielded a sample of 485 smokers. The sample provided a diverse cross-section of Atlanta smokers well-suited to exploring our research questions regarding the factors associated with persistent smoking. Compared to national data reported by the Centers for Disease Control and Prevention, the study sample included more women and was better educated. Otherwise, the sample reflected the characteristics of smokers nationally (CDC, 2008).

Measures Used

The principal variable of interest in this paper is a scale measure assessing the number of times that people reported seriously having tried to quit or cut down on their smoking. This was a continuous measure with a considerable skew in its distribution. To make it more suitable for analysis, we performed a data transformation procedure whereby we converted this item to a 1+log value, which is a standard way of handling continuous measures that have a skewed distribution (Sokal & Rohlf, 1995; Zar, 2009).

Three types of measures were examined for their relevance to understanding the number of times that people had tried to quit or cut down on their smoking: demographic characteristics, measures of psychological and psychosocial functioning, and smoking-related items. These will be discussed in turn.

Nine demographic characteristics items were used. These included gender (male versus female), age (continuous measure), race/ethnicity (Caucasian,

African American, all others), marital status ("involved" with someone versus not "involved"), sexual orientation (heterosexual versus gay, lesbian, or bisexual), income (continuous measure), educational attainment (high school or less, some college, college graduate or more), religiosity (continuous scale measure, Cronbach's alpha = 0.79), and employment status (employed full-time, employed part-time, unemployed).

Six measures assessing psychological and psychosocial functioning were used. The first was an 11-item sociability scale, with higher scores indicating greater sociability in social settings involving interactions with other people (Cronbach's alpha = 0.89). Sociability was examined because previous studies have established a link between sociability or perceived sociability and tobacco use (MacFadyen, Amos, Hastings, & Parkes, 2003; Spigner, Shigaki, & Tu, 2005; Zuckerman & Kuhlman, 2000). The second was self-consciousness in social situations, which was assessed using an 8-item scale. This scale was found to be reliable (Cronbach's alpha = 0.83). It was included in this study because other researchers have reported an association between self-consciousness in public situations and smoking behaviors (Raichle, Christensen, Ehlers, Moran, Karnell, & Funk, 2001). The third measure examined social isolation because, once again, other studies have shown this construct to be related to adults' smoking practices (Lauder, Mummery, Jones, & Caperchione, 2006). Social isolation was measured using an 11-item scale (Cronbach's alpha = 0.87). Fourth, we examined participants' locus of control, or the degree to which people considered life's events to occur randomly and unpredictably rather than in an orderly and systematic fashion. This was assessed with a 12-item scale (Cronbach's alpha = 0.75), which was included in the present study due to published reports establishing a relationship between locus of control and individuals' ability to quit smoking (Giskes, Van Lenthe, Turrell, Brug, & Mackenbach, 2006; Steptoe & Wardle, 2001). Fifth, respondents' depression levels were assessed using the *Center for Epidemiologic Studies Depression (CES-D)*'s 20-item scale (Cronbach's alpha = 0.90) (Radloff, 1977). A link between depression and tobacco use has been well-established in the scholarly literature (Cranford, Eisenberg, & Serras, 2009; Khaled, Bulloch, Exner, & Patten, 2009; Pedersen & Von Soest, 2009), hence warranting its inclusion here. Finally, Rosenberg's (1965) 10-item self-esteem scale was used as well (Cronbach's alpha = 0.86). Self-esteem was included in the present study because numerous previous studies have shown it to be related, typically inversely, with smoking behaviors (Croghan, Bronars, Patten, Schroeder, Nirelli *et al.*, 2006; Kendler, Neale, Sullivan, Corey, Gardner, & Prescott, 1999).

Several smoking-related measures were examined as well, because we hypothesized them to be related to people's likelihood of having attempted to quit or cut down on their smoking behaviors. The first such measure was the number of cigarettes the person smoked per week (continuous measure), which was expected to be related positively to their smoking cessation/ reduction attempts. The second item here was the number of reasons people expressed for wanting to quit or cut down on their smoking. This scale was comprised by 12 items (Cronbach's alpha = 0.84), and our hypothesis was that more actual attempts to quit or cut down on smoking would be undertaken by people who expressed a greater number of reasons for wanting to quit or cut down on their tobacco use (behavioral intention → actual behaviors). Third, the frequency of experiencing various smoking dependency symptoms (e.g., need cigarettes to function, making special trips to get cigarettes, chain smoking, smoking more than intended) was examined. Our hypothesis was that having more problems of these types would correspond with more numerous attempts to quit or cut down on one's smoking. Fourth, we analyzed the extent to which people perceive themselves and/or their smoking negatively, with the expectation that more negative the person's perceptions were, the more times he/she was likely to have tried to quit or cut down on his/her smoking. This construct was measured using a highly-reliable (Cronbach's alpha = 0.87) 32-item scale. Similarly, we also included one scale assessing people's perceptions of the negative things that have happened to them as a result of their smoking (four items, Cronbach's alpha = 0.82) and one assessing the positive benefits that they perceived themselves to derive from their tobacco use (16 items, Cronbach's alpha = 0.81). Additionally, people's general attitudes toward quitting smoking were examined here using an 18-item scale (Cronbach's alpha = 0.71). The hypothesis was that more attempts to quit or cut down on smoking would be reported by people whose attitudes toward quitting smoking were more favorable to quitting (pertinent attitudes → actual behaviors).

Several individual items capturing information about people's exposure to smokers or to people who have suffered from adverse consequences of smoking were also examined. Living with anyone who smokes (yes/no) was one such measure used in this paper. Our hypothesis here was that people who did not live with any other smokers would be less likely to have tried to quit or cut down on their smoking than their counterparts who did live with at least one other tobacco user. Having any family members who are currently ill (yes/no) as a result of smoking was another such measure. A third measure of this type was whether or not people had any friends who smoke, and a fourth was whether or not people have friends who commented negatively to them about their smoking.

Analysis

After the 1+log data transformation of the dependent variable, the number of times having tried to quit or cut down on one's smoking remained a continuous variable, but one with a far more normal distribution than was the case pre-transformation. In the first part of the analysis, we examined bivariate differences in trying to quit or cut down on one's smoking based on the demographic, psychological/psychosocial, and smoking-related measures described above. Whenever the independent variable was dichotomous (e.g., gender, sexual orientation), Student's *t* tests were performed. Whenever the independent variable was continuous in nature (e.g., depression level, number of cigarettes smoked per week), correlation coefficients were computed, with Pearson's *r* values being reported.

In the second part of the analysis, we developed a multivariate model to ascertain which items helped to explain the number of times people had tried to quit or cut down on their smoking, when the effects of the other measures were taken into account. Only items that were statistically significant in the first part of the analysis were considered here. These items were entered simultaneously into a multivariate equation, and then removed in a stepwise fashion until only statistically-significant multivariate predictors remained. To make sure that the order of entry into the equation was not affecting the outcome obtained, a forward selection approach was also employed. No differences were found based on which method of selection/elimination was used. Throughout this paper, differences are reported as being statistically significant whenever $p<.05$.

Results

Sample Characteristics

Slightly more than half (56.8%) of the study participants were male. They ranged in age from 18 to 70, with a mean age of 36.4 (median = 34, *s.d.* = 12.3). Most of the study participants were either Caucasian (54.6%) or African American (39.0%). Although most were heterosexual (83.5%), there was good representation of people self-identifying as gay, lesbian, or bisexual (16.5%). Overall, this was a fairly well-educated research sample, with only 25.2% of the people having completed no more than a high school education. Of those who had attended college, nearly half (34.2% of the total sample) were college graduates or people with post-graduate education. About half of the study participants were employed on a full-time basis at the time of their interview (55.1%); about one-third (32.9%) were employed on a part-time basis; and most of the remaining people (12.0%) were unemployed. On balance, this was a relatively low-income sample, with annual median income being approximately $21,500 (mean = $30,475, *s.d.* = $28,183, range = $0 to $216,000).

Attempts to Quit or Cut Down on Smoking

Approximately 1 person in 11 (9.1%) who took part in this study said that he/she had never made a serious attempt to quit or cut down on his/her smoking. Among persons who ***had*** tried, the median number of attempts was seven (range = 1 to 1,001, mean = 14.4, *s.d.* = 51.1). In the analyses that follow, only people who reported at least one previous serious attempt to quit or cut down on their smoking are examined.

Bivariate Analysis–Demographic Characteristics

There were no differences in the number of times that men and women reported having tried to quit or cut down on their smoking. African Americans acknowledged approximately 50% more quit/reduction attempts than other persons did ($p<.05$). The older people were, the more times they reported having tried to quit or cut down on their tobacco use ($p<.001$). All three of the socioeconomic status measures–educational attainment, employment status, and income–were found to be unrelated to the number of times study participants said they had attempted to quit/reduce their tobacco use. The same was true for marital/relationship status and sexual orientation. Finally, the more religious people were, the more times they had tried to quit or cut down on their tobacco use ($p<.01$).

Bivariate Analysis–Psychological and Psychosocial Functioning

All of the psychological and psychosocial functioning measures examined were found to be unrelated to the number of times people reported having tried to quit or cut down on their tobacco use. This was true for sociability, self-consciousness in social situations, social isolation, locus of control regarding daily occurrences, depression, and self-esteem alike.

Bivariate Analysis–Smoking Measures

Several of the smoking-related measures were related to the number of times that study participants had tried to quit or cut down on their tobacco use, and several were not. Regarding the latter, the number of cigarettes that people smoked each week was found to be unrelated to the number of times they had tried to quit or cut down on their smoking. Similarly, all four of the exposure to smokers or to people who have suffered from adverse consequences of smoking measures examined were found to be unrelated to quit/reduction attempts.

In contrast, however, the more reasons people reported for wanting to quit or cut down on their smoking, the more times they had, in fact, tried to do so ($r = 0.32$, $p < .001$). Additionally, the more frequently people experienced tobacco dependency symptoms, the more they tended to have tried to quit or cut down on their smoking ($r = 0.14$, $p < .01$). Moreover, the more negatively people viewed themselves as a result of smoking and/or the more negatively they viewed their smoking, the greater the number of quit/reduction attempts they reported ($r = 0.22$, $p < .001$). Neither the number of positive benefits they perceived themselves to derive from smoking nor the number of negative smoking-related consequences they perceived themselves to have experienced was found to be related to the number of times study participants reported having tried to quit or cut down on their tobacco use. Finally and counterintuitively, the better their overall attitudes toward quitting smoking were, the fewer the number of times people actually tried to quit or cut down on their smoking ($r = -0.12$, $p < .01$).

Multivariate Analysis

Table 1 presents the main findings obtained for the multivariate analysis. Three similar models are presented, each explaining 14-15% of the total variance. Models 1 and 2 contain only statistically-significant predictors. Model 3, which explains somewhat more variance than the other two, retains one independent variable that does not quite attain statistical significance but nearly does.

All three models have two items in common. One of these is the number of reasons people cited for wanting to quit or cut down on their smoking, which was related strongly ($p<.001$) and directly to the number of times they reported having tried to quit or cut down on their smoking. The other was age, which also was related directly to the number of times they had attempted to terminate or curtail their tobacco use. In Model 1, having a negative view of oneself as a result of one's smoking and/or having a negative view of one's tobacco-using behaviors was related to the number of times people had tried to quit or cut down on their tobacco use. In Model 3, this item narrowly failed to attain statistical significance. In Models 2 and 3, the number of smoking-related dependency symptoms people reported experiencing was associated with the number of times they had tried to cease/reduce their smoking.

Table 1. Multivariate Findings for the Number of Times That People Tried to Quit or Cut Down on Their Smoking.

	b	β	p<|x|
MODEL 1 $R^2 = 0.140$			
Number of reasons for wanting to quit or cut down on smoking	0.10	0.28	.001
Age	0.01	0.13	.01
Perceiving oneself and/or one's smoking negatively	0.31	0.12	.01
MODEL 2 $R^2 = 0.141$			
Number of reasons for wanting to quit or cut down on smoking	0.11	0.30	.001
Age	0.01	0.16	.001
Number of smoking dependency symptoms experienced	0.01	0.13	.01
MODEL 3 $R^2 = 0.149$			
Number of reasons for wanting to quit or cut down on smoking	0.10	0.28	.001
Age	0.01	0.14	.01
Perceiving oneself and/or one's smoking negatively	0.23	0.09	.054
Number of smoking dependency symptoms experienced	0.01	0.10	.05

Discussion

One interesting finding to come out of the present research is the small percentage of adult persistent smokers who said that they had never made a serious attempt to curtail their tobacco use. One smoker in eleven said this. Although numerous reports in the scientific literature discuss the fact that most smokers have tried to quit smoking at least once–typically several times (Foldes, Carlson, Alesci, Chen, Kinney *et al.*, 2001)–little has been documented about the "exceptions to the rule," those persons who have never made a serious effort to reduce or cease their use of tobacco. Sparse though they are, published reports suggest that smokers who have never tried to quit smoking comprise approximately 19% of the tobacco-using population (News-Journal.com, 2009). Evidence suggests that such individuals may be less knowledgeable about smoking than their peers who have made attempts to stop smoking (Cummings, Hyland, Giovino, Hastrup, Bauer, & Bansal, 2004). Learning more about smokers who have never made a bonafide effort to stop smoking or to reduce their tobacco use is an area well worth exploring in future research, particularly if these persons do, indeed, comprise a sizable proportion of all current smokers.

Not too surprisingly, the present study found that attempts to quit smoking increased with advancing age. One possible explanation of this is that a generational effect could be in operation here, such that currently younger smokers are more intractable in their tobacco use than their older counterparts are. There is little evidence in the scientific literature to support such an interpretation of the data. More likely, however, the relationship identified here reflects the passage of time and a greater number of opportunities to quit/reduce tobacco use that comes with more time passing. That is, it seems likely to us that our age-related finding reflects the fact that younger people who smoke have had fewer years of smoking during which they might try to stop when compared to their older counterparts, who by virtue of their advanced age have had more years of smoking during which they could try to curtail their tobacco use.

If that interpretation of the age-related association we obtained for quit/reduction attempts is accurate, then there are two important implications of this finding. First, it indicates a need to target younger smokers and to try to work with them to develop strategies that can help them to reduce their nicotine intake and/or cease smoking altogether. It will be important for such programs to take age into account as they develop and implement their anti-tobacco educational, prevention, and intervention programs with younger adults; and other authors have commented on the need for anti-smoking campaigns to be designed in an age-appropriate manner (Hanewinkel, Wiborg, Isensee, Nebot, & Vartiainen, 2006; Ruchlin, 1999; Stoddard, Sussman, Dent, Donaldson, & Severson, 1997). Second, this finding highlights the importance of persistence and continued commitment to helping older adults in their efforts to curtail their tobacco use. Despite what is, for many of them, repeated failures to stop smoking, many middle-aged and older adult smokers continue to want to quit or cut down on their tobacco use; and many of these individuals continue to try to stop/reduce smoking even as they age. Helping these people to avoid feelings of discouragement, and providing them with previously-untried (by them) strategies that can be adopted to maximize their chances of success, may be key ways of enhancing their likelihood of attaining their cessation-related goals. Some studies have addressed approaches that have–or have not–worked with this population segment (Fu, Okuyemi, Partin, Ahluwalia, Nelson, Clothier, & Joseph, 2008; Messer, Trinidad, Al-Delaimy, & Pierce, 2008; Tait, Hulse, Waterreus, Flicker, Lautenschlager, Jamrozik, & Almeida, 2007), and more needs to be learned about approaches that can be particularly successful with older adults who want to reduce their tobacco intake or stop using tobacco altogether.

Another not surprising, yet important, finding emanating from the present research is the fact that more attempts to quit or cut down on smoking were reported by smokers who endorsed the most reasons for wanting to quit or cut down. While this may seem commonsensical (and indeed in many respects, it is), it is also an important manifestation of the core tenets of the Health Belief Model "in action." This theoretical paradigm posits that people's behaviors can be understood, at least in part, based on their behavioral intentions. The Health Belief Model advocates the position that, if interventionists wish to have an impact upon a particular population's behaviors, then those interventionists would be behooved to target the beliefs and attitudes that underlie the behaviors in question. If interventionists are successful in reshaping belief structures and attitudes, then they have an increased chance of affecting how people will act. Applied to the present study's findings, we obtained strong support for a link between smoking-related behavioral intentions (as measured here by the item "reasons for wanting to quit or cut down on one's smoking) and smoking-related behaviors (as measured here by the number of times people actually tried to quit or cut down on their smoking).

From a health promotion point of view, the main implication of our finding is that anti-smoking campaigns need to devise ways to make smokers want to quit smoking, and to give them an increasing number of personally-applicable reasons to do so. One approach often advocated for people who are seriously planning to or interested in curtailing their tobacco use is to have these persons write down a list of reasons they continue to smoke alongside a list of reasons they wish to quit smoking. The present study's finding suggests that this approach is well-advised. Moreover, it highlights the need for anti-tobacco interventionists to work with persistent tobacco users to think of more and more reasons why it would be beneficial to them to cut back (or stop altogether) on their tobacco use. McKee, O'Malley, Salovey, Krishnan-Sarin, & Mazure (2005) have provided an interesting and on-point discussion of behavioral intentions and quitting smoking, and we encourage interested readers to consult this work. Additionally, some authors have discussed the applicability of the Health Belief Model's tenets to smoking cessation efforts (Chassin, Presson, Sherman, & Kim, 2002; Krosnick, Chang, Sherman, Chassin, & Presson, 2006), and their work, which is quite relevant to the present study's findings, may interest some readers as well.

Coinciding with our finding regarding the number of reasons people reported for wanting to quit or cut down on their smoking is our finding pertaining to perceiving oneself negatively as a result of one's smoking behaviors and/or perceiving one's smoking in a negative manner. In our research, these negative perceptions were associated with more attempts to quit or cut down on one's smoking. Once again, this type of finding is consistent with the main tenets of the Health Belief Model, which would hypothesize a relationship between negative perceptions about a particular behavior (in this case, using tobacco) and subsequent efforts to modify that behavior (here, reducing tobacco use or quitting smoking). Our finding suggests that one approach to reducing or eliminating tobacco use among persistent smokers might be to emphasize the ways that smoking is affecting them adversely and to help them to understand more about and focus on the negative aspects of being a tobacco user. When as a result of these focus-on-the-negative efforts smokers come to adhere to a more oppositional viewpoint regarding their ongoing use of tobacco, we would expect them to be increasingly willing to modify their behaviors. Recent research has shown that a negative mindset with regard to continued tobacco use is, indeed, predictive of subsequent attempts to stop smoking (Chassin, Presson, Sherman, & Kim, 2002; McCaul, Mullens, Romanek, Erickson, & Gatheridge, 2007; Moorman & Van Den Putte, 2008).

In conclusion, this study has shown that the large majority of adult persistent smokers have made serious attempts to quit or cut down on their smoking. Indeed, most of these individuals have made numerous such attempts. Based on the present research, several factors appear to be related to the number of times people have tried to quit or cut down on their tobacco use. One such factor is age, with older adults reporting having tried to quit or cut down more times than their younger counterparts. Another such factor is the number of reasons people have for wanting to reduce/cease their use of tobacco. A third factor is the extent to which people's smoking behaviors cause them to have a negative self-view, with a more negative self-perception being associated with a greater number of attempts to quit/cut down. Also relevant is the extent to which people exhibited smoking dependency symptoms/behaviors, such as making special trips to purchase cigarettes, chain smoking, needing cigarettes in order to function, and smoking more than originally intended.

Potential Limitations

We would like to acknowledge three potential limitations of this research. First, the data collected as part of this study of adult persistent smokers were all based on uncorroborated self-reports. Therefore, the extent to which respondents underreported or overreported their involvement in various smoking-related behaviors is unknown. In all likelihood, the self-reported data can be trusted, as numerous authors have noted that persons in their smoking studies have provided reasonably accurate information about their tobacco-using behaviors (Johnson & Mott, 2001; Klein, Thomas, & Sutter, 2007; Stanton, Papandonatos, Lloyd-Richardson, & Niaura, 2007).

A second possible limitation pertains to recall bias. Respondents were asked to report about their beliefs, attitudes, and behaviors during the past 30 days or the past year, depending upon the measure in question. These time frames were chosen specifically (1) to incorporate a large enough amount of time in the risk behavior questions' time frames so as to facilitate meaningful variability from person to person, and (2) to minimize recall bias. The exact extent to which recall bias affected the data cannot be assessed although other researchers collecting various types of smoking-related data have reported that recall bias is sufficiently minimal that its impact upon study findings is likely to be small (Pomerleau, Pomerleau, Mehringer, Snedecor, & Cameron, 2005).

A third possible limitation of these data comes from the sampling strategy used. All interviews were conducted in the Atlanta, Georgia metropolitan area. There may very well be local or regional influences or subcultural differences between these persons and those residing elsewhere that could affect the generalizability of the data. Additionally, the chain referral sampling approach used to identify study participants is not a random sampling strategy, and there may be inherent biases in who was/not identified as potential study participants in this research. A good discussion of the issues pertinent to this issue may be found in Heckathorn (1997), along with strategies that can be employed to minimize any bias that could result from the use of a chain-referral sampling approach.

ACKNOWLEDGMENTS

This research was supported by a grant from the National Institute on Drug Abuse (grant #R01 DA015707).

REFERENCES

Banyard, P. (2002). *Psychology in practice: Health.* London: Hodder and Stoughton

Centers for Disease Control and Prevention (2002a). Cigarette smoking among adults–UnitedStates 2000. *Morbidity and Mortality Weekly Report*, *51*, 642-645.

Centers for Disease Control and Prevention (2002b). *Early release of selected estimates based on data from the 2001 NHIS.* Found on the internet at *http://www.cdc.gov/nchs/about/major/nhis/released200207.htm*, last retrieved on June 10, 2009.

Centers for Disease Control and Prevention (2008). *Early release of selected estimates based on data from the 2007 NHIS.* Found on the internet at *http://www.cdc.gov/nchs/about/major/nhis/released200806.htm*, last retrieved on June 10, 2009.

Chassin, L., Presson, C. C., Sherman, S. J. & Kim, K. (2002). Long-term psychological sequelae of smoking cessation and relapse. *Health Psychology*, *21*, 438-443.

Clark, M. A., Hogan, J. W., Kviz, F. J. & Prohaska, T. R. (1999). Age and the role of symptomatology in readiness to quit smoking. *Addictive Behaviors*, *24*, 1-16.

Cranford, J. A., Eisenberg, D. & Serras, A. M. (2009). Substance use behaviors, mental health problems, and use of mental health services in a probability sample of college students. *Addictive Behaviors*, *34*, 134-145.

Croghan, I. T., Bronars, C., Patten, C. A., Schroeder, D. R., Nirelli, L. M., Thomas, J. L., Clark, M. M., Vickers, K. S., Foraker, R., Lane, K., Houlihan, D., Offord, K. P. & Hurt, R. D. (2006). Is smoking related to body image satisfaction, stress, and self-esteem in young adults? *American Journal of Health Behavior*, *30*, 322-333.

Foldes, S., Carlson, C. L., Alesci, N. L., Chen, X., Kinney, A., Rode, P., Zupan, B. A., Epstein, H., Geber, G. & Jensen, J. (2001). *Quitting smoking: Nicotine addiction in Minnesota*. St. Paul, MN: Minnesota Partnership for Action Against Tobacco.

Fu, S. S., Okuyemi, K. S., Partin, M. R., Ahluwalia, J. S., Nelson, D. B., Clothier, B. A. & Joseph, A. M. (2008). Menthol cigarettes and smoking cessation during an aided quit attempt. *Nicotine and Tobacco Research*, *10*, 457-462.

Giskes, K., Van Lenthe, F. J., Turrell, G., Brus, J. & Mackenbach, J. P. (2006). Smokers living in deprived areas are less likely to quit: A longitudinal follow-up. *Tobacco Control: An International Journal*, *15*, 485-488.

Hanewinkel, R., Wibord, G., Isensee, B., Nebot, M. & Vartiainen, E. (2006). 'Smoke-free class competition': Far-reaching conclusions based on weak data. *Preventive Medicine*, *43*, 150-151.

Harris, J. B., Schwartz, S. M. & Thompson, B. (2008). Characteristics associated with self- identification as a regular smoker and desire to quit among college students who smoke cigarettes. *Nicotine and Tobacco Research*, *10*, 69-76.

Haviland, L., Thornton, A. H., Carothers, S., Hund, L., Allen, J. A., Kastens, B., Wojciak, A., Hamasaka, L. & Healton, C. G. (2004). Giving infants a great start: Launching a national smoking cessation program for pregnant women. *Nicotine and Tobacco Research*, *6*, s181-s188.

Hebert, R. (2004). What's new in *Nicotine and Tobacco Research*? *Nicotine and Tobacco Research*, *6*, 279-283.

Hebert, R. (2008). What's new in *Nicotine and Tobacco Research*? *Nicotine and Tobacco Research*, *10*, 399-405.

Heckathorn, D. D. (1997). Respondent-driven sampling: A new approach to the study of hidden populations. *Social Problems*, *44*, 174-199.

Hyland, A., Rezaishiraz H., Bauer, J., Giovino, G. A. & Cummings, K. M. (2005). Characteristics of low-level smokers. *Nicotine and Tobacco Research*, *7*, 461-468.

Johnson, T. P. & Mott, J. A. (2001). The reliability of self-reported age of onset of tobacco, alcohol, and illicit drug use. *Addiction*, *96*, 1187-1198.

Kendler, K. S., Neale, M. C., Sullivan, P., Corey, L. A., Gardner, C. O. & Prescott, C. A. (1999). A population-based twin study in women of smoking initiation and nicotine dependence. *Psychological Medicine*, *29*, 299-308.

Khaled, S. M., Bulloch, A., Exner, D. V. & Patten, S. B. (2009). Cigarette smoking, stages of change, and major depression in the Canadian population. *Canadian Journal of Psychiatry*, *54*, 204-208.

Klein, J. D., Thomas, R. K. & Sutter, E. J. (2007). Self-reported smoking in online surveys: Prevalence estimate validity and item format effects. *Medical Care*, *45*, 691-695.

Krosnick, J. A., Chang, L. C., Sherman, S. J., Chassin, L. & Presson, C. (2006). The effects of beliefs about the health consequences of cigarette smoking on smoking onset. *Journal of Communication*, *56*, s18-s37.

Lauder, W., Mummery, K., Jones, M. & Caperchione, C. (2006). A comparison of health behaviours in lonely and non-lonely populations. *Psychology, Health, and Medicine*, *11*, 233-245.

MacFadyen, L., Amos, A., Hastings, G. & Parkes, E. (2003). 'They look like my kind of people'–Perceptions of smoking images in youth magazines. *Social Science and Medicine*, *56*, 491-499.

McCaul, K. D., Mullens, A. B., Romanek, K. M., Erickson, S. C. & Gatheridge, B. J. (2007). The motivational effects of thinking and worrying about the effects of smoking cigarettes. *Cognition and Emotion*, *21*, 1780-1798.

McKee, S. A., O'Malley, S. S., Salovey, P., Krishnan-Sarin, S. & Mazure, C. M. (2005). Perceived risks and benefits of smoking cessation: Gender-specific predictors of motivation and treatment outcome. *Addictive Behaviors*, *30*, 423-435.

Messer, K., Trinidad, D. R., Al-Delaimy, W. K. & Pierce, J. P. (2008). Smoking cessation rates in the United States: A comparison of young adult and older smokers. *American Journal of Public Health*, *98*, 317-322.

Milberger, S. M., Davis, R. M. & Holm, A. L. (2009). Pet owners' attitudes and behaviours related to smoking and second-hand smoke: A pilot study. *Tobacco Control: An International Journal*, *18*, 156-158.

Moorman, M. & Van Den Putte, B. (2008). The influence of message framing, intention to quit smoking, and nicotine dependence on the persuasiveness of smoking cessation messages. *Addictive Behaviors*, *33*, 1267-1275.

News-Journal.com (2009). *Illustrated health encyclopedia: Tobacco use–smoking and smokeless tobacco.* Found on the internet at: *http://www.news-journal.com/search/healthfd/shared/health/adam/ency/article/002032.html*. Last retrieved on June 10, 2009.

Pederson, W. & Von Soest, T. (2009). Smoking, nicotine dependence and mental health among young adults: A 13-year population-based longitudinal study. *Addiction*, *104*, 129-137.

Pomerleau, O. F., Pomerleau, C. S., Mehringer, A. M., Snedecor, S. M. & Cameron, O. G. (2005). Validation of retrospective reports of early experiences with smoking. *Addictive Behaviors*, *30*, 607-611.

Radloff, L. S. (1977). The CES-D scale: A self-report depression scale for research in the general population. *Applied Psychological Measurement*, *1*, 385-401.

Raichle, K. A., Christensen, A. J., Ehlers, S., Moran, P. J., Karnell, L. & Funk, G. (2001). Public and private self-consciousness and smoking behavior in head and neck cancer patients. *Annals of Behavioral Medicine*, *23*, 120-124.

Rosenberg, M. (1965). *Society and the adolescent self-image.* Princeton, NJ: Princeton University Press.

Ruchlin, H. S. (1999). An analysis of smoking patterns among older adults. *Medical Care*, *37*, 615-619.

Sokal, R. R. & Rohlf, F. J. (1995). *Biometry: The principles and practice of statistics in biological research (3rd edition).* New York: W.H. Freeman.

Spigner, C., Shigaki, A. & Tu, S. P. (2005). Perceptions of Asian American men about tobacco cigarette consumption: A social learning theory framework. *Journal of Immigrant Health*, *7*, 293-303.

Stanton, C. A., Papandonatos, G., Lloyd-Richardson, E. E. & Niaura, R. (2007). Consistency of self-reported smoking over a six-year interval from adolescence to young adulthood. *Addiction*, *102*, 1831-1839.

Steptoe, A. & Wardle, J. (2001). Locus of control and health behaviour revisited: A multivariate analysis of young adults from 18 countries. *British Journal of Psychology*, *92*, 659-672.

Stoddard, J. L., Sussman, S., Dent, C. W., Donaldson, S. I. & Severson, H. H. (1997). Characteristics of tobacco use in the lumber industry. *American Journal of Health Behavior*, *21*, 91-99.

Substance Use and Mental Health Services Administration (1998). *Results from the 1997 National Household Survey on Drug Abuse.* Rockville, MD: U.S. Government Printing Office.

Substance Use and Mental Health Services Administration (2008). *Results from the 2007 National Survey on Drug Use and Health: National Findings.* NSDUH series H-34, DHHS publication number SMA 08-4343. Rockville, MD: U.S. Government Printing Office.

Tingen, M. S., Waller, J. L., Smith, T. M., Baker, R. R., Reyes, J. & Treiber, F. A. (2006). Tobacco prevention in children and cessation in family members. *Journal of the American Academy of Nurse Practitioners, 18*, 169-179.

Tong, E. K., Ong, M. K., Vittinghoff, E. & Perez-Stable, E. J. (2006). Nondaily smokers should be asked and advised to quit. *American Journal of Preventive Medicine, 30*, 23-30.

Watters, J. & Biernacki, P. (1989). Targeted sampling: Options for the study of hidden populations. *Social Problems, 36*, 416-30.

Willemsen, M. C. (2005). The new EU cigarette health warnings benefit smokers who want to quit the habit: Results from the Dutch Continuous Survey of Smoking Habits. *European Journal of Public Health, 15*, 389-392.

Yong, H. H., Borland, R. & Siahpush, M. (2005). Qutting-related beliefs, intentions, and motivations of older smokers in four countries: Findings from the international tobacco control policy evaluation survey. *Addictive Behaviors, 30*, 777-788.

Zar, J. H. (2009). *Biostatistical analysis (5th edition).* Upper Saddle River, NJ: Prentice Hall.

Zuckerman, M. & Kuhlman, D. M. (2000). Personality and risk-taking: Common biosocial factors. *Journal of Personality, 68*, 999-1029.

In: Smoking Relapse: Causes, Prevention ... ISBN: 978-1-60876-580-5
Editors: J. Egger and M. Kalb

Chapter 5

CONTRIBUTION OF DRUG CUE, PRIMING, AND STRESS TO REINSTATEMENT OF NICOTINE-SEEKING BEHAVIOR IN A RAT MODEL OF RELAPSE

Xiu Liu *

Department of Psychiatry and Human Behavior, University of Mississippi Medical Center, Jackson, Mississippi, USA.

ABSTRACT

Exposure to drug-associated environmental stimuli (cue), drug priming, and stress have been thought of as the major risk factors contributing to relapse in abstinent subjects. Our recent animal studies along with reports from other laboratories have demonstrated that nicotine cues reliably reinstate nicotine-seeking behavior. However, investigation of nicotine-seeking elicited by nicotine priming and stress exposure as well as their combination with nicotine cues is limited. This study, using a response-reinstatement procedure, examined the motivational effects of a nicotine-associated cue, nicotine priming, pharmacological stress, and combination of the cue with priming or stress. Male Sprague-Dawley rats were trained in 30 daily 1-h sessions to

* Corresponding author: Department of Psychiatry and Human Behavior, University of Mississippi Medical Center, 2500 North State Street, Jackson, MS 39216, Tel: (601) 984-2875; Fax: (601) 984-5899, Email: xliu@psychiatry.umsmed.edu

intravenously self-administer nicotine (0.03 mg/kg/infusion, free base) on an FR5 schedule and associate an auditory/visual cue with each nicotine administration. Then, lever responding was extinguished by saline substitution of nicotine and omission of the cue. After rats reached an extinction criterion, reinstatement tests were conducted under five conditions: cue re-presentation, nicotine priming, stress, cue+priming, and cue+stress. Nicotine (0.25 mg/kg, s.c.) priming, stress (yohimbine, 2 mg/kg, i.p.), and response-contingent re-presentation of the cue significantly reinstated the extinguished nicotine-seeking behavior with cue producing the most robust effect. Combination of cue with either priming or stress did not produce additive effect. These results confirm the motivational effects of nicotine cue, priming, and stress in the present animal model of relapse and demonstrate the most robust ability of cue exposure to elicit nicotine-seeking after extinction. The present findings suggest that re-exposure to smoking-related environmental cues may play a critical role in the high recidivism rates of smoking and thereby lend support for the continued effort on cue management as a strategy for the treatment and prevention of smoking relapse.

INTRODUCTION

Tobacco smoking and nicotine dependence, like addiction to other drugs of abuse, is a chronic relapsing disorder. Without aids, only 4-7% of adult smokers who try to quit may successfully remain abstinent (Fiore et al. 2008). Although there have been several pharmacological treatments available, i.e. nicotine replacement therapy, bupropion, and recently varenicline, long-term abstinence rates still remain quite low. The 1-year abstinence rates are 14.6-16.1% for bupropion, 12.9-20.3% for nicotine replacement and 21.9-26.1% for varenicline (Aubin et al. 2008; Bala et al. 2008; Gonzales et al. 2006; Jorenby et al. 2006; Oncken et al. 2006). The high rates of resumption to cigarette smoking in abstinent smokers always present a central and formidable challenge for long-term success of smoking cessation treatment. To develop more effective strategies for prevention of relapse, it is important to fully understand the environmental and neurobiological basis of resumption of smoking behavior in abstinent smokers.

Exposure to drug-associated environmental stimuli (cues), stressful life events, and drug-priming have been thought of as the three major risk factors critically contributing to drug relapse in humans (Cooney et al. 1997; O'Brien et al. 1998; Sinha 2001; Stewart 2000). Among these factors, exposure to environmental stimuli previously associated with drug intake might be more liable for the craving for cigarette smoking given that smoking may involve more frequent pairings between the environmental cues and nicotine intake (cigarette puffs, approximately 70,000 times each year) than any other drug-taking behavior, i.e., cigarette smoking may be particularly effective in establishing the incentive properties of nicotine-associated environmental stimuli (cues), such as the smell and taste of cigarettes or contexts within which smoking occurs (Balfour et al. 2000; Caggiula et al. 2001; Goldberg et al. 1981; Rose and Levin 1991). Facing stressful life events and nicotine priming (a lapse to smoking) usually result in relapse of cigarette smoking and thereby decrease the abstinence rates among smokers (Cook et al. 2007; Juliano et al. 2006; Shiffman et al. 2006; Shiffman and Waters 2004; Swan et al. 1988). In animal studies, although ample evidence has been accumulated showing that these risk factors individually reinstate drug-seeking responding across a wide range of drugs of abuse (Epstein et al. 2006; Shaham et al. 2003 for comprehensive reviews), there has been relatively little effort to characterize resumption of nicotine-seeking behavior in animal models of relapse. Nevertheless, the limited reports on reinstatement of nicotine-seeking in animals have consistently demonstrated the motivational effect of nicotine-associated cues. We (Liu et al. 2008; Liu et al. 2006) as well as others (Cohen et al. 2005; LeSage et al. 2004; Paterson et al. 2005) have shown that reintroduction of nicotine cues after extinction resulted in increased responding on the lever previously reinforced by nicotine delivery. Footshock stress has been documented to reinstate nicotine-seeking in rats (Buczek et al. 1999; Zislis et al. 2007). The relapse-eliciting effect of nicotine priming has been reported in some studies (Andreoli et al. 2003; Chiamulera et al. 1996) but this effect is not consistent (LeSage et al. 2004).

The resumption of addictive behavior including nicotine-seeking during abstinence in humans is often associated with the presence of multiple risk factors (McKay 1999; Swan et al. 1988; Zhou et al. 2009). However, the significance of interactions among these factors for drug-seeking behavior has received little experimental attention. To the best of our knowledge, there have been only a few attempts in animal research. Our previous work has shown that the combination of alcohol-related cue with footshock stress produced an additive effect on the reinstatement of alcohol-seeking responding in rats (Liu and Weiss 2002). In another study, stress produced by yohimbine administration was found to potentiate the cue-induced reinstatement of cocaine-seeking responses (Feltenstein and See 2006). In terms of nicotine-seeking, there has been no attempt to examine whether stress and cue interact to produce stronger effect. An enhanced effect by the combination of nicotine priming and nicotine cue exposure was observed in one study (Shoaib 2008) but not in the other (LeSage et al. 2004).

After systemically characterizing the conditioned incentive properties of nicotine-associated cues (Liu et al. 2008; Liu et al. 2006; Liu et al. 2007a; Liu et al. 2009), in this study, we further compared the motivational effects of nicotine cue, nicotine priming, and pharmacological stress as well as explored the effects of combination of cue exposure with nicotine priming or stress in rats. The stressor employed was an anxiogenic drug yohimbine. It is a α_2 adrenergic receptor antagonist. It increases activity of noradrenergic systems including neural structures implicated in stress response (Abercrombie et al. 1988; Aghajanian and VanderMaelen 1982; Chopin et al. 1986; Uhde et al. 1984) and produces anxiety- and stress-like states in humans and laboratory animals (Bremner et al. 1996a; b; Charney et al. 1983; Davis et al. 1979; Holmberg and Gershon 1961; Lang and Gershon 1963). It has been increasingly used as a pharmacological stressor, especially in the field of drug addiction research (Feltenstein and See 2006; Funk et al. 2006; Ghitza et al. 2006; Le et al. 2005; Lee et al. 2004; Nair et al. 2006; Schroeder et al. 2003; Shepard et al. 2004; Zarrindast et al. 2000). Importantly, yohimbine-induced reinstatement of drug-seeking behavior in a response-reinstatement model of relapse appears to be more robust than that elicited by footshock stress (Bossert et al. 2005; Le and Shaham 2002; Lu et al. 2003; Shaham et al. 2000).

MATERIALS AND METHODS

Subjects

Twenty two male Sprague-Dawley rats (Harlan) weighing 225–250 g upon arrival were used. Animals were individually housed in a humidity- and temperature-controlled (21-22 °C) vivarium on a reversed light/dark cycle (lights on 7:00 PM; off 7:00 AM) with unlimited access to water. After one week habituation to the colony room, rats were placed on a food-restriction (20 g chow/day) regimen throughout the experiment. Training and experimental sessions were conducted during the dark phase at the same time each day (9:00 AM-3:00 PM). All experimental procedures were carried out in accordance with the *National Institutes of Health Guide for the Care and Use of Laboratory Animals*.

Self-Administration Apparatus

Operant training and reinstatement tests were conducted in operant chambers located inside sound-attenuating, ventilated cubicles (Med Associates, St. Albans, VT). The chambers were equipped with two retractable levers on one side panel and with a 28-V white light above each lever as well as a red chamber light on the top of the chambers. Between the two levers was a food pellet trough. Intravenous nicotine injections were delivered by a drug delivery system with a syringe pump (Med Associates, model PHM100-10 rpm). Experimental events and data collection were automatically controlled by an interfaced computer.

Food Training

One day after the start of the food-restriction regimen, food training sessions began. During the 1-h sessions, lever pressing responses were rewarded with delivery of food pellets (45 mg). Rats could earn a maximum delivery of 45 food pellets first on a fixed-ratio (FR) 1 and then on a FR5 schedule. Successful food training was achieved within 3-5 sessions.

Surgery

After food training, the rats were anesthetized with isoflurane (1-3%) and implanted with jugular catheters. Animals were allowed at least 7 days to recover from surgery. During the recovery period catheters were flushed once/day with 0.1 ml of sterile saline containing heparin (20 U/ml), timentin (10 mg/ml) to maintain catheter patency and prevent infection. Thereafter, the catheters were flushed with the heparinized (20 U/ml) saline prior to and after the experimental sessions throughout the experiment.

Nicotine Self-Administration/Conditioning

After recovery from surgery, rats were trained to intravenously self-administer nicotine (0.03 mg/kg/infusion, free base) and associate an auditory/visual cue with nicotine delivery. In the training sessions, animals were placed in the operant conditioning chambers and connected to a drug delivery system. The daily 1-h sessions were initiated by introduction of the two levers with illumination of the red chamber light. Once the FR requirement on the active lever was met, an infusion of nicotine was dispensed in a volume of 0.1 ml in approximately 1 s. Each nicotine infusion was paired with a presentation of the cue consisting of a 5 s tone and illumination of the lever light for 20 s. The latter signaled a 20 s timeout period, during which time responses were recorded but not reinforced. Responses on the inactive lever had no consequence. An FR1 schedule was used for days 1-5, an FR2 for days 6-8 and an FR5 for remainder of the experiments. All rats received 30 daily self-administration/conditioning sessions.

Extinction

After completion of the self-administration/conditioning phase, rats were subjected to daily extinction sessions. During the extinction sessions, lever responding was extinguished by withholding nicotine and the cue. Specifically, the daily 1-h extinction sessions began with introduction of the levers and illumination of the red chamber light. Responses on the active lever resulted in the delivery of saline rather than nicotine and the cue presentation was omitted. The criterion for extinction was 3 consecutive days in which the number of responses/session was less than 20% of the (averaged) number of responses/session that occurred during the last 3 days of nicotine self-administration.

Reinstatement Tests

One day after the extinction criterion was met, the reinstatement tests were conducted. During the test sessions, responses on the active lever resulted in saline infusion (no availability of nicotine) on the FR5 schedule with a 20 s timeout period. The re-presentation or absence of the cue depending on testing conditions is described below. The tests were scheduled with an interval of 2 days, during which time the daily extinction sessions were performed in order to assure the extinction baseline.

1. Effects of Nicotine Priming, Cue, and their Combination

Eleven rats were used for these tests. To test the effect of nicotine priming, rats received a subcutaneous administration of nicotine (0.25 mg/kg in a volume of 1 ml/kg) 5 min before the test session. During the session, there was no cue presentation. To test the effect of cue exposure, the session was conducted with response-contingent re-presentation of the cue. To test the effect of combination of nicotine priming with cue exposure, the session was performed 5 min after nicotine (0.25 mg/kg in a volume of 1 ml/kg, s.c.) priming injection and with response-contingent re-presentation of the cue during the session.

2. Effect of Stress, Cue, and their Combination

Eleven rats were used for these tests. To test the effect of stress, rats received an intraperitoneal administration of yohimbine (2 mg/kg in a volume of 1 ml/kg) 30 min before the test session. During the session, there was no cue presentation. Then, the effect of cue exposure was tested as described above. To test the effect of combination of stress with cue exposure, the test session was performed 30 min after yohimbine (2 mg/kg in a volume of 1 ml/kg) injection and with response-contingent re-presentation of the cue during the session.

Data Analyses

Data were presented as the mean (±SEM) number of lever responses. One-way ANOVA was used to separately analyze the data obtained from the two sets of rats (one set for the priming/cue/their combination tests and the other for stress/cue/their combination tests). Differences among individual means in each set of rats were verified by subsequent Newman-Keuls *post hoc* tests.

RESULTS

Nicotine Self-Administration/Conditioning and Extinction

By the end of the 30 daily 1-h self-administration training, rats developed stable operant responding for intravenous nicotine infusions (Figure 1). Averaged across the last 3 sessions, response rates were 83.0±2.9 on the active lever and 9.7±0.9 on the inactive lever, resulting in 14.9±0.5 nicotine infusions per 1-h session. In the first extinction session, rats emitted 68.1±6.4 responses on the active lever and 6.5 ±1.1 on the inactive lever. During the following extinction sessions, lever responses gradually decreased. All rats reached the extinction criterion within 10 daily sessions. Since rats were divided into two sets for the reinstatement tests in a counterbalanced manner, there was no difference in the number of lever responses and nicotine infusions (data not shown).

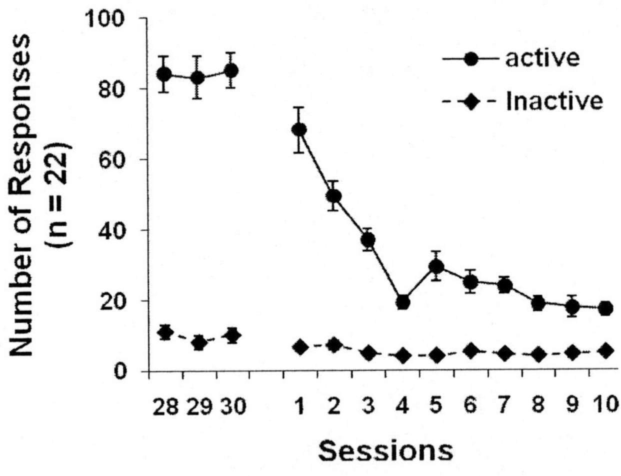

Figure 1. Lever responses made in the last three sessions (sessions 28, 29, 30) of nicotine self-administration/conditioning and during subsequent extinction sessions.

Effects of Nicotine Priming, Cue Re-presentation, and their Combination in the Reinstatement Tests

A one-way ANOVA on the number of responses emitted on the active lever in the reinstatement test sessions yielded a significant effect of testing condition [$F(3,40)=7.10$, $p<0.001$]. Further Newman-Keuls *post hoc* tests revealed a significant increase in the number of responses under both the cue exposure ($p<0.01$) and the cue+priming combination ($p<0.05$) conditions above extinction baseline as well as under the cue ($p<0.05$) over the priming condition (Figure 2). The increase of the active lever responses under the priming condition above the extinction baseline marginally reached statistical significance ($p=0.0602$). However, responses on the inactive lever remained low and indistinguishable between testing conditions.

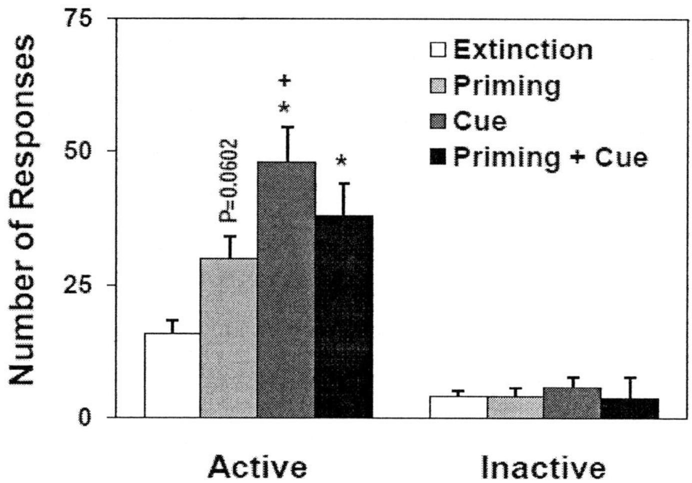

Figure 2. Lever responses in the reinstatement test sessions under the nicotine priming, cue exposure, and their combination conditions. The number of responses is presented as the mean±SEM (n=11). * $p < 0.05$ different from Extinction; + $p < 0.05$ different from Priming.

Effects of Stress, Cue Re-presentation, and their Combination in the Reinstatement Tests

A one-way ANOVA on the number of active lever responses collected in the reinstatement test sessions produced a significant effect of testing condition [$F(3,40)=3.97$, $p<0.05$]. Subsequent Newman-Keuls *post hoc* tests showed a significant ($p<0.05$) increase in the number of responses under all three conditions above extinction baseline (Figure 3). However, responses on the inactive lever remained low and indistinguishable between testing conditions.

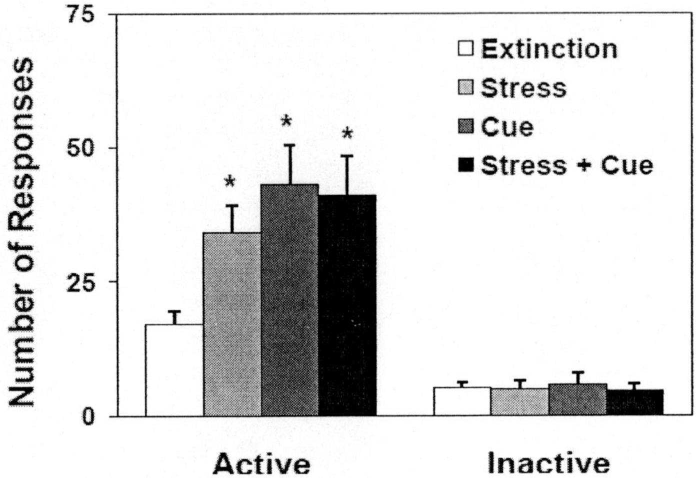

Figure 3. Lever responses in the reinstatement test sessions under the stress, cue exposure, and their combination conditions. The number of responses is presented as the mean±SEM (n=11). * $p < 0.05$ different from Extinction.

DISCUSSION

This study simultaneously examined the motivational effects of the three major risk factors (cue, priming, and stress) under one experimental setting of the response-reinstatement model of relapse and further investigated the issue of whether these factors could interact in reinstating nicotine-seeking behavior. The results demonstrated that re-presentation of the nicotine-associated cue, pharmacological stress produced by yohimbine administration, and nicotine priming injection effectively reinstated extinguished nicotine-seeking behavior in rats. In comparison, re-presentation of the nicotine cue showed the most robust motivational effect. Combination of cue with either priming or stress did not show additive effect.

The issue of whether the cue-induced reinstatement of lever-pressing responses represents conditioned nicotine-seeking behavior needs to be discussed. In the present response-reinstatement paradigm, like in most cases using similar procedures (Shaham et al. 2003 for a review), both nicotine and its associated stimulus (cue) were omitted during extinction after self-administration/conditioning training and re-presented in the reinstatement test to determine the conditioned incentive properties of the cue without further nicotine availability. In light of the fact that recent animal studies have shown that some particular sensory stimuli have intrinsic reinforcing values and thereby support moderate levels of operant responding such as lever-pressing (Chaudhri et al. 2007; Cohen et al. 2005; Donny et al. 2003; Liu et al. 2007b; Palmatier et al. 2006), it is speculated that the increase of responding during re-presentation of the cue might be attributable to the possible reinforcing value of the stimulus regardless of its association with nicotine; this might then be misinterpreted as response-reinstatement induced by the conditioned incentive properties of the stimulus. To address this concern, in a recent study (Liu et al. 2008) a control group was included that received procedures exactly the same as other experimental groups with the exception that saline rather than nicotine was available during self-administration/conditioning training. Since the stimulus, albeit the same as in other groups, was never associated with nicotine delivery and subjective actions of nicotine, it did not acquire conditioned reinforcement value. Responding on the active lever in this control group remained low and constant across the self-administration/conditioning, extinction, and reinstatement phases. This finding indicates that the specific stimulus used in that procedure had very little, if any, intrinsic reinforcing value. Particularly convincing was the observation that removal of the stimulus during extinction in this saline control group did not impact the level of responding. Therefore, the recovery of extinguished responding of nicotine groups during the reinstatement tests resulted from the conditioned incentive value of the stimulus (cue) due to its prior repeated association with nicotine infusion and pharmacological actions. Indeed, by using a procedure that employed criteria established by Mackintosh (1974) for demonstrating conditioned reinforcement, it was verified that self-administered nicotine endowed its associated stimulus with conditioned reinforcing value (Palmatier et al. 2007). Therefore, it should be no doubt that in the present study nicotine-associated cue-elicited reinstatement of nicotine-seeking responding was solely due to the acquired conditioned incentive properties of the cue because the stimulus cue was exactly the same as in that study (Liu et al. 2008).

As observed in our previous studies (Liu et al. 2008; Liu et al. 2006; Liu et al. 2007a; Liu et al. 2009), response-contingent re-presentation of the nicotine cue after extinction significantly reinstated responding on the active lever previously reinforced by nicotine. This effect cannot be attributed to the nonspecific arousal effects of reintroduction of the cue because responding on the inactive lever remained at extinction levels. Thus, the reinstatement of responding on the active lever was selectively controlled by the cue that had been associated with delivery and reinforcing actions of nicotine during self-administration/conditioning training. These data lend support for a pioneer endeavor showing that exposing rats to the self-administration training chambers after 21 drug-free days, during which time the rats remained in home cages, resulted in recovery of lever pressing (Shaham et al. 1997). The results are in line with increasing evidence in animal studies showing the behavioral significance of nicotine-related cues (Chiamulera et al. 2008; Cohen et al. 2005; LeSage et al. 2004; Paterson et al. 2005). Taken together, it is indicated that the environmental stimuli associated with availability and subjective actions of nicotine may play an important role in relapse to tobacco smoking in abstinent smokers. Thus, these animal studies lend support for clinical observations that smoking-related cues enhance desire to smoke (Drobes and Tiffany 1997; Droungas et al. 1995; Lazev et al. 1999; McDermut and Haaga 1998; Perkins et al. 1994). It has been hypothesized that when compared to other drugs of abuse, environmental stimuli associated with nicotine intake play a more important role in maintaining nicotine self-administration and tobacco smoking (Balfour et al. 2000). Consistent with this view, tobacco smoking or nicotine self-administration is particularly effective in establishing the incentive properties of accompanying environmental stimuli (Balfour et al. 2000; Caggiula et al. 2001; Goldberg et al. 1981; Rose and Levin 1991) because smoking may involve more frequent pairings between the environmental cues and nicotine intake (cigarette puffs, approximately 70,000 times each year) than any other drug-taking behavior. Moreover, since the reinstatement tests dissociate the motivation to engage in nicotine-seeking behavior from the direct reinforcing properties of nicotine, the procedures used in the present study may be useful for understanding the factors involved in nicotine relapse and the neurobiological mechanisms involved in nicotine-seeking behavior and relapse to tobacco smoking.

Increasing human studies have indicated that a lapse or slip to drug use is one of the best predictors of a full blown relapse to drug abuse including cigarette smoking (Brandon et al. 1990; Garvey et al. 1992; Kenford et al. 1994; Marlatt et al. 1988; Nides et al. 1995; Norregaard et al. 1993). In several animal studies nicotine priming has been documented to reinstate nicotine-seeking responses (Andreoli et al. 2003; Chiamulera et al. 1996; Shram et al. 2008). The present data add to the literature supporting the notion that priming with nicotine leads to recovery of nicotine-seeking. Interestingly, nicotine doses used for the priming tests varied across a wide range from 0.001 mg/kg (intravenous) up to 0.3 mg/kg (subcutaneous). This laboratory dosing matches with clinical definition of lapse that could be any amount of smoking including even only a single puff (e.g., Brandon et al. 1990; Shiffman et al. 1996).

Together, it is argued that in these priming tests nicotine acts as an occasion setter or discriminative stimulus as long as the injected doses are above a threshold that produces pharmacological actions. This stand could get support from our recent observation showing that self-administered nicotine across a dose range of 0.015-0.06 mg/kg/infusion could endow its associated stimulus similar strength of the conditioned incentive value in rats (Liu et al. 2008). However, one study failed to find the response-reinstating effect of priming by intravenous nicotine at 0.01-0.06mg/kg (LeSage et al. 2004). Although detailed procedural differences in the latter study from other experiments may help explain the inability of nicotine priming to reinstate nicotine-seeking responding, systemic investigation into this issue deserves future efforts.

In the animal model of relapse that tests the effects of stress, footshock has been widely used as a means to induce drug-seeking (Erb et al. 1996; Lu et al. 2003; Shaham et al. 2000; Stewart 2000). Recently, however, a pharmacological stress produced by administration of yohimbine has been increasingly employed instead (Feltenstein and See 2006; Funk et al. 2006; Ghitza et al. 2006; Le et al. 2005; Lee et al. 2004; Nair et al. 2006; Schroeder et al. 2003; Shepard et al. 2004; Zarrindast et al. 2000) because yohimbine via blockade of the presynaptic α_2 adrenergic receptors increases activity of noradrenergic systems including neural structures implicated in stress response and thereby produces anxiety- and stress-like states in humans and laboratory animals (Bremner et al. 1996a; b; Charney et al. 1983; Davis et al. 1979; Holmberg and Gershon 1961; Lang and Gershon 1963). In the present study, the yohimbine-produced stress states effectively reinstated extinguished nicotine-seeking responding. This finding is consistent with previous reports that employed footshock as stress (Buczek et al. 1999; Zislis et al. 2007). Moreover, the fact that yohimbine has a long half-life (7-8 h) ensured prolonged stress states throughout the whole reinstatement session. That could guarantee the overlap between stress and nicotine cue exposure during the reinstatement sessions.

In contrast to our previous observation showing that stress and ethanol cue interacted to produce additive effect in reinstating ethanol-seeking (Liu and Weiss 2002) and a similar report showing additive response-reinstating effect between yohimbine stress and cocaine cue in reinstating cocaine-seeking (Feltenstein and See 2006), combined exposure to stress and nicotine cue in the present study failed to produce an enhanced motivational effect. The magnitude of reinstatement of nicotine-seeking responding under the stress and cue combination was similar to that elicited by nicotine cue alone. The major reason for this discrepancy may reside in the different categories of the drugs of abuse tested across these experiments. In this respect, it is necessary for future work to elucidate the biological mechanisms underlying this discrepancy between nicotine and ethanol or cocaine. Nevertheless, together with the inability of nicotine priming and cue combination to produce a stronger effect above that elicited by nicotine cue alone, these results indicate that re-exposure to smoking-related environmental cues may play a critical role in the high recidivism rates of smoking, and therefore, lend support for the continued effort on cue management as a strategy for the treatment and prevention of smoking relapse.

ACKNOWLEDGMENTS

This work was supported by NIH grant DA017288 from the National Institute on Drug Abuse. The author would like to thank Mrs. Maysa Gharib and Sheri Booth at the University of Pittsburgh and Mrs. Courtney Jernigan at the University of Mississippi Medical Center for their technical assistance.

REFERENCES

Abercrombie, E. D., Keller, R. W. Jr. & Zigmond, M. J. (1988). Characterization of hippocampal norepinephrine release as measured by microdialysis perfusion: pharmacological and behavioral studies. *Neuroscience*, *27*, 897-904.

Aghajanian, G. K. & VanderMaelen, C. P. (1982). alpha 2-adrenoceptor-mediated hyperpolarization of locus coeruleus neurons: intracellular studies in vivo. *Science*, *215*, 1394-6.

Andreoli, M., Tessari, M., Pilla, M., Valerio, E., Hagan, J. J. & Heidbreder, C. A. (2003). Selective antagonism at dopamine D3 receptors prevents nicotine-triggered relapse to nicotine-seeking behavior. *Neuropsychopharmacology*, *28*, 1272-80.

Aubin, H. J., Bobak, A., Britton, J. R., Oncken, C., Billing, C. B. Jr., Gong, J., Williams, K. E. & Reeves, K. R. (2008). Varenicline versus transdermal nicotine patch for smoking cessation: Results from a randomised, open-label trial. Thorax.

Bala, M. M., Lesniak, W. & Strzeszynski, L. (2008). Efficacy of pharmacological methods used for treating tobacco dependence: meta-analysis. *Pol Arch Med Wewn*, *118*, 20-8.

Balfour, D. J., Wright, A. E., Benwell, M. E. & Birrell, C. E. (2000). The putative role of extra-synaptic mesolimbic dopamine in the neurobiology of nicotine dependence. *Behav Brain Res*, *113*, 73-83.

Bossert, J. M., Ghitza, U. E., Lu, L., Epstein, D. H. & Shaham, Y. (2005). Neurobiology of relapse to heroin and cocaine seeking: an update and clinical implications. *Eur J Pharmacol*, 526, 36-50.

Brandon, T. H., Tiffany, S. T., Obremski, K. M. & Baker, T. B. (1990). Postcessation cigarette use: the process of relapse. *Addict Behav*, *15*, 105-14.

Bremner, J. D., Krystal, J. H., Southwick, S. M. & Charney, D. S. (1996a). Noradrenergic mechanisms in stress and anxiety: I. Preclinical studies. *Synapse*, *23*, 28-38.

Bremner, J. D., Krystal, J. H., Southwick, S. M. & Charney, D. S. (1996b). Noradrenergic mechanisms in stress and anxiety: II. Clinical studies. *Synapse*, *23*, 39-51.

Buczek, Y., Le, A. D., Stewart, J. & Shaham, Y. (1999). Stress reinstates nicotine seeking but not sucrose solution seeking in rats. *Psychopharmacology (Berl)*, *144*, 183-8.

Caggiula, A. R., Donny, E. C., White, A. R., Chaudhri, N., Booth, S., Gharib, M. A., Hoffman, A., Perkins, K. A. & Sved, A. F. (2001). Cue dependency of nicotine self-administration and smoking. *Pharmacol Biochem Behav*, *70*, 515-30.

Charney, D. S., Heninger, G. R. & Redmond, D. E. Jr. (1983). Yohimbine induced anxiety and increased noradrenergic function in humans: effects of diazepam and clonidine. *Life Sci*, *33*, 19-29.

Chaudhri, N., Caggiula, A. R., Donny, E. C., Booth, S., Gharib, M., Craven, L., Palmatier, M. I., Liu, X. & Sved, A. F. (2007). Self-administered and noncontingent nicotine enhance reinforced operant responding in rats: impact of nicotine dose and reinforcement schedule. *Psychopharmacology (Berl)*, *190*, 353-62.

Chiamulera, C., Borgo, C., Falchetto, S., Valerio, E. & Tessari, M. (1996). Nicotine reinstatement of nicotine self-administration after long-term extinction. *Psychopharmacology (Berl)*, *127*, 102-7.

Chiamulera, C., Tedesco, V., Zangrandi, L., Giuliano, C. & Fumagalli, G. (2008). Propranolol transiently inhibits reinstatement of nicotine-seeking behaviour in rats. *J Psychopharmacol, (Epub ahead of print, PMID: 18832430).*

Chopin, P., Pellow, S. & File, S. E. (1986). The effects of yohimbine on exploratory and locomotor behaviour are attributable to its effects at noradrenaline and not at benzodiazepine receptors. *Neuropharmacology*, *25*, 53-7.

Cohen, C., Perrault, G., Griebel, G. & Soubrie, P. (2005). Nicotine-associated cues maintain nicotine-seeking behavior in rats several weeks after nicotine withdrawal: reversal by the cannabinoid (CB1) receptor antagonist, rimonabant (SR141716). *Neuropsychopharmacology*, *30*, 145-55.

Cook, J. W., McFall, M. M., Calhoun, P. S. & Beckham, J. C. (2007). Posttraumatic stress disorder and smoking relapse: A theoretical model. *J Trauma Stress*, *20*, 989-98.

Cooney, N. L., Litt, M. D., Morse, P. A., Bauer, L. O. & Gaupp, L. (1997). Alcohol cue reactivity, negative-mood reactivity, and relapse in treated alcoholic men. *J Abnorm Psychol*, *106*, 243-50.

Davis, M., Redmond, D. E. Jr. & Baraban, J. M. (1979). Noradrenergic agonists and antagonists: effects on conditioned fear as measured by the potentiated startle paradigm. *Psychopharmacology (Berl)*, *65*, 111-8.

Donny, E. C., Chaudhri, N., Caggiula, A. R., Evans-Martin, F. F., Booth, S., Gharib, M. A., Clements, L. A. & Sved, A. F. (2003). Operant responding for a visual reinforcer in rats is enhanced by noncontingent nicotine: implications for nicotine self-administration and reinforcement. *Psychopharmacology (Berl)*, *169*, 68-76.

Drobes, D. J. & Tiffany, S. T. (1997). Induction of smoking urge through imaginal and in vivo procedures: physiological and self-report manifestations. *J Abnorm Psychol*, *106*, 15-25.

Droungas, A., Ehrman, R. N., Childress, A. R. & O'Brien, C. P. (1995). Effect of smoking cues and cigarette availability on craving and smoking behavior. *Addict Behav*, *20*, 657-73.

Epstein, D. H., Preston, K. L., Stewart, J. & Shaham, Y. (2006). Toward a model of drug relapse: an assessment of the validity of the reinstatement procedure. *Psychopharmacology (Berl)*, *189*, 1-16.

Erb, S., Shaham, Y. & Stewart, J. (1996). Stress reinstates cocaine-seeking behavior after prolonged extinction and a drug-free period. *Psychopharmacology (Berl)*, *128*, 408-12.

Feltenstein, M. W. & See, R. E. (2006). Potentiation of cue-induced reinstatement of cocaine-seeking in rats by the anxiogenic drug yohimbine. *Behav Brain Res*, *174*, 1-8.

Fiore, M. C., Jaen, C. R., Baker, T. B., et. al. (2008). Treating tobacco use and dependence: 2008 update. *Clinical practice guideline*. Rockville, MD: USDHHS.

Funk, D., Li, Z. & Le, A. D. (2006). Effects of environmental and pharmacological stressors on c-fos and corticotropin-releasing factor mRNA in rat brain: Relationship to the reinstatement of alcohol seeking. *Neuroscience*, *138*, 235-43.

Garvey, A. J., Bliss, R. E., Hitchcock, J. L., Heinold, J. W. & Rosner, B.(1992). Predictors of smoking relapse among self-quitters: a report from the Normative Aging Study. *Addict Behav*, *17*, 367-77.

Ghitza, U. E., Gray, S. M., Epstein, D. H., Rice, K. C. & Shaham, Y. (2006). The anxiogenic drug yohimbine reinstates palatable food seeking in a rat relapse model: a role of CRF1 receptors. *Neuropsychopharmacology*, *31*, 2188-96.

Goldberg, S. R., Spealman, R. D. & Goldberg, D. M. (1981). Persistent behavior at high rates maintained by intravenous self-administration of nicotine. *Science*, *214*, 573-5.

Gonzales, D., Rennard, S. I., Nides, M., Oncken, C., Azoulay, S., Billing, C. B., Watsky, E. J., Gong, J., Williams, K. E. & Reeves, K. R. (2006). Varenicline, an alpha4beta2 nicotinic acetylcholine receptor partial agonist, vs sustained-release bupropion and placebo for smoking cessation: a randomized controlled trial. *Jama*, *296*, 47-55.

Holmberg, G. & Gershon, S. (1961). Autonomic and psychic effects of yohimbine hydrochloride. *Psychopharmacologia*, *2*, 93-106.

Jorenby, D. E., Hays, J. T., Rigotti, N. A., Azoulay, S., Watsky, E. J., Williams, K. E., Billing, C. B., Gong, J. & Reeves, K. R. (2006). Efficacy of varenicline, an alpha4beta2 nicotinic acetylcholine receptor partial agonist, vs placebo or sustained-release bupropion for smoking cessation: a randomized controlled trial. *Jama*, *296*, 56-63.

Juliano, L. M., Donny, E. C., Houtsmuller, E. J. & Stitzer, M. L. (2006). Experimental evidence for a causal relationship between smoking lapse and relapse. *J Abnorm Psychol*, *115*, 166-73.

Kenford, S. L., Fiore, M. C., Jorenby, D. E., Smith, S. S., Wetter, D. & Baker, T. B. (1994). Predicting smoking cessation. Who will quit with and without the nicotine patch. *JAMA*, *271*, 589-94.

Lang, W. J. & Gershon, S. (1963). Effects of psychoactive drugs on yohimbine induced responses in conscious dogs. A proposed screening procedure for anti-anxiety agents. *Arch Int Pharmacodyn Ther*, *142*, 457-72.

Lazev, A. B., Herzog, T. A. & Brandon, T. H. (1999). Classical conditions of environmental cues to cigarette smoking. *Exp Clin Psychopharmacol*, *7*, 56-63.

Le, A. & Shaham, Y. (2002). Neurobiology of relapse to alcohol in rats. *Pharmacol Ther*, *94*, 137-56.

Le, A. D., Harding, S., Juzytsch, W., Funk, D. & Shaham, Y. (2005). Role of alpha-2 adrenoceptors in stress-induced reinstatement of alcohol seeking and alcohol self-administration in rats. *Psychopharmacology (Berl)*, *179*, 366-73.

Lee, B., Tiefenbacher, S., Platt, D. M. & Spealman, R. D. (2004). Pharmacological blockade of alpha2-adrenoceptors induces reinstatement of cocaine-seeking behavior in squirrel monkeys. *Neuropsychopharmacology*, *29*, 686-93.

LeSage, M. G., Burroughs, D., Dufek, M., Keyler, D. E. & Pentel, P. R. (2004). Reinstatement of nicotine self-administration in rats by presentation of nicotine-paired stimuli, but not nicotine priming. *Pharmacol Biochem Behav*, *79*, 507-13.

Liu, X., Caggiula, A. R., Palmatier, M. I., Donny, E. C. & Sved, A. F. (2008). Cue-induced reinstatement of nicotine-seeking behavior in rats: effect of bupropion, persistence over repeated tests, and its dependence on training dose. *Psychopharmacology (Berl)*, *196*, 365-75.

Liu, X., Caggiula, A. R., Yee, S. K., Nobuta, H., Poland, R. E. & Pechnick, R. N. (2006). Reinstatement of nicotine-seeking behavior by drug-associated stimuli after extinction in rats. *Psychopharmacology (Berl)*, *184*, 417-25.

Liu, X., Caggiula, A. R., Yee, S. K., Nobuta, H., Sved, A. F., Pechnick, R. N. & Poland, R. E. (2007a). Mecamylamine attenuates cue-induced reinstatement of nicotine-seeking behavior in rats. *Neuropsychopharmacology*, *32*, 710-8.

Liu, X., Palmatier, M. I., Caggiula, A. R., Donny, E. C. & Sved, A. F. (2007b). Reinforcement enhancing effect of nicotine and its attenuation by nicotinic antagonists in rats. *Psychopharmacology (Berl)*, 194, 463-73.

Liu, X., Palmatier, M. I., Caggiula, A. R., Sved, A. F., Donny, E. C., Gharib, M. & Booth, S. (2009). Naltrexone attenuation of conditioned but not primary reinforcement of nicotine in rats. *Psychopharmacology (Berl)*, *202*, 589-98.

Liu, X. & Weiss, F. (2002). Additive effect of stress and drug cues on reinstatement of ethanol seeking: exacerbation by history of dependence and role of concurrent activation of corticotropin-releasing factor and opioid mechanisms. *J Neurosci*, *22*, 7856-61.

Lu, L., Shepard, J. D., Hall, F. S. & Shaham, Y. (2003). Effect of environmental stressors on opiate and psychostimulant reinforcement, reinstatement and discrimination in rats: a review. *Neurosci Biobehav Rev*, *27*, 457-91.

Mackintosh, N. J. (1974). *The psychology of animal learning*. Academic, New York.

Marlatt, G. A., Curry, S. & Gordon, J. R. (1988). A longitudinal analysis of unaided smoking cessation. *J Consult Clin Psychol*, *56*, 715-20.

McDermut, W. & Haaga, D. A. (1998). Effect of stage of change on cue reactivity in continuing smokers. *Exp Clin Psychopharmacol*, *6*, 316-24.

McKay, J. R. (1999). Studies of factors in relapse to alcohol, drug and nicotine use: a critical review of methodologies and findings. *J Stud Alcohol*, *60*, 566-76.

Nair, S. G., Gray, S. M. & Ghitza, U. E. (2006). Role of food type in yohimbine- and pellet-priming-induced reinstatement of food seeking. *Physiol Behav*, *88*, 559-66.

Nides, M. A., Rakos, R. F., Gonzales, D., Murray, R. P., Tashkin, D. P., Bjornson-Benson, W. M., Lindgren, P. & Connett, J. E. (1995). Predictors of initial smoking cessation and relapse through the first 2 years of the Lung Health Study. *J Consult Clin Psychol*, *63*, 60-9.

Norregaard, J., Tonnesen, P. & Petersen, L. (1993). Predictors and reasons for relapse in smoking cessation with nicotine and placebo patches. *Prev Med*, *22*, 261-71.

O'Brien, C. P., Childress, A. R., Ehrman, R. & Robbins, S. J. (1998). Conditioning factors in drug abuse: Can they explain compulsion? *J. Psychopharmacol.*, *12*, 15-22.

Oncken, C., Gonzales, D., Nides, M., Rennard, S., Watsky, E., Billing, C. B., Anziano, R. & Reeves, K. (2006). Efficacy and safety of the novel selective nicotinic acetylcholine receptor partial agonist, varenicline, for smoking cessation. *Arch Intern Med*, *166*, 1571-7.

Palmatier, M. I., Evans-Martin, F. F., Hoffman, A., Caggiula, A. R., Chaudhri, N., Donny, E. C., Liu, X., Booth, S., Gharib, M., Craven, L. & Sved, A. F. (2006). Dissociating the primary reinforcing and reinforcement-enhancing effects of nicotine using a rat self-administration paradigm with concurrently available drug and environmental reinforcers. *Psychopharmacology (Berl)*, *184*, 391-400.

Paterson NE, Froestl W, Markou A (2005). Repeated administration of the GABAB receptor agonist CGP44532 decreased nicotine self-administration, and acute administration decreased cue-induced reinstatement of nicotine-seeking in rats. *Neuropsychopharmacology 30*, 119-28.

Palmatier, M. I., Liu, X., Matteson, G. L., Donny, E. C., Caggiula, A. R. & Sved, A. F. (2007). Conditioned reinforcement in rats established with self-administered nicotine and enhanced by noncontingent nicotine. *Psychopharmacology (Berl)*, *195*, 235-43.

Perkins, K. A., Grobe, J. E., Fonte, C., Goettler, J., Caggiula, A. R., Reynolds, W. A., Stiller, R. L., Scierka, A. & Jacob, R. G. (1994). Chronic and acute tolerance to subjective, behavioral and cardiovascular effects of nicotine in humans. *J Pharmacol Exp Ther*, *270*, 628-38.

Rose, J. E. & Levin, E. D. (1991). Inter-relationships between conditioned and primary reinforcement in the maintenance of cigarette smoking. *Br J Addict*, *86*, 605-9.

Schroeder, B. E., Schiltz, C. A. & Kelley, A. E. (2003). Neural activation profile elicited by cues associated with the anxiogenic drug yohimbine differs from that observed for reward-paired cues. *Neuropsychopharmacology*, *28*, 14-21.

Shaham, Y., Adamson, L. K., Grocki, S. & Corrigall, W. A. (1997). Reinstatement and spontaneous recovery of nicotine seeking in rats. *Psychopharmacology (Berl)*, *130*, 396-403.

Shaham, Y., Erb, S. & Stewart, J. (2000). Stress-induced relapse to heroin and cocaine seeking in rats: a review. *Brain Res Brain Res Rev*, *33*, 13-33.

Shaham, Y., Shalev, U., Lu, L., De Wit, H. & Stewart, J. (2003). The reinstatement model of drug relapse: history, methodology and major findings. *Psychopharmacology (Berl)*, *168*, 3-20.

Shepard, J. D., Bossert, J. M., Liu, S. Y. & Shaham, Y. (2004). The anxiogenic drug yohimbine reinstates methamphetamine seeking in a rat model of drug relapse. *Biol Psychiatry*, *55*, 1082-9.

Shiffman, S., Ferguson, S. G. & Gwaltney, C. J. (2006). Immediate hedonic response to smoking lapses: relationship to smoking relapse, and effects of nicotine replacement therapy. *Psychopharmacology (Berl)*, *184*, 608-18.

Shiffman, S., Paty, J. A., Gnys, M., Kassel, J. A. & Hickcox, M. (1996). First lapses to smoking: within-subjects analysis of real-time reports. *J Consult Clin Psychol*, *64*, 366-79.

Shiffman, S. & Waters, A. J. (2004). Negative affect and smoking lapses: a prospective analysis. J Consult Clin Psychol 72, 192-201.

Shoaib M (2008). The cannabinoid antagonist AM251 attenuates nicotine self-administration and nicotine-seeking behaviour in rats. *Neuropharmacology*, *54*, 438-44.

Shram, M. J., Funk, D., Li, Z. & Le, A. D. (2008). Nicotine self-administration, extinction responding and reinstatement in adolescent and adult male rats: evidence against a biological vulnerability to nicotine addiction during adolescence. *Neuropsychopharmacology*, *33*, 739-48.

Sinha, R. (2001). How does stress increase risk of drug abuse and relapse? *Psychopharmacology (Berl)*, *158*, 343-59.

Stewart, J. (2000). Pathways to relapse: the neurobiology of drug- and stress-induced relapse to drug-taking. *J Psychiatry Neurosci*, *25*, 125-36.

Swan, G. E., Denk, C. E., Parker, S. D., Carmelli, D., Furze, C. T. & Rosenman, R. H. (1988). Risk factors for late relapse in male and female ex-smokers. *Addict Behav*, *13*, 253-66.

Uhde, T. W., Boulenger, J. P., Post, R. M., Siever, L. J., Vittone, B. J., Jimerson, D. C. & Roy-Byrne, P. P. (1984). Fear and anxiety: relationship to noradrenergic function. *Psychopathology*, *17 Suppl 3*, 8-23.

Zarrindast, M. R., Homayoun, H., Babaie, A., Etminani, A. & Gharib, B. (2000). Involvement of adrenergic and cholinergic systems in nicotine-induced anxiogenesis in mice. *Eur J Pharmacol*, *407*, 145-58.

Zhou, X., Nonnemaker, J., Sherrill, B., Gilsenan, A. W., Coste, F. & West, R. (2009). Attempts to quit smoking and relapse: factors associated with success or failure from the ATTEMPT cohort study. *Addict Behav*, *34*, 365-73.

Zislis, G., Desai, T. V., Prado, M., Shah, H. P. & Bruijnzeel, A. W. (2007). Effects of the CRF receptor antagonist D-Phe CRF(12-41) and the alpha2-adrenergic receptor agonist clonidine on stress-induced reinstatement of nicotine-seeking behavior in rats. *Neuropharmacology*, *53*, 958-66.

In: Smoking Relapse: Causes, Prevention … ISBN: 978-1-60876-580-5
Editors: J. Egger and M. Kalb

Chapter 6

SMOKING RELAPSE PREVENTION: AN UPDATE

A.Nikolakopoulou and C.Christodoulou
Oncology Dept., Metropolitan Hospital, Faliro, Greece

INTRODUCTION

A number of interventions can help people who smoke to quit. These include pharmacological treatments, such as nicotine replacement therapies, antidepressants and the lately developed nicotine receptor partial agonists. Behavioural approaches are also continiously tried, either delivered individually or in groups.

However, a significant proportion of initially successful quitters relapse over time and more commonly within the first two years after having stopped smoking. It is estimated that 50-80% of quitters relapse within the first year. The causes of relapse are beyond the scope of this article. We are rather focusing on the existing ways of preventing it.

It is well known nowdays that smoking is a chronic condition or better described a chronic illness that relapses over time if left untreated. This notion is mirrored in the current guidelines for smoking cessation. The famous "5 As "approach in these guidelines refers to follow up contacts and relapse prevention as one of the five key components of a succesfull cessation.

Smoking relapse can be defined as the resumption of smoking at any time after the quit date so a relapse prevention intervention can not clearly be distinct from an extended cessation programme.

Relapse prevention studies have been using two major tools. Either psychological treatments usually combined with the "skills approach" for coping with high risk situations for relapse, either pharmacological treatments.

A huge body of literature have been published so far on the subject concerning all sorts of the above mentioned interventions being mainly observational studies. The truth is that limited effort has been devoted so far on developing and then evaluating relapse prevention interventions.

Special interest has been shown for certain subpopulations as pregnant women or respiratory patients. Many trials have focused on pregnant women and the invaluable meaning of keeping them off smoking before or after giving birth to their children, as well as on people with respiratory diseases. These patients who continue smoking face difficulties in the management of their disease and have augmented morbidity and mortality risk.

Non-Pharmacological Interventions

It was almost a decade ago when a meta-analytic review on the efficacy of relapse prevention was published in the Journal of Consulting and clinical Phychology[1]. This review addressed all sorts of addictions (alcohol, substance use, smoking) and concluded that relapse prevention is a worthwile intervention as a cognitive and behavioral treatment. However the intervention was more succesfull when applied for alcohol or polysubstance use and less effective in the case of smoking.

For years and years the behavioral approach, first introduced back in 1985, was monopolizing all studies. Two main axes were used. One was teaching smokers how to identify high risk situations and then provide them with the behavioral or cognitive skills to cope with them so as not to relapse. The other was the notion of extended sessions that were continued long after the quit date either as phonecalls or as relapse prevention material sent to succesfull quitters.

In order to clarify the conflicting results of different studies Hajek P and co-workers from the Tobacco Dependence Research Center of UCL conducted a systematic review of the Cochrane Tobacco Addiction Group trials database[2]. The review was first published in 2006 and it was recently up-dated and published in the Cochrane Library 2009 1st issue.

The authors retrieved a total of 54 studies that met their inclusion criteria being mainly randomized controlled trials with a minimum follow up of 6 months. They included trials that compared relapse prevention interventions to a no intervention control, or trials that compared a cessation programme with additional relapse prevention components to a cessation programme alone.

The main results of the review answer with reasonable certainty the question of the role of behavioral interventions. No significant effect was detected for the skills-based methods which was the commonest approach across most studies. This negative result applied to all different population subgroups as for women who had quit smoking during pregnancy or smokers quitting during hospitalization or military training. Although studies had limited power to detect small differences the authors conclude that "there is insufficient evidence to support the use of any specific behavioral intervention for helping smokers who quit to avoid relapse".

Several trials are still being conducted on the subject. In the non-pharmacologic field there is an interesting ongoing trial that started in June 2007 and is designed to stop recruitment in June 2010[3].The study is conducted by the U. S National Institute of Health and is a randomized trial testing hypnosis as a relapse prevention intervention. The hypothesis of the trial is that hypnosis is at least as effective as behavioral counseling and is estimated to enroll more than 500 current smokers. The primary measure will be the prevalence of smoking status at 9, 26 and 52 weeks.

However, it needs to be mentioned at this point that the danger of relapse is greater the first two years after quitting but there is a continuing rate of relapse of 2% to 4% per year until the 6th year that goes down to 1% only after 10 years of abstinence[4]. These figures leave us with the need to design studies of relapse intervention with long- term follow up before we can decide which measure is more effective. We should also all physicians keep in mind that as in any other chronic illness a relapse is part of a dynamic process and that we are obliged to give our patients a second opportunity to quit smoking by giving them another therapy plan.

In 2008, an article published in the Nicotine and Tobacco Research Journal focused on symptoms of withdrawal among 137 female smokers to conclude that there is an escalation of withdrawal symptoms during abstinence of smoke that drives people back to their smoking habits[5]. This finding seems to be clinically important as close symptom monitoring could be crucial for the selection of time for a succesfull intervention relapse and should be taken into account in future studies.

PHARMACOLOGICAL INTERVENTIONS

There are a number of 1st and 2nd line medications that have been used so far for smoking cessation and then have been assessed for their efficacy to prevent relapse. Among them the nicotine replacement therapies (patch, gum , nicotine inhaler, nasal spray e.t.c) and the antidepressant bupropion were the most widely used. Varenicline, a recently developed and launched in the market nicotine receptor partial agonist is also intensively tested.

In most studies these pharmacotherapies were first used for smoking cessation and then their extended use for preventing relapse was tested either using each medication alone or in combination. Follow up lasted from 6 months up to one year. In randomized trials the time of randomization was mostly set before quitting smoking and again pharmacotherapies were tried on different subgroup populations.

Collected data in the recent Cochrane systematic review [2] offers a complete picture of our current conception for the use of pharmacotherapy.

Author's main conclusions were that:

(1) Bupropion failed to show any significant long-term benefit (risk ratio 1.17;95% confidence interval 0.99 to 1.39). Given the sufficient body of literature on bupropion authors believe that bupropion is unlikely to show any effect in future studies.
(2) extended treatment with varenicline, a nicotine receptor partial agonist, was the only pharmacological intervention showing significant reduction in relapse rates (risk ratio 1.18,95% confidence interval 1.03 to 1.36).

Results on nicotine replacement therapies were conflicting so the authors suggest that such studies with extended NRT are urgently needed.

In April 2008 a very interesting press release from the Independent Pharmaceutica AB announced the initiation of a multicenter phase II trial with Niccine[6]. This Swedish vaccine is directed against nicotine dependence as the vaccine induces the production of antibodies that bind nicotine and the nicotine-antibody complex formed prevents nicotine from reaching the brain. The trial will have a one year duration and its primary goal is to prevent relapse in former smokers. Future plans will test the vaccine as a smoking cessation intervention as well.

A number of clinical trials are also currently recruiting smokers for all the above mentioned pharmacotherapies trying different therapeutic combinations or different timing for a succesfull intervention.

As genetic studies come into play more and more the last years interesting genetic variations between smokers come to light. Smokers have different genetic background concerning their smoking behavior or level of addiction. Genetic polymorphisms have been found concerning the rate of metabolism of nicotine by hepatic enzymes as well as in genes involved in the dopamine or serotonin pathways[7]. As it is known these pathways are involved in nicotine's rewarding effects. In the light of these findings a number of studies have recently explored the success rate of pharmacotherapies between smokers with different genetic variations. It is hoped that through this approach tailored therapies for different people will be plausible and success rates will rise.

CONCLUSION

Tobacco smoking is documented to be the largest preventable cause of disease. It is estimated that there are currently over 1.2 billion smokers worldwide and this number is expected to rise up to 1.6-1.9 billion by 2025.

Although there has been a significant progress in cessation interventions we seem to have failed so far in preventing relapse. Neither behavioral techniques nor existing pharmacotherapies achieve a long-term abstinence from the smoking habit. This is probably a result of under-investigation as so far most of physician's efforts where turned towards cessation. Now that smoking is well recognized as a chronic illness, intensive care should be given towards preventing people of going back to a habit that in most cases equals with their death penalty.

REFERENCES

[1] Irvin, Jennifer, E; et al. *Journal of Consulting and Clinical Psychology*. Vol 67(4), Aug 1999, 563-570.

[2] Hajek, P; Stead, LF; West, R; Jarvis, M; Lancaster, T. *Relapse prevention interventions for smoking cessation(Review)*, Cochrane Library 2009, Issue 1.

[3] Hypnosis for smoking Relapse Prevention, ClinicalTrials.gov.

[4] Elizabeth A. Krall; Arthur J.Garvey; Raul, I. Garcia; Smoking relapse after 2 years of abstinence: findings from the VA Normative Aging Study; *Nicotine and tobacco Research*, 2002, 4(1), 95-100.

[5] Sharon S. Allen; Tracy Bade; et al. Craving, Withdrawal, and Smoking urges on days immediately prior to smoking relapse, *Nicotine and tobacco Research*, 2008, 10(1), 35-45.

[6] Smoking vaccine against smoking enters clinical trial phase II, Press Release April 2008.

[7] Quaak, M; van Schayck, CP; Knaapen, AM; van Schooten, FJ. Genetic variation as a predictor of smoking cessation success. A promising preventive and intervention tool for chronic respiratory diseases? *Eur Respir J*, 33, 468-480.

In: Smoking Relapse: Causes, Prevention ... ISBN: 978-1-60876-580-5
Editors: J. Egger and M. Kalb

Chapter 7

TOBACCO CONTROL IN A "FLAT WORLD" – GLOBALIZATION AND NEW PUBLIC HEALTH PERSPECTIVES

John E. Snyder
University of North Carolina School of Medicine,
SEAHEC Department of Internal Medicine

In his insightful 2005 book *The World is Flat: A Brief History of the Twenty-First Century*, Thomas Friedman described how the digital age, transportation, political change, and economic influences have hastened "globalism" – an intermingling and unification of people from all countries and walks of life [1]. One can simply pick up a phone and join a conference call between the United States, China, and South Africa. In a mere instant, information can be digitally transmitted from one part of the world to another. And within hours, a person can travel from one end of the globe to another. These technologies are advancing at a lightning pace, and their impact on the world is just in the beginning stages. As people from diverse backgrounds and cultures become interconnected, the peace, health, and well-being of people from different nations are also joined [2]. From the public health perspective, the implications can be enormous. If someone with an infectious disease, like Severe Acute Respiratory Syndrome (SARS), gets on a plane from Beijing to New York, an illness can quickly transform from outbreak to epidemic and pandemic proportions [3]. The World Health Organization has had, as a result, to form a Global Outbreak Alert & Response Network to adjust to such problems [4]. The health problems of previously distant parts of the world are no longer so isolated and ignorable has they have been considered to be in the past [2].

Some critics of *The World is Flat* claim that the world is, in the current economic climate, not flat but "tilted" in the favor of large corporations who exploit nations where labor costs are low and greater profits can be acquired [5]. Other tactics of such corporations can have major impacts on public health. Take "Big Tobacco" as an example: in countries where health policy is not as progressive or established as it is in Western nations, transnational tobacco companies have found a way to reap huge profits and offset the declines in tobacco product consumption observed in more developed areas [6]. Enormous marketing campaigns over the last two decades have promoted tobacco use in these countries, and the health implications of this advertising are enormous. It is anticipated that by the year 2030, there will be 7 million deaths annually in developing countries that are attributable to tobacco use [7]. Up to 18.3% of pregnant women in Latin American countries are active smokers, and second-hand smoke exposure rates are high as well, affecting both maternal and child health [8]. The effectiveness of cessation aids in developing nations is not known, and the cost of such aids in these countries may be prohibitive [9].

Whether you believe that the world is "flat" or if it's "tilted," both theories come to the same conclusion about the health implications of tobacco dependence in an increasingly "globalized" world. Tobacco companies are finding alternative means for profit – and countless lives are being lost as a result. Few public health problems are rooted in such a profit-hungry business model, and "Big Tobacco" must be stopped. We must no longer ignore the health of developing nations. We are connected to and dependent on their welfare as much as they are on ours. International efforts are clearly going to be necessary to reverse the pandemic-like spread of tobacco-related disease across other nations. Policy initiatives to prevent tobacco-related disease must occur globally, locally, and everywhere in between.

REFERENCES

[1] Friedman, T. The World is Flat: A Brief History of the Twenty-First Century. New York: Farrar, Straus and Giroux; 2005.

[2] Spencer, DC. The neurology world is flat. Neurology. 2007 Oct 23;69(17):E16-7. Comment on: *Neurology*. 2007 Oct 23;69(17):1715-8.

[3] Severe Acute Respiratory Syndrome (SARS). Retrieved June 13, 2009 from: http://www.who.int/csr/sars/en/index.html.

[4] Global Outbreak Alert & Response Network. Retrieved June 13, 2009 from:

http://www.who.int/csr/outbreaknetwork/en/.

[5] Aronica, R; Ramdoo, M. *The World Is Flat?: A Critical Analysis of New York Times Bestseller by Thomas Friedman*. Meghan-Kiffer Press;2006.

[6] Stebbins, KR. Going like Gangbusters: Transnational Tobacco Companies "Making a Killing" in South America. *Medical Anthropology Quarterly*, New Series. 15(2): 147-170, Jun 2001.

[7] Dobson, R. Annual tobacco deaths in poor countries to reach 7 million by 2030. *BMJ*. 329: 71, July 10, 2004.

[8] Bloch, M; Althabe, F; Onyamboko, M; Kaseba-Sata, C; Castilla, EE; Freire, S; Garces, AL; Parida, S; Goudar, SS; Kadir, MM; Goco, N; Thornberry, J; Daniels, M; Bartz, J; Hartwell, T; Moss, N; Goldenberg, R. Tobacco Use and Secondhand Smoke Exposure During Pregnancy: An Investigative Survey of Women in 9 Developing Nations. *American Journal of Public Health*. 98: 1833-1840, October 2008.

[9] Abdullah, ASM; Husten, CG. Promotion of smoking cessation in developing countries: a framework for urgent public health interventions. *Thorax*.59:623-630, 2004.

In: Smoking Relapse: Causes, Prevention ... ISBN: 978-1-60876-580-5
Editors: J. Egger and M. Kalb

Chapter 8

A BRIEF HISTORY OF SCHOOL-BASED SMOKING PREVENTION RESEARCH: A PENDULUM EFFECT CASE STUDY

Steve Sussman**, David S. Black, and Louise A. Rohrbach
University of Southern California, Keck School of Medicine

ABSTRACT

School-based cigarette smoking prevention has experienced a brief but active history, which was initiated shortly after the first Surgeon General's Report in 1964. This paper highlights a sequence of events by which school-based tobacco use prevention research developed as an active science, and illustrates a pendulum effect, with confidence in tobacco use prevention increasing and decreasing at different points in time. Suggestions are offered to advance school-based smoking prevention research.

Key words: History, pendulum effect school-based, smoking, prevention research

---

* Address correspondence and reprint requests to: Steve Sussman, Ph.D., Professor of Preventive Medicine and Psychology, Institute for Health Promotion and Disease Prevention Research, University of Southern California, Department of Preventive Medicine, Keck School of Medicine, 1000 S. Fremont Avenue, Unit 8, Building A-5, Suite #5228, Alhambra, CA 91803-4737, Email: ssussma@usc.edu (email can be used in print)

INTRODUCTION

The "pendulum effect" in the context of history or planning has been defined as "something that swings back and forth from one course, opinion, or condition to another" (http://www.answers.com/topic/pendulum; accessed on September 1, 2009; also see Hall, 2005; Leversee & Pearson, 2001). The pendulum effect may reflect a public-level attitude that an innovation is useful or not useful, healthy or unhealthy, and such an effect may also reflect the way that science progresses, or at times a pendulum effect may impede progress in cumulative knowledge. "Swung" to the right generally intends to refer to the public attitude that science is advancing in a particular arena (public confidence is increasing); whereas movement to the left intends to refer to the attitude that science has been side tracked by going down a particular direction (public confidence is decreasing). Movement to another particular scientific course may be asserted. School-based smoking prevention research has had a relatively brief scientific history yet appears to illustrate operation of the pendulum effect. This chapter will illustrate this effect as it applies to the evolution of school-based smoking prevention research in the U.S.

SMOKING PREVENTION BEGINNINGS: TO THE RIGHT AND THEN SLIGHTLY TO THE LEFT, 1964-1976

The pendulum of smoking prevention research (or practice) at first appeared to exhibit a "powerful" swing to the right, followed by a brief retreat. Early smoking and other drug education prevention efforts which served as the foundation of smoking prevention research emphasized information provision (e.g., physical consequences of smoking) and values clarification (Thompson, 1978; Flay, 1985; Sussman & Ames, 2008; U.S. DHHS, 2005). These efforts originated primarily after the first Surgeon General's report in 1964, which spent only one-half page addressing the general topic of tobacco prevention (U.S. DHHS, 1964). Many anti-smoking programs for youth were implemented, and a subset of these programs was evaluated. Programs designed for youth involved school-wide antismoking campaigns (e.g., smoking consequences demonstrations, assemblies, school newspaper articles), youth-to-youth programs (older peer instruction of younger peers), as well as classroom-based efforts. While initially fueled with optimism, these early efforts failed to show notable empirical effects, or were not evaluated rigorously. Among 35 youth-based studies reviewed by

Thompson (1978), for example, only one study of teen male apprentices in a machine factory in Switzerland, that was quite intensive, focused on ill effects of smoking, and utilized a variety of learning modalities nested within a comprehensive health program found lasting effects (41% difference in smoking prevalence comparing control and program groups at four-years post-baseline). It looked to some researchers that school-based tobacco use prevention did not have a future. The pendulum swung to the right after 1964, but then seemed to be swinging to the left by 1974.

SMOKING PREVENTION ADVANCES TO THE RIGHT: 1976-1990

Richard Evan's pioneer work was mentioned briefly by Thompson (1978) as a study that was not yet evaluated. However, Evans and colleagues from 1976 through the 1980s demonstrated great promise in their work through use of a social influence approach; the idea being to inoculate youth (primarily in the classroom) against social pressures related to initiating and increasing levels of smoking (Evans, 1976; Flay, 1985; Sussman et al., 1995). The pendulum swung to the right again, with a change in program content focus. Through the end of the 1970's and over the following decade, advances in school-based smoking prevention research accumulated including using a larger number of school (or other community) units, using randomized control designs, combining school-based programming with other modalities (e.g., mass media), and considering other substantive additions to programming such as life skills material (Flay, 1985; Sussman et al., 1995). However, there remained several wide gaps in scientific knowledge. These included a lack of understanding the mediating effects of the social influences program approach. At the time, it was presumed that mediators included alteration of youths' perceptions of social influences, actual social network influences, and tobacco use outcome expectancies (e.g., Sussman, 2001).

The pendulum continued to move even farther to the right in terms of advancing the social influences approach, possibly bypassing a solid understanding of program effects mediation. In 1989, the National Cancer Institute (NCI) convened a Consensus Conference under the leadership of Peter Greenwald and Joe Cullen, in which a panel of experts identified social influences-oriented school-based smoking prevention programs as a promising solution among youth and they also recommended a new emphasis on dissemination research (Glynn, 1989; Glynn & Cullen, 1989, U.S., DHHS, 1990). This recommendation closely followed a request for grant proposals (National Cancer Institute, 1987) and led to subsequent funding of several studies on the dissemination of school-based social influences-oriented prevention programs (e.g., Parcel et al., 1989; Steckler et al., 1992).

THE CONTINUED SWING TO THE RIGHT: 1990-2000

By 1996, NCI's commitment to smoking prevention effectiveness and dissemination research was evident in the support of the large-scale study, Project ASSIST. This project was launched in 1991, and involved multiple smoking prevention and control modalities that were implemented and evaluated in 17 states involving 255 state and local coalitions with more than 2,900 members (U.S., DHHS, 2005). However, contrary to expectations, the Project ASSIST intervention failed to show substantial effects, purportedly due in part to tobacco industry opposing efforts (e.g., legal and regulatory actions, public relations tactics) and admittedly perhaps due to an overly ambitious leap forward in translation (U.S. DHHS, 2005).

Concurrent with the implementation of Project ASSIST, in 1997, the Safe and Drug Free Schools and Communities Act, which has provided the majority of funds for tobacco and other substance use prevention programs in schools nationwide since 1986, began to require that the programs supported by Safe and Drug Free School funds be "guided by research or best practices" (DOE, 1998). At this time, several agencies, including the federal Department of Education, developed methods to evaluate and generate lists of programs that met certain evaluation criteria (Petrosino, 2003). Although a fair amount of variability was noted in these criteria (Gandhi et al., 2007; Petrosino, 2003), some consensus began about which smoking prevention programs should be implemented within schools (Petrosino, 2003). For example, a meta-analysis of 207 universal school-based tobacco and other drug prevention programs examined 138 prevention programs that included social influence components, and provided strong support for the efficacy of social influence programming on smoking at 1-year post-program (Tobler et al., 2000).

THE PENDULUM SWINGS BACK TO THE LEFT AGAIN: 2000-2008

During the early 2000s, however, skepticism surfaced regarding the validity of efficacy studies for some of the school-based tobacco use prevention programs included in these lists, in part because replication studies often had shown varying results (e.g., Gorman, 2003a; Gorman, 2003b; Weiss, Murphy-Graham, & Birkeland, 2005). In addition, several limitations in the data analyses of these studies were observed including the use of multiple subgroup analyses, post hoc analyses, omission of baseline data in attrition calculations, lack of consistency in data analytic techniques used across replication studies, and modification of outcome measures (Gorman, 2003a; Gorman, 2003b).

In 2000, the outcomes paper for the Hutchinson Smoking Prevention Project (HSPP) was published (Peterson et al., 2000). The HSPP was a well-designed trial that was conducted from 1984 to 1999. The intervention tested was social influences-based, and was delivered to cohorts of youth from grades 3 to 12 in 40 randomly assigned school districts (n=8388). The analyses indicated that no significant overall differences were found in prevalence rates of smoking between students in program and control districts in 12th grade and 2 years after high school. The HSPP article, accompanying editorial (Clayton, Scutchfield, & Wyatt, 2000) and published media accounts (Kaufman, 2002; Los Angeles Times, 2002) possibly influenced the public to conclude that school-based prevention programming, or at least the social influences approach, is ineffective (Botvin, Sussman, & Biglan, 2001; Sussman et al., 2001).

There was some resistance to this pendulum swing to the left. Scientists in the field postulated that sentiments of school-based program ineffectiveness should be considered with caution both by the general public and scientific community. For example, Sussman and colleagues (2001) suggested that the results of HSPP needed to be interpreted within the context of all other studies, which collectively provided compelling evidence that some school-based prevention approaches are effective. Moreover, researchers offered rationale for the inconsistent findings in the field. For example, HSPP was conducted at small schools in primarily rural settings with primarily white youth, and did not include several currently discussed elements of the social influences approach that might be important to the achievement of prevention effects, such as listening and communication skills, decision making, and making a commitment (Botvin, 2000; Sussman et al., 2001).

However, a subsequent review by Wiehe and colleagues (Wiehe et al., 2005a; Wiehe et al., 2005b) which included only 8 studies due to the exclusion and inclusion criteria used, concluded that school-based tobacco use prevention programming does not work (i.e., only 1 of 8 studies found effects). Unfortunately, quasi-experiments and subjects who were younger than 18 years of age by the end of the study were excluded. If one enters into the meta-analysis only randomized controlled trials but reduces the end-point age to 17 for inclusion, then 4 studies from their search pool find effects. Slight changes in their criteria lead to changes in conclusions (Flay, 2009a; Flay, 2009b).

Despite warnings by some researchers, the pendulum continued to swing back to the left. Research statements had become more consensually negative toward social influences-based tobacco use prevention programming, particularly school-based work. As recently described by Flay (2009a; 2009b) some recent reviews have not included school-based prevention as an important component in broad-based tobacco control, or have considered it relevant only in combination with other components such as media-based work (e.g., Glantz & Mandel, 2005). Flay argues that relatively comprehensive reviews do find that school-based tobacco use prevention is effective particularly if (a) delivery methods are interactive, (b) a social influences model is used including components on norms, commitment not to use, training and practice in social and life skills, (c) peer leaders are used to assist in implementation, (d) community components are added, and (e) if programs consist of perhaps 15 or more sessions and are boosted into high school. He does caution that dissemination of programming may be difficult to accomplish due to differences between the context of the original implementation and new settings of implementation. Some groups of prevention scientists have begun to promote the adoption of uniform standards for identifying effective prevention programs and policies (Flay et al., 2005).

Conclusions and Future Directions: Will the Pendulum Swing to the Right Again?

Researchers are in a process of continuing to refine how to measure and evaluate smoking prevention outcomes appropriately and, as time passes, measurement tools may advance and change. Overall, the history of research pertaining to the efficacy of school-based tobacco use prevention programs remains mixed. School-based programs such as social influences-oriented tobacco use prevention programming appear to work at least 60% of the time in research studies (see Skara & Sussman [2003] and Thomas & Perera [2006]). There are several plausible reasons for the inconsistency of results, and future researchers may need to consider the following implications while developing and implementing future school-based prevention programs and evaluation methods. Each implication may lead the pendulum to move to the right or to the left.

First, it is possible that programming needs to be tailored for different specific recipient populations. For example, in the HSPP trial there seemed to be some school districts that showed positive effects while others showed negative effects relative to controls; hence, the program did appear have an impact (positive or negative) in certain subgroup contexts (Peterson et al., 2000). However, this trial did not intend to examine differential findings by sociocultural characteristics (see Johnson et al., 2007). Thus, further work on the extent to which teen population variations mediate and/or moderate prevention program effects is needed. Then again, inherent in the notion of sociocultural-specific findings may be limitations in translation. For example, flexibility would need to be built into programming for it to be applicable across numerous groups. Moreover, engaging in post-hoc subgroup analyses becomes limited by the potential to obtain chance findings. Researchers should maintain sound scientific practices by including important mediators and moderators into measurements and analyses of subgroup effects, conduct appropriate statistical analyses that adjust for post-hoc sample refinement, and encourage numerous replication efforts. Group-specific programming may be difficult to institutionalize compared to a "one size fits all" type of public health approach, and one might anticipate some frustration among researchers and a pendulum swing to the left, particularly if efforts are independent and competitive.

Second, school-based smoking prevention programs are typically implemented within a larger context of community-wide and state-wide tobacco control efforts, and these endeavors may show greater effectiveness when used comprehensively. For example, comprehensive school-based smoking prevention efforts might be maximized when they reflect expert input, community ownership, and involve multiple additional community modalities (e.g., mass media efforts; Flay, 2009a; Flay, 2009b). However, this type of coordination is very difficult to implement and research attempts are few in number. Still, such approaches may be able to move the pendulum to the right if carefully conducted with consistent community buy-in.

Finally, few studies have examined the variables that affect implementation fidelity and maintenance of school-based tobacco prevention programs. Fidelity of program implementation is predicted by factors related to the organizational context in which the program is implemented, characteristics of the program itself, factors related to the program provider, and adequate training and technical assistance (Hopkins et al., 2001; Rohrbach et al., 1996).Weakness in any of these factors may lead to poor implementation, and, in turn, to lack of program effectiveness. Without a careful examination of implementation-related factors, one may incorrectly conclude that a program has failed because of its content or modality of delivery, rather than due to incomplete implementation. Of course, it is possible that program adaptation is inevitable and even essential to meet the needs of different program providers and recipients (Rohrbach et al., 2006). On the other hand, it has been suggested that any departure from an exact replication of an evidence-based program will most likely decrease its effectiveness (Backer, 2001). Thus, studies are needed to determine whether and under what conditions adaptation might enhance outcomes, and under what conditions it might result in a loss of program effectiveness (Elliott & Mihalic, 2004). Perhaps a return to smaller scale studies that "fit" programming into contexts could lead to a future swing of the pendulum to the left initially but then to the right in a new, evidence-grounded direction.

The future of research in school-based tobacco use prevention, and the resulting public reaction and "pendulum swings" are not known, and our statements are speculative as such. Extreme pendulum swings to the left or right do appear to impede consideration of the full breadth of research in tobacco use prevention, and it is possible that these extreme swings have been occurring. On the other hand, one positive aspect of these pendulum swings is to raise awareness of the need for further methodologically rigorous studies. Rigorous studies, empirical reviews, and meta-analyses have assisted to continue to pave the route of school-based smoking prevention. Overall, the history and recent events in the study of school-based tobacco prevention indicate that much has been learned since the first Surgeons General's Report and that the field can gain much from further research. The field may have a bright future as long as the pendulum continues to move (research continues).

ACKNOWLEDGMENT

This paper was supported by grants from the National Institute on Drug Abuse (#sDA13814, DA016090, and DA020138)

References

Backer, T.E. (2001). Finding the balance: Program fidelity in substance abuse prevention: A state-of-the-art review. Rockville, MD: Center for Substance Abuse Prevention, *Substance Abuse and Mental Health Services Administration*, Conference Edition.

Botvin, G.J. (2000). Preventing drug abuse in schools: Social and competence enhancement approaches targeting individual level etiologic factors. *Addictive Behaviors,* 25, 887-97.

Botvin, G.J., Sussman, S., & Biglan, A. (2001). The Hutchinson Smoking Prevention Project: A lesson on inaccurate media coverage and the importance of prevention advocacy. *Prevention Science*, 2, 67-70.

Clayton, R.R., Scutchfield, D.F., & Wyatt, S.W. (2000). Hutchinson Smoking Prevention Project: A new gold standard in prevention science requires new transdisiplinary thinking (editorials). *Journal of the National Cancer Institute*, 92, 1964.

Elliott, D.S., & Mihalic, S. (2004). Issues in disseminating and replicating effective prevention programs. *Prevention Science,* 5, 47-53.

Evans, R.I. (1976) Smoking in children: Developing a social psychological strategy of deterrence. *Preventive Medicine,* 5, 122-27.

Flay, B.R. (1985). Psychosocial approaches to smoking prevention: A review of findings. Health Psychology, 4, 449-88.

Flay, B.R. (2009a). School-based smoking prevention programs with the promise of long-term effects. *Tobacco Induced Diseases,* 5:6, 18 pages.

Flay, B.R. (2009b). The promise of long-term effectiveness of school-based smoking prevention programs: a critical review of reviews. *Tobacco Induced Diseases*, 5:7, 12 pages.

Flay, B.R., Biglan, A., Boruch, R.F., Castro, F.G., Gottfredson, D., Kellam, S., et al. (2005). Standards of evidence: criteria for efficacy, effectiveness, and dissemination. *Prevention Science,* 6, 151-75.

Gandhi, A.G., Murphy-Graham, E., Petrosino, A., Chrismer, S.S., Weiss, C.H. (2007). The devil is in the details: Examining the evidence for proven school-based drug abuse prevention programs. *Evaluation Review,* 31, 43-74.

Glantz, S.A., & Mandel, L.L. (2005). Since school-based tobacco prevention programs do not work, what should we do? *Journal of Adolescent Health,*, 36, 157-59.

Glynn, T.J. (1989). Essential elements of school-based smoking prevention programs. *Journal of School Health,* 59, 181-88.

Glynn, T.J., & Cullen, J.W. (1989). Health promotion through smoking prevention and cessation–the need for a selective research agenda. Health Education Research, 4, 5-11.

Gorman, D.M. (2003a). The best of practices, the worst of practices: The making of science-based primary prevention programs. *Psychiatric Services*, 54, 1087-89.

Gorman, D.M. (2003b). Assessing outcomes of prevention interventions (in reply). *Psychiatric Services*, 54, 1548.

Hall, J. (2005). Health care workforce planning: can it ever work? *Journal of Health Services Research & Policy*, 10, 65-66.

Hopkins, D.P., Briss, P.A., Ricard, C.J., Husten, C.G., Carande-Kulis, V.G., Fielding, J.E., et al. (2001). Reviews of evidence regarding interventions to reduce tobacco use and exposure to environmental tobacco smoke. *American Journal of Preventive Medicine,* 20(2S),16-66.

Johnson, C.A., Cen, S., Gallaher, P., Palmer, P.H., Xiao, L., Ritt-Olson, A., & Unger, J.B. (2007). Why smoking prevention programs sometimes fail. Does effectiveness depend on sociocultural context and individual characteristics? *Cancer Epidemiology Biomarkers and Prevention*, 16, 1043-49.

Kaufman, M. (2002). *Anti-smoking units failed to stop teens*. The Washington Post. Dec 20; Sect. A (p.3).

Leversee, T. & Pearson, C. (2001). Eliminating the pendulum effect: a balanced approach to the assessment, treatment, and management of sexually abusive youth. *Journal of the Center for Families, Children, & The Courts,* 45-57.

Los Angeles Times. (2002). *School anti-smoking programs ineffective, study says.* Article reprinted from The Washington Post. Dec 20; Sect. A (p.6).

National Cancer Institute. (1987). Integrating tobacco education into the school system: *Request for research grant proposals*. Bethesda, MD: Author.

Parcel, G.S., Erickson, M.P., Lovato, C.Y., Gottlieb, N.H., Brink, S.G., Green, L.W. (1989). The diffusion of school-based tobacco-use prevention programs: project description and baseline data. *Health Education Research*, 4, 111-24.

Peterson, A.V., Kealey, K.A., Mann, S.L., Marek, P.M., Sarason, I.G. (2000). Hutchinson Smoking Prevention Project: Long-term randomized trial in school-based tobacco use prevention-results on smoking. *Journal of the National Cancer Institute,* 92, 1979-91.

Petrosino, A. (2003). Standards for evidence and evidence for standards: The case of school-based drug prevention. *The Annals of the American Academy of Political and Social Sciences,* 587, 180-207.

Rohrbach, L.A., D'Onofrio, C.N., Backer, T.E., & Montgomery, S.B. (1996). Diffusion of school-based substance abuse prevention programs. *American Behavioral Scientist*, 39, 919-34.

Rohrbach, L.A., Grana, R., Sussman, S., & Valente, T.W. (2006). Type II translation: Transporting prevention interventions from research to real-world settings. *Evaluation & the Health Professions*, 29, 302-33.

Skara, S.N., & Sussman, S. (2003). A review of 25 long-term adolescent tobacco and other drug use prevention program evaluations. *Preventive Medicine*, 37, 451-74.

Steckler, A., Goodman, R.M., McLeroy, K.R., Davis, S., & Koch, G. (1992). Measuring the diffusion of innovative health promotion programs. *American Journal of Health Promotion,* 6, 214-24.

Sussman, S. (2001). School-based tobacco use prevention and cessation: Where are we going? *American Journal of Health Behavior*, 25, 191-99.

Sussman, S., & Ames, S.L. (2008). *Drug abuse: Concepts, prevention and cessation*. West Nyack: NY: Cambridge University Press.

Sussman, S., Dent, C.W., Burton, D., Stacy, A.W., & Flay, B.R. (1995). *Developing school-based tobacco use prevention and cessation programs.* Thousand Oaks, CA: Sage.

Sussman, S., Hansen, W.B., Flay, B.R., & Botvin, G.J. (2001). Re: Hutchinson Smoking Prevention Project: Long-term randomized trial in school-based tobacco use prevention-results on smoking. *Journal of the National Cancer Institute,* 93, 1267.

Thomas, R., & Perera, R. (2006). School-based programs for preventing smoking. *Cochrane Database of Systematic Reviews;3: Art*. No. CD001293.

Thompson, E.L. (1978). Smoking education programs 1960-1976. *American Journal of Public Health*, 68, 250-257.

Tobler, N.S., Roona, M.R., Ochshorn, P., Marshall, D.G., Streke, A.V., & Stackpole, K.M. (2000). School-based adolescent drug prevention programs: 1998 Meta-analysis. *Journal of Primary Prevention,* 20, 275-336.

U.S. Department of Education. (1998). Safe and Drug Free Schools Program; notice. *Federal Register*, 63(104):29901-6.

U.S. Department of Health and Human Services (US DHHS). (1964). Smoking and Health: Report of the advisory Committee to the Surgeon General of the Public Health Service. Washington, DC: *US DHHS*; Pub. No. 1103.

U.S. Department of Health and Human Services (US DHHS). (1990). Smoking, Tobacco, and Cancer Program: 1985-1989 Status Report. Washington, DC: National Institutes of Health; *NIH Pub*. No. 90-3107.

U.S. Department of Health and Human Services (US DHHS). (2005). ASSIST: Shaping the future of tobacco prevention and control. Tobacco Control Monograph No. 6. Bethesda, MD: National Institutes of Health, National Cancer Institute; *NIH Pub.* No. 05-5645.

Weiss, C.H., Murphy-Graham, E., & Birkeland, S. (2005). An alternate route to policy influence: how evaluations affect D.A.R.E. *American Journal of Evaluation*, 26, 12-20.

Wiehe, S., Garrison, M., Christakis, D., Ebel, B.E., & Rivara, F.P. (2005a). A systematic review of school-based smoking prevention trials with long-term follow-up. *Journal of Adolescent Health*, 36,162-69.

Wiehe, S.E., Garrison, M.M., Christakis, D.A., Ebel, B.E., Rivara, F.P. (2005b). The author's reply (letters to the editor). *Journal of Adolescent Health,* 37, 6-7.

In: Smoking Relapse: Causes, Prevention ... ISBN: 978-1-60876-580-5
Editors: J. Egger and M. Kalb

Chapter 9

EVALUATION OF A SMOKING RELAPSE PREVENTION PROGRAM FOR CARDIOVASCULAR PATIENTS*

Warren R. Stanton[1,2,†], John B. Lowe[3], Kevin P. Balanda[4] and Christopher B. Del Mar[5]

[1]Cancer Prevention Research Centre, School of Population Health, University of Queensland.
[2]Division of Physiotherapy, School of Health and Rehabilitation Sciences, University of Queensland.
[3]Department of Community and Behavioral Health, College of Public Health,University of Iowa.
[4]Institute of Public Health, Redmond's Hill, Dublin.
[5]Centre for General Practice, Department of Social and Preventive Medicine, University of Queensland.

---

* A version of this chapter was also published in *Cancer Prevention Research Compendium Volume 1*, edited by Thomas H. Conway, published by Nova Science Publishers. It was submitted for appropriate modifications in an effort to encourage wider dissemination of research.

† Corresponding author: School of Health and Rehabilitation Science, University of Queensland, St. Lucia, Queensland 4006, AUSTRALIA.

Abstract

Smoking cessation reduces both the mortality and re-infarction rate amongst smokers who have experienced a myocardial infarction (MI). Smoking cessation programs have tended to be conducted with post-operative or seriously ill patients. In this study, we examined the efficacy of a relapse prevention program for hospital cardiovascular patients who did not require operative procedures or extensive hospitalization. A pre-post, two groups, control trial involving 208 patients (103 in the intervention group) recruited from three coronary care units in large metropolitan hospitals was used to assess the effect of the intervention. Smoking status of self-reported quitters were verified using CO concentrations in expired air. Complete follow-up was obtained from 129 (62.0%) of initial participants. At three months after discharge, the self-report quite rate in the intervention group was 19.4%, significantly higher than in the control group (7.6%) ($p = 0.046$). This difference persisted at nine months after discharge, when the self reported quit rate was 27.3% in the intervention group and 12.9% in the control group ($p = 0.043$). A behavior-based smoking cessation program was effective for less serious cardiovascular patients and the effect persisted for nine months after discharge.

Keywords: Smoking; relapse-prevention; cardiovascular.

Smoking is a risk factor in half the major causes of death for older adults, in particular heart disease (Orleans, Jepson, Resch & Rimer, 1994; Guilmette, Motta, Shadel, Mukand & Niaura, 2001). An increased risk of myocardial infarction (MI) is associated with an increase in amount smoked, and is considerably elevated for heavy smokers (Rosenburg & Shapiro, 1990). By comparison to post MI non-smokers, post MI smokers have more non-fatal MI's, increased arteriosclerosis peripheral vascular disease and more severe and extensive atherosclerosis of the aorta and coronary arteries (Chowdhury, Lasker & Dyer, 1999; Milei & Grana, 1998). Cessation of smoking reduces both mortality and re-infarction rate by 50% (Burling, Singleton, Bigelow, Baile & Gottlieb 1984; Jajich, Ostfeld & Freeman, 1984; Squires, Gau, Miller, Allison & Lavie, 1990). After 5 - 10 years of cessation (less than 5 years according to Rosenberg et al, 1990 and Gottlieb, 1992), ex-smokers exhibit coronary heart disease mortality ratios similar to that of non-smokers (Burling et al, 1984). Opportunities to quit and the availability of suitable resources are therefore essential for all patients who have had a myocardial infarction.

The immediate post-hospitalisation period is a critical stage of rehabilitation (Moller, Pedersen, Villebro, et al., 2003). Patients are receptive to changes in lifestyle and are motivated by a clear recollection of the acute event (Squires et al, 1990). A longer period of smoking cessation has been found to be associated with higher severity of the MI, previous heart problems, higher degree of perceived threat, smoking history, belief that smoking contributed to their cardiac problem, extent of the disease, age and occupation, being married and male (Baile, Bigelow, Gottlieb, Stitzer & Sacktor, 1982; Ockene et al, 1985a, 1985b; Scott & Lamparski, 1985; Havik & Maeland, 1988; Frid et al, 1991; Rice et al, 1994). In these first few weeks, relapse is strongly associated with anxiety and depression; later it is primarily associated with poorer general cardiac knowledge and understanding of smoking as a risk factor (Havik & Maeland, 1988). Long-term quitting is related to steady gain in basic cardiac knowledge.

There are a variety of behavioural reasons for relapse by smokers. Smokers may start smoking again because of the presence and frequency of smoking in their environment (learning theory), because smoking is used as a behaviour to cope with stress (stress-coping theories), or because of the relationship between attitudes and behaviour itself (cognitive - attitudinal theories eg. health belief model) (Oldenburg & Pope, 1990). In the immediate post-quitting phase, which for many smokers occurs when they are admitted to hospital with MI, behavioural programs should include social support, reinforcement and coping skills. In the later phase of long-term maintenance, emphasis can be given to ongoing monitoring and vigilance, lifestyle change, cue exposure, stress management and weight control (Oldenburg & Pope, 1990) Multi-component, self-management packages have been found to consistently aid smoking control (Kamarck & Lichtenstein, 1985).

A number of studies have examined the behaviour of smokers after myocardial infarction. Factors such as personality traits and perceived self control (Maiani, Callegari & Sanavio, 1990) smoking history, health beliefs and demographic characteristics (Baile et al, 1982) are unrelated to cessation or relapse in this population group. In the absence of an intervention program, between 16% and 32% of MI patients stop smoking initially for part of the first 12 months after hospitalisation (Scott & Lamparski, 1985; Rigotti, Singer, Mulley & Thibault, 1991; Emmons & Goldstein, 1992). Positive health beliefs are associated with post-MI cessation maintenance, though experience of the MI was seen as the main motivational factor (Marshall, 1990). (Scott & Lamparski, 1985) concluded that the best time to intervene was immediately after a patient's first cardiac event.

Smoking interventions for MI patients have yielded different levels of success. The short-term cessation rate (5-6 weeks) for hospitalised post-operative patients given three structured cessation sessions and follow-up phone calls over 5 weeks, was 12% higher than the 'usual care' group in a study by Wewers, Bowen, Stanislaw & Desimone (1994). A nurse-managed program which consisted of a manual focussing on identification and coping with high risk situations and follow-up phone calls, resulted in a 12-month cessation rate which was 29% higher in the intervention group compared to the 'usual care' group (Taylor, Houston-Miller, Killen & Debusk, 1990). A more recent and rigorous randomised control trial conducted by the same group (Miller et al, 1997) incorporated a nurse-mediated, behaviourally-oriented, relapse prevention counselling with follow-up telephone calls, and produced a more modest effect size of 7%. A study by Rice et al, (1994) found that nurse-patient interactions were more effective than self-help materials, but they also found a higher 12-month cessation rate among the non-intervention group (possibly due to other group differences). A behavioural multi-component intervention delivered to seriously ill MI patients Ockene et al, (1985a), achieved an 11% increase in cessation compared to a group who received advice only. The cessation rates for validated smoking status were 45% and 34% respectively.

Studies to date have generally been conducted with post-operative or seriously ill patients and have produced varied levels of success. The aim of this study is to examine the efficacy of a relapse prevention program for cardiovascular patients with less serious illness, who were hospitalised with heart problems that did not require operative procedures or an extensive period of hospitalisation. This group may be less motivated to quit smoking and provide a more conservative test of the efficacy of a behavioural program for cardiovascular patients.

METHODS

Sample

The eligible sample consisted of patients admitted to the coronary care unit of three Brisbane hospitals, who had been regular smokers and had smoked in the month prior to hospitalisation. The criteria for inclusion of smokers in the eligible sample included those with myocardial infarction, ischemic heart problems or unstable angina. Patients who required oxygen or narcotic pain control (or other drugs potentially inhibiting cognitive function) were excluded from the sample. Over the recruitment period of four years, which was required to achieve a sufficiently large sample size to detect an estimated 20% effect size with 80% power at the 5% level of significance allowing for loss to follow-up, 208 patients were enrolled in the project (105 in the control group and 103 in the intervention group).

The socio-demographic characteristics of the enrolled sample was as follows: 75% male, 25% female; 63% married or de facto, 21% separated or divorced, 7% widowed, 9% single; 56% skilled or professional, 36% semi-skilled, 8% unskilled; age range 20-76 years (mean = 53.6, standard deviation = 11.0).

Procedure

After ethical approval was obtained from the hospitals, two focus group interviews were conducted with 12-15 coronary care patients, in order to gauge the range of issues relevant to patients who were smokers and to obtain information that would inform the development of the intervention. The intervention was developed from a cognitive behavioural approach fostering individuals' responsibility for their behavioural choices. The theoretical basis of the intervention was drawn from Roger's Protection Motivation Theory (Rogers, 1983), which holds that for behaviour change to occur the individual must be sufficiently motivated, but also hold a high belief in their ability to achieve the desired change, that is high self-efficacy to quit smoking (Maddux & Rogers, 1983). Components of the intervention were developed in accord with other cited smoking prevention programs delivered to cardiovascular patients.

Each morning of the recruitment period, coronary care units of the participating hospitals were contacted or made contact with the research team, and patients who were admitted in the past 24 hours and had been regular smokers were identified. If a past or current smoker had been admitted, a registered nurse visited the hospital, screened the patient for eligibility in the study, and if eligible, sought written informed consent and administered a baseline self-completed questionnaire (assisted by the nurse blind to group allocation, if the patient was having difficulty). Information was obtained about a range of topics including socio-demographic characteristics, their admission and prognosis, past and current health status, smoking history and environment, history and opinions about quitting cigarette smoking and knowledge of the health risks of smoking. The cardiologist of each patient enrolled in the study was informed of their patient's participation in order to ensure that the program was suitable for their medical condition.

The study was conducted as a two group, pre-post, control design. Allocation to the int`ervention group was based on alternate week blocks of eligible admissions, which in combination with low weekly recruitment rates effectively minimised the possibility of contamination. Patients allocated to the control group received the usual care of the hospitals and were provided with an efficacious self-help, smoking cessation booklet (Balanda, Lowe & O'Connor-Fleming, 1999). Patients allocated to the intervention group received the program described below.

Delivery of the intervention was based on two sessions with the patient in hospital where they were not permitted to smoke, and weekly follow-up phone calls for a month post-discharge. The content of each session, based on commonly used behavioural strategies, was as follows:

Session 1 was designed to develop the patient's motivation and self-efficacy to stop smoking. The material included two audio-tapes of motivational and educational material produced by the research team. The content for the tapes was drawn from the results of the focus groups and findings reported in the relevant literature. The first tape dealt with ambivalence towards quitting as well as the known positive and negative factors related to quitting, discussed by a group of blue-collar workers during a work break. The second tape encouraged positive attitudes and exemplified appropriate strategies, in a scene of a doctor discussing with an intern doctor the approach to be taken with patients wishing to quit smoking. After listening to the tapes, patients completed a self-administered quiz (Situational Competency Test) which allowed patients to identify high-risk situations, viewed a booklet containing cognitive strategies targeting each of these situations, and signed a "Stop Smoking" contract designed to develop the patient's commitment to not smoking while in hospital.

Session 2 continues to build the patient's motivation and self-efficacy and teach the patient skills for dealing with high risk situations for smoking relapse. The material consisted of an audio-taped discussion of cardiac patients views on quitting and the difficulties they encountered, a self-scored quiz (Behavioural Competency Test) dealing with behavioural issues related to high risk situations, a booklet providing behavioural activities which complemented the cognitive strategies developed in Session 1, a 'daily plan' to deal with these situations during the week following discharge which incorporated (a) gradually revealing hidden messages as a reward for each day of success and (b) a self nominated reward for staying quit for the week, and a letter requesting support sent to a nominated friend or partner. A letter was also sent to their General Practitioner informing them of the patients involvement in the project.

After discharge from hospital, a series of 4 follow-up phone calls were conducted weekly in order to provide the patient with continued support following discharge. The nurse enquired as to their progress in staying quit, provided support for positive activities and encouragement to quit if they had lapsed, and asked about use of the components of the intervention (cognitive and behavioural strategies booklets, daily plan completed in hospital, and support by friend and partner).

Among the 208 patients enrolled in the study 138 (66.3%) were followed up at 3 months after discharge from hospital (T2); among the remainder 52 did not return the questionnaire after 3 contacts from research staff, 12 could not be contacted and 6 had died. At 9 month follow-up (T3) 129 (62.0%) were surveyed; 43 did not reply, 30 could not be contacted and 6 had died. Similar proportions of participants in the two intervention groups were followed up. A number of patients (n=16) who did not participate.at T2 did so at T3. Self-reported quit rates were calculated on the basis of triangulating answers to three questions; “Have you changed your level of smoking since you were admitted to hospital with your heart problem” (answered ‘stopped altogether’) and “Have you had even one puff of a cigarette since you left hospital” (answered ‘no’) and “How long is it since you have smoked (even a puff)” (where the number of reported days was greater than the days to follow-up assessment). In addition, internal consistency for the group identified as quitters at T2 was obtained by a requirement that the number of days between the recorded discharge date and the follow-up date was less than the number of days since they reported they last smoked. Those who were self reported smokers at T2 but became non-smokers were coded as ‘quitters’ at T3. A subset of the participants who indicated they had quit smoking (50 at T2 and 44 at T3) were tested for verification of self report by a measure of carbon monoxide in expired air. Those contacted who refused to provide a measure of CO or had readings above 9ppm were classed as smokers.

RESULTS

Data from the baseline questionnaire showed that the intervention and control groups were statistically similar across the broad range of variables examined in the study, including socio-demographics (gender, age, education and occupation), rating of current health, family history of heart disease, advice to stop smoking from GP, smoking history, partners who smoke, intentions to stay quit, amount smoked in the week before admission, number of previous admissions and length of hospital stay ($p>0.05$).

A 'process' survey conducted with the 70 intervention cases followed up at 3 months indicated that the program was well received. Questions about each component of the program showed that two-thirds of the intervention group thought the tape recordings, cognitive and behavioural quiz with resource booklets, contract and daily plan were helpful to them in their efforts to quit. A larger proportion (more than 80%) thought the conversations with the nurse while in hospital and follow-up phone calls after discharge were helpful.

At 3 month follow-up, complete data was obtained from 133 participants (67 from the intervention group). Chi-square analysis of self-report of quitting (based on the 4 criteria described above), indicated that 7.6% of the comparison group had quit smoking completely, compared to 19.4% of the intervention group (X^2=3.97, df=1, p=.046). Apart from those who had quit, a notable trend was evident in which 23.2% of the intervention group indicated they had puffed on a cigarette since they left hospital but had stopped again, compared with only 3.0% of the comparison group. Examination of CO readings for the subset of 50 quitters (and 3 refusals) whose smoking status was verified or assumed to be a smoker, confirmed that approximately 92% of both groups were non-smokers, the adjusted quit rates based on 'intention to treat' were 4.8% and 12.6% respectively.

At 9 month follow-up, complete data was obtained from 128 participants (66 from the intervention group). The rate of self-reported quitting was 12.9% in the comparison group and 27.3% in the intervention group (X^2=4.3, df=1, p=.043). The effect across groups of a different level of quitting after a lapse was not evident at 9 month follow-up. Verification of smoking status for 44 quitters (and 5 refusals) confirmed that 90% were not smoking, and was similar for both groups the adjusted quit rates based on 'intention to quit' were 7.6% and 17.5% respectively.

Table 1. Correlates of patient's reports of number of weeks since smoking or puffing a cigarette, at three month follow-up (T2) and nine month follow-up (T3), adjusted for the factor of 'group.

Variable	Correlates of more weeks without smoking at T2	Correlates of more weeks without smoking at T3
1. How important are each of the following for you continuing to smoke. (4 point Likert scale, 1 = very, 4 = not at all)		
a) Enjoyment	.20*	.31*
b) Social reasons; family and friends do	.20*	.18
c) Relieve stress	.27*	.41*
d) Addicted to cigarettes	.28*	.43*
e) fills in time when bored	.16	.36*
2. How would you describe your state of health at the moment? (7 point scale; 1 = extremely poor, 7 = extremely good)	.03	.07
3. How serious do you think your current condition is? (4 point scale: 1 = very serious, 4 = not at all serious)	-.20*	.01
4. How frightening was your heart problem at stay in hospital? (4 point scale; 1 = not at all frightening, 4 = the most frightening experience ever)	.13	.13
5. How hard or easy do you think it will be to stay off cigarettes now that you have left hospital? (4 point scale; 1 = very easy, 4 = very hard)	-.24*	-.64*
6. How sure are you that you can stay off cigarettes? (4 point scale; 1 = very unsure, 4 = very sure)	.32*	.52*
7. Have you asked your family or friends to help you stop smoking (1 = No, 2 = Yes)	-.03	.25*
8. How much encouragement have you been getting from family to stop smoking (4 point scale; 1 = none at all, 4 = very much)	.04	.19*

*=p<.05

A loglinear analysis (multiway contingency) with a saturated model was used to test for change in smoking status between 3 month and 9 month followup for 108 participants who provided complete data at both follow-up assessments. Results of the analysis indicated that a significant proportion of respondents changed their smoking status (χ^2=5.6, df=1, p=.018). Among those who were smokers at 3 months follow-up (T2), proportionally more of the intervention group (26.1%) than the comparison group (10.4%) quit smoking between the 3 month and 9 month follow-up assessments.

Variables in the baseline survey which were significantly ($p<.05$) correlated with 'number of weeks since they had smoked or puffed on a cigarette' at 3 month follow-up were; GP had advised them to stop smoking (r=.19), greater confidence staying quit after leaving hospital (r=.21) and perception of self as a non-smoker (r=.24). Variables from the baseline questionnaire which predicted 'more weeks without smoking' at 9 month follow-up were; the amount of pain experienced before admission (r=.24), GP had offered help to stop smoking (r=.22) and perceived ease of staying quit (r=.21). The rates of quitting were not sufficiently high to examine a dichotomous measure of quitting. The factor of 'group' was partialled out of these reported correlations.

Correlations of the measure of quitting with variables from the follow-up surveys are shown in Table 1. A range of variables were correlated with quitting, but knowledge of the health risks of smoking and ratings of helpfulness of each of the components of the program (intervention group only) were not related to quitting, and are not listed in the table. Notably, perceived 'state of health', 'seriousness of condition' (T3) and rating of heart problem and hospital stay as a 'frightening experience', were not related to the variable of 'number of weeks without smoking' ($p>.05$).

DISCUSSION

Results of previous studies of smoking cessation among cardiovascular patients have produced inconsistent results, in part because the seriousness of the illness may have an impact on the outcome of smoking relapse prevention programs. This study indicated that a behavioural-based program is effective for patients not requiring operative procedures for heart problems. A multi-component program containing motivational material, cognitive restructuring, cognitive and behavioural skills development, social support and use of behavioural strategies including reinforcement, was effective in producing a quit rate significantly higher than achieved with 'usual care' which included a self-help quit book. The impact of the program was evident at 3 months (T2) and 9 months (T3) post discharge and also resulted in an increased quit rate after the 3 month period. Confirmation of non-smoking status by measurement of CO in expired air indicated that self-report of quitting was reliable.

The predictors of quitting identified in the study provide a profile of the type of patient who may benefit from this type of program. Variables such as 'education level', 'perceived difficulty staying quit' and 'age of onset of smoking' are supported by the results of previous research, but the significance of a number of variables such as 'self perception as a non-smoker' and 'GP offered assistance with quitting' provide avenues for new initiatives which would support this type of behavioural program. Notably, variables related to perceived severity of the health problem predicted patients efforts to quit. Commonly reported reasons for wanting to continue smoking were also related to failed quit efforts (Table 1).

The program as presented by the study nurse appears to be of assistance in helping patients remain abstinent from smoking. Further research needs to be conducted to determine whether the program as currently designed can continue to be effective when delivered by nursing staff in the wards. Recent debate about nicotine replacement therapy (NRT) for patients with cardiovascular disease favours its use (McRobbie & Hajek, 2001; Joseph & Fu, 2003) and should be included in future behavioural-based programs. In addition, as this was principally an efficacy trial, cost data was not collated. Further research needs to incorporate a comprehensive cost study to determine whether the addition of this program to the cost of the health care system can be measured against the possible cost saving of maintaining this group of high risk patients smoke free.

Acknowledgments

The authors wish to acknowledge the contribution of Michelle Willis, Romana Madl and Sandra Chippindall to this project. The authors also thank the hospital staff and patients for their participation. This project was funded by the National Heart Foundation of Australia.

REFERENCES

Baile, W. F., Bigelow, G. E., Gottlieb, S. H., Stitzer, M. L. & Sacktor, J. D. (1982). Rapid resumption of cigarette smoking following myocardial infarction: Inverse relation to MI severity. *Addictive Behaviours*, *7*, 373-380.

Balanda, K. P., Lowe, J. B. & O'Connor-Fleming, M. L. (1999). Which booklet to use: A comparison of two self-help smoking cessation booklets. *Tobacco Control*, *8*, 57-61.

Burling, T. A., Singleton, E. G., Bigelow, G. E., Baile, W. F. & Gottlieb, S. H. (1984). Smoking following myocardial infarction: A critical review of the literature. *Health Psychology*, *3*, 83-96.

Chowdhury, T. A., Lasker, S. S. & Dyer, P. H. (1999). Comparison of secondary prevention measures after myocardial infarction in subjects with and without diabetes mellitus. *Journal of Internal Medicine*, *254*, 565-570.

Emmons, K. M. & Goldstein, M. G. (1992). Smokers who are hospitalized: A window of opportunity for cessation interventions. *Preventive Medicine*, *21*, 262-269.

Frid, D., et al. (1991). Severity of angiographically proven artery disease predicts smoking cessation. *American Journal of Preventive Medicine*, *7*, 131-135.

Gottlieb, S. O. (1992). Cardiovascular benefits of smoking cessation. *Heart Disease and Stroke*, *1*, 173-175.

Guilmette, T. J., Motta, S. I., Shadel, W. G., Mukand, J. & Niaura, R. (2001). Promoting smoking cessation in the rehabilitation setting. *American Journal of Physical Medicine and Rehabilitation*, *80*, 560-562.

Havik, O. E. & Maeland, J. G. (1988). Changes in smoking behavior after myocardial infarction. *Health Psychology*, *7*, 3-20.

Jajich, C. L., Ostfeld, A. M. & Freeman, D. H. (1984). Smoking and coronary heart disease mortality in the elderly. *Journal of the American Medical Association*, *252*, 2831-2834.

Joseph, A. M. & Fu, S. S. (2003). Safety issues in pharmacotherapy for smoking in patients with cardiovascular disease. *Progress in Cardiovascular Diseases*, *45*, 429-441.

Kamarck, T. W. & Lichtenstein, E. (1985). Current trends in clinic-based smoking control. *Annals of Behavioural Medicine*, *7*, 19-23.

Maddux, J. E. & Rogers, R. W. (1983). Protection motivation and self-efficacy: A revised theory of fear appeals and attitude change. *Journal of Expermental Social Psychology*, *19*, 469-479.

Maiani, G., Callegari, S. & Sanavio, E. (1990). Smoking after myocardial infarction. *New Trends in Experimental Clinical Psychiatry*, *6*, 207-215.

Marshall, P. (1990). "Just one more...!" A study into the smoking attitudes and behavior of patients following first myocardial infarction. *International Journal of Nursing Studies*, *27*, 375-387.

McRobbie, H. & Hajek, P. (2001). Nicotine replacement therapy in patients with cardiovascular disease: Guidelines for health professionals. *Addiction*, *2001*, 1547-1551.

Milei, J. & Grana, D. R. (1998). Mortality and morbidity from smoking-induced cardiovascular diseases: the necessity of the cardiologist's involvement and commitment. *International Journal of Cardiology*, *67*, 95-109.

Miller, N. H., et al. (1997): Smoking cessation in hospitalized patients. Results of a randomized trial. *Archives of Internal Medicine*, *157*, 409-415.

Moller, A. M., Pedersen, T., Villebro, N., Schnaberich, A., Haas, M. & Tonnesen, R. (2003). A study of the impact of long-term tobacco smoking on postoperative intensive care admission. *Anaesthesia*, *58*, 55-59.

Ockene, J., et al. (1985b). Smoking cessation and severity of disease: the Coronary Artery Smoking Intervention Study. *Health Psychology*, *11*, 119-126.

Ockene, J. K., et al. (1985a). Factors affecting cigarette smoking status in patients with ischemic heart disease. *Journal of Chronic Disease*, *38*, 985-994.

Oldenburg, B. & Pope, J. (1990): A critical review of determinan0ts of smoking cessation. *Behavior Change*, *7*, 101-109.

Orleans, C. T., Jepson, C., Resch, N. & Rimer, B. K. (1994). Quitting motives and barriers among older smokers. The 1986 Adult Use of Tobacco Survey revisited. *Cancer*, *74(7 suppl)*, 2055-2061.

Rice, V. H., et al. (1994). A comparison of nursing interventions for smoking cessation in adults with cardiovascular health problems. *Heart and Lung*, *23*, 473-486.

Rigotti, N. A., Singer, D. E., Mulley, A. G. & Thibault, G. E. (1991). Smoking cessation following admission to a coronary care unit. *Journal of General Internal Medicine*, *6*, 305-311.

Rogers, R. W. (1983). Cognitive and physiological processes in fear appeals and attitude change: A revised theory of protection motivation. *In: Cacioppo & Petty, eds. Social Psychophysiology*, New York;

Rosenberg, L. P. & Shapiro, J. R. (1990). Decline in the risk of myocardial infarction among women who stop smoking. *New England Journal of Medicine*, *322*, 213-217.

Scott, R. R. & Lamparski, D. (1985). Variables related to long-term smoking status following cardiac events. *Addictive Behaviours*, *10*, 257-264.

Squires, R. W., Gau, G. T., Miller, T. D., Allison, T. G. & Lavie, L. J. (1990). Cardiovascular rehabilitation status. *Mayo Clinic Proceedings*, *65*, 731-755.

Taylor, C. B., Houston-Miller, N., Killen, J. D. & Debusk, R. F. (1990). Smoking cessation after acute myocardial infarction: Effects of a nurse-managed intervention. *Annals of Internal Medicine*, *113*, 118-123.

Wewers, M. E., Bowen, J. M., Stanislaw, A. E. & Desimone, V. B. (1994). A nurse-delivered smoking cessation intervention among hospitalized postoperative patients--influence of a smoking-related diagnosis: A pilot study. *Heart and Lung*, *23*, 151-156.

INDEX

B

D

E

F

G

J

N

O

P

Q

R

S

T

U

V

W

Y